# BRIGHT IDEAS

# Inspirations for TECHNOLOGY

Published by Scholastic Publications Ltd,
Villiers House,
Clarendon Avenue,
Leamington Spa,
Warwickshire CV32 5PR

© 1992 Scholastic Publications Ltd
Reprinted 1993

Written by Colin Lever
Edited by Juliet Gladston
Sub-edited by Jenny Lawson
Designed by Elizabeth Harrison
Series designed by Juanita Puddifoot
Illustrated by Ann Johns and Chris Saunderson
Cover design by Joy White
Cover artwork by Richard Wetherill

Designed using Aldus Pagemaker
Processed by Pages Bureau, Leamington Spa
Artwork by Salvo Design and Print, Leamington Spa
Printed in Great Britain by Ebenezer Baylis & Son, Worcester

**British Library Cataloguing in Publication Data**
A catalogue record for this book is available from the British Library.

ISBN 0-590-53028-3

Every attempt has been made to trace copyright holders of works quoted in this book. The publishers apologise for any omissions.

All rights reserved. This book is sold subject to the condition that it shall not, by way of trade or otherwise, be lent, hired out or otherwise circulated without the publisher's prior consent in any form of binding or cover other than that in which it is published and without a similar condition, including this condition, being imposed upon the subsequent purchaser.

No part of this publication may be reproduced, stored in a retrieval system, or transmitted, in any form or by any means, electronic, mechanical, photocopying, recording or otherwise, without the prior permission of the publisher, except where photocopying for educational purposes within a school or other educational establishment is expressly permitted in the text.

# CONTENTS

| | | |
|---|---|---|
| **Introduction** | | 5 |
| **Chapter 1** | *Food* | 15 |
| **Chapter 2** | *Textiles* | 39 |
| **Chapter 3** | *Wood* | 63 |
| **Chapter 4** | *Environments* | 89 |
| **Chapter 5** | *Systems* | 115 |
| **Chapter 6** | *Energy and control* | 139 |
| **Chapter 7** | *A framework for assessment* | 161 |
| **Attainment target chart** | | 163 |
| **Photocopiable pages** | | 165 |

To my wife Elaine and my
children Matthew and Aidan.

The author wishes to acknowledge
the following: special thanks to Jean
Robinson and pupils of Birtle View
School, Rochdale; thanks to the staff
and pupils of St Vincent's Roman
Catholic Primary School, Rochadale;
St Margaret's C of E Primary School,
Heywood; Bullough Moor Primary
School, Heywood; Darnhill County
Primary School, Heywood; Heap
Bridge Primary School, Heywood;
Heywood Community School,
Heywood; Rochdale TVEI; Pauline
Ellery; Julie Entwistle and *Junior
Education*.

# INTRODUCTION

## Technology

If you were to ask most people what their perception of technology is, they would probably say 'computers' or 'applied science'; but technology covers many areas and many skills. Craft teachers would likely view technology as being part of their 'domain'. Artists might see what they do as teaching in the context of using materials to enhance style and shape; to create effect and dictate fashion. To a scientist, technology may be about electronics, computers, developing new materials and chemicals in order to tackle problems faced by human need.

Home economists often view technology as part of their brief. Indeed, food technology is big business – involving the development of 'fast foods' and equipment to 'speed up' cooking times, and the designing of special diets. The involvement of home economists in textiles can also be said to be a branch of technology. From choosing the 'best' material to fulfil a certain role (denim for jeans, viscose rubber for wet suits) to the development and use of chemicals to colour materials in different, exciting ways – the person working with textiles is involved with technology.

The economists, too, with an eye on markets and finance, not only use technological hardware and software, but have more than just a passing interest in technology. They are continually trying to cut production times while maintaining productivity, open new markets with new products and enhance sales by creating positive attitudes to products, for example, environmentally friendly, more hygienic, less wasteful and so on. In doing this, economists feel that technology is also part of their domain. Indeed, just about every person from every walk of life can claim 'technology' as belonging, at least in part, to them.

Technology 5

# BACKGROUND

## What is technology?

So what is technology? Can it be pigeon-holed with science or craft subjects or engineering or business studies? To put a finite definition on technology will result in disagreement from one quarter or another. If you put it in a pigeon-hole with science, you negate the influence of style and design; pigeon-hole it with craft and you skew it in favour of working with a few materials, ignoring less traditional materials such as electronics and excluding concepts such as 'control' and 'systems'.

To develop technology as a subject in its own right, we must endeavour to include all players in the field – the scientist, the artist, the craftsperson, the food technician and the economist. All of them play a crucial role in technology as an educational subject and in technological developments as a whole.

Clearly some aspects of technology will have a bias one way or another, but over a period of time a balance has to be effected so that all contributions are seen playing their part to the full.

## Design within technology

Using design as an educational tool can prove to be a highly successful way for children to learn. When participating in design activities children are forced to apply their knowledge, exploring and filling the gaps, and ultimately leading to a better understanding of the subject matter involved.

Design is a style and a methodology not limited by subject boundaries and in this way is totally cross-curricular. Historically, however, design like technology, has always been seen as merely part of other subjects, such as art (art and design), craft (CDT), and home economics.

In terms of developments within education therefore, design and technology have similar roots. In many ways they are integral to each other and often difficult to separate. Any attempt at defining technology implies the use of design. For example, from the term 'applied science' one infers that ideas for practical uses for scientific knowledge are being developed. This in itself has strong design connotations.

## Design and technology as a process

Little, if anything, is ever designed just for the sake of designing. There is always another reason, whether implicit or explicit, for designing. Similarly, few technological advances ever emerge from nothing, and inadvertent discoveries tend to be the exception rather than the norm.

Most design and technological developments evolve in an attempt to meet the ever-changing demands of society. These developments, in turn, often end up shaping society. For example, the development of the internal combustion engine has shaped the whole transportation system – vehicles, roads, travel and so on. It has also contributed greatly to

environmental damage, on both a local and global scale. This, in turn, has created new needs, from a more environmentally aware society, for technological advances to counter the problems created.

These demands and necessities are referred to as *needs* and *opportunities*. We can identify what is needed and we can seek out opportunities for designing and making. In a classroom setting this identification process will probably not be anything as sophisticated as a recognition of the need to modify the internal combustion engine; but rather a simple idea to address classroom needs. The stimulus may come from structured play, for example, the need to make a play tent, or a container in which to carry liquids. Older children may think of things to design and make as part of their topic work. For example, they may design and make castles or armour as part of a history project or create a new waste disposal system to help reduce waste in their local community as part of a topic related to the environment.

Once an idea has formed, it should be investigated, researched and studied in detail. The reason for this is to define and clarify the ideas. In the early years this might be done through conversation or by using simple sketches, but later on, children can provide developmental drawings and plans showing more detail. Putting pencil to paper not only allows the designer to see what her ideas look like, but also, in educational terms, provides the teacher with an insight into the child's thought processes thereby facilitating assessment. The final plans are termed *design proposals*.

From the design proposals the object can be made. In the early years, children are likely simply to go ahead and make. However, older children should be encouraged to plan how they are going to carry out their manufacture before they do so. This means being organised – listing equipment, working out times, and so on. 'Making skills' do not necessarily mean having the ability to construct dovetail joints or doing complicated embroidery; they are more likely to involve work in paper and card and the use of colouring media, scissors and sticky tape.

Once a product has been made, it should be assessed to see how effective it is. For children in the early years, their opinions are likely to be egocentric. Do they like what they have made? How well do they think everything went? In later years however, children should be encouraged to seek out the opinions of others – perhaps their peers, teachers or, most importantly, the person or people for whom their design was intended. This process is known as *evaluation*.

This four-part strategy, taking an idea, developing it, making it and then evaluating it, when viewed as a whole, gives a design and technological process.

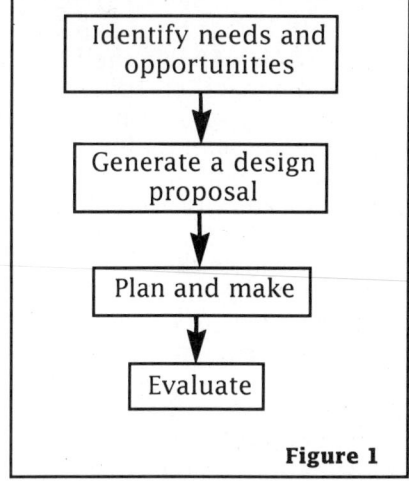

**Figure 1**

This process, illustrated in Figure 1, is not without its problems. For many children, trying to come up with ideas by looking for needs and opportunities is difficult, particularly if the subject matter is not conducive to design and technology, for example, musical theory, foreign languages, basic mathematics. Assuming a start was made at this point, the children might run into serious

problems at the design stage, or more likely, at the making stage. This is because their ideas and general creativity is likely to outstrip their basic skills in manufacture, for example, they might want to bake a cake but not actually have the skills to carry out the task. To counter these problems the design and technology process is better represented as a cyclical process (see Figure 2).

The advantage of this model is that children can enter the cycle at various points for example, they might first be taught – through skill development work – how to make something. They might then evaluate it – and identify needs and opportunities for its use. This in turn may generate new ideas for improving and changing its design. Finally, the new design can be planned and made, after a lot of initial skill development input.

Evaluating other people's designs is often an easier, more fruitful starting point. There is a wealth of artefacts, systems and environments to look at, not only within a child's own sphere of experience, but from other times and cultures. The use of traditional ethnic styles in cooking, clothing and fashion in general is evidence of cultural influences and much technological development has come from modifying ancient or existing, outdated technology, for example, windmills have been used to harness energy and compost as a way of recycling waste (Figure 3).

However, design and technology as a process is in reality, much less clearly defined than either Figures 2 or 3 imply. As a child plans,

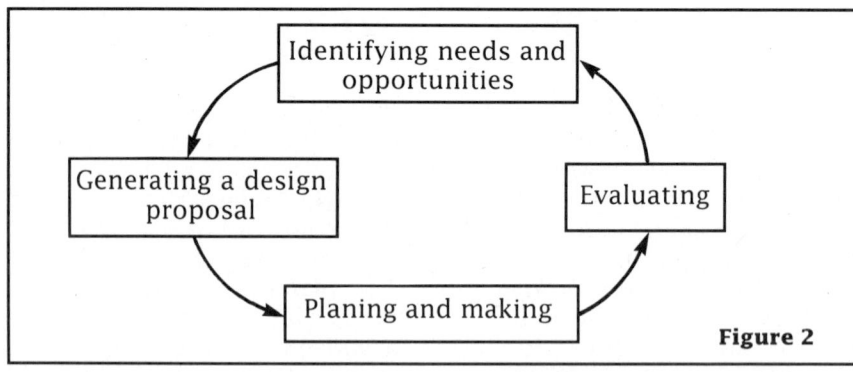

Figure 2

makes, develops, designs and identifies needs and opportunities, he is constantly evaluating his efforts. This evaluation may be overt or it may simply be reflective thought. Similarly, making as an instructional activity may lead to the identification of new ideas for designs or development of existing designs. These ideas may then be evaluated and from this work a final proposal may ensue. The whole process is therefore, much more interactive (see Figure 4).

For design and technology to function all four parts should be viewed as a *holistic process*, to be visited at least once during the work. If a product is merely researched and ideas developed, all that will emerge is a design, while

making without designing is merely craftwork. All four stages must feed into and complement each other so that children gain maximum benefit from the activity.

## *The language of technology*

All curricular subjects have their own language and jargon, and technology is no exception. Therefore, it is probably worth providing a brief explanation of a few of the more common terms at this point.

### *Defining the end product*

As distinct from simple craftwork, the end product of technology can be several forms:
• an artefact;

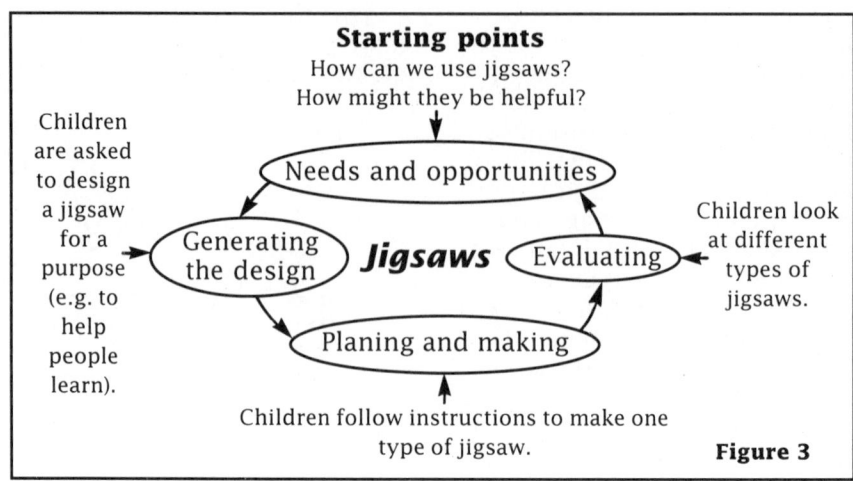

Figure 3

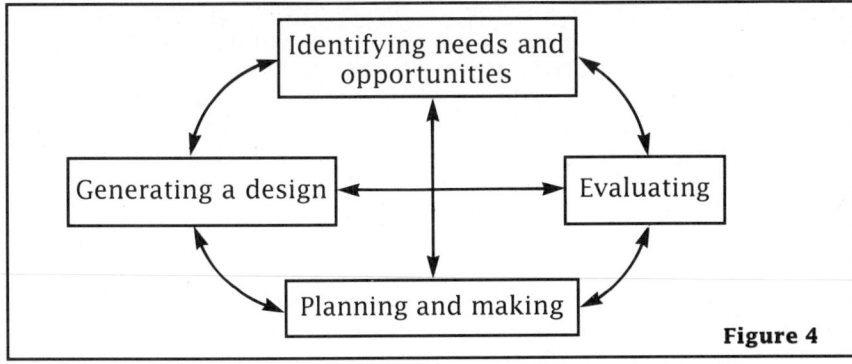

**Figure 4**

- a system;
- an environment.

An artefact is defined generally as 'an object made by people'. This can be clarified by thinking of such an object as being 'passive', for example, a chair, a poster and so on.

A system can be described as 'sets' of objects or activities which together perform a 'task'. Clearly, the performance of a task indicates an 'active' product, not a passive one, and so distinguishes an artefact from a system. 'Hard' technologists such as those people who work with computers and electronic hardware engineers, electronic buffs and computer users, may add that a system also has input(s) and output(s) linked together by processes. It is interesting to note the inclusion of the word 'activities' in the definition. This implies manual performance for example, people working as a team doing different jobs, as well as mechanical and/or electronic tasks.

An environment is defined in the DES document *Technology in the National Curriculum* (HMSO, 1990) as 'surroundings made or developed by people' (p.19) and environmental design is likely to include artefacts and systems, but is principally about how (and for what reason) the environment is organised and designed.

Look at the following examples and try to ascertain whether each is an artefact, a system or an environment:
- a house;
- a clockwork toy;
- baking a cake;
- a shoe;
- a garden.

## Materials

The word 'materials' usually conjures up visions of working with wood or metal. In technological terms however, materials range from wood and metal, through food and textiles to much more easily available items such as card, paper and 'junk' materials. Indeed it is important that children are given an experience of working in different mediums during their time in the primary school. The following provides an overview of the possible range of materials:
- food;
- wood;
- plastic;
- metal;
- fabrics;
- construction kits;
- electronics;
- potters clay;
- modelling clay;
- paints;
- photographic media;
- paper and card.

The nature of the activity will sometimes dictate what material is used. Equally, if it is seen as a priority to work in one material as opposed to any other, then such a constraint will affect what the children can physically make.

Early work with wood might, for example, involve

hammering nails, simple sawing or drilling, and finally painting. A more advanced approach might tackle gluing pieces together and beginning to shape or work using angles and joints.

Simple work with paper might consist of cutting and sticking. A more developed approach would include the use of a compass or ruler, or perhaps folding and bending in order to change the properties of the paper.

The activities found later on in this book focus on some of the more 'common' technological materials.

### Tools and equipment

The same principle of breadth applies to tools and equipment. By all means use saws and hammers, but there is also a need to develop skills in the use of scissors, kitchen utensils, sewing equipment, computers, rulers, paints and so on.

We are familiar, through traditional craftwork, with specific vocabulary such as measure, mark, cut, shape, join, assemble and finish – words used for a long time by the woodworker and metalworker. However, these same words are also applicable to work with textiles, food and materials such as clay, paper and card. Measuring and marking out may mean either using a ruler and pencil or scales and a knife. Cutting may involve slicing food in different ways, for example, chipping and grating or perhaps the use of pinking shears with textiles. Assembling may refer to the use of G-clamps – or to pins. Indeed, the number of ways which fabrics can be joined is exhaustive (try to list them all).

Paper and card also have many ways in which they can be joined. Finishing off a product may involve the use of paint, varnish or glaze (food and pottery). Finishing may also include snipping away loose threads and trimming rough edges.

### Modelling

Modelling uses a wide variety of components, materials and equipment, most of which are readily available in the classroom. The traditional perception of modelling is perhaps in the context of construction kits and following specific instructions.

The problem with asking the children simply to follow instructions, is that it does not constitute technology. Following instructions to create an end product is craftwork. However, construction kits can provide useful demonstrators of scale, proportion, movement and other scientific principles. In this capacity, they may serve a purpose in a fuller technological exercise. For example, a child may study mechanisms using a modelling kit. This will help to develop knowledge of the principles of levers, pulleys or gears. The knowledge introduced can then be applied to constructing in another medium, perhaps paper, card or wood, or it may be used to redesign something to suit new needs and opportunities.

Construction kits are common items in many primary schools, but are often under-used. They tend to be perceived as 'toys', which means that they are often relegated to be used as play things on wet days or as time fillers for when other classwork has been completed.

Modelling clay is another medium through which ideas can be developed. Scale models of people, animals, vehicles and buildings can all be made using modelling clay and it is also useful when

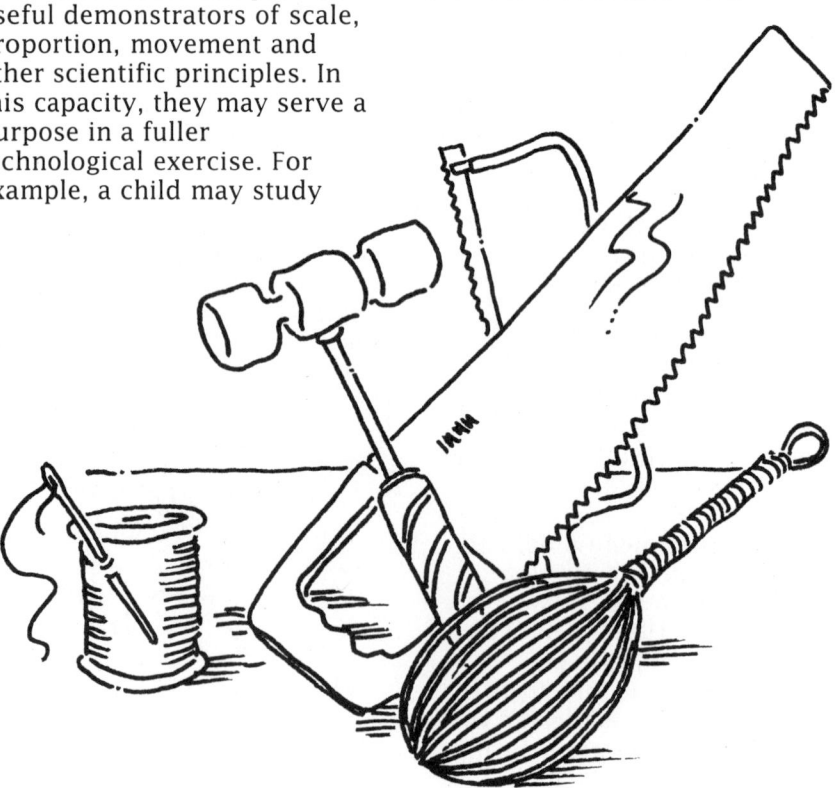

exploring joints. Objects can be modelled in clay to explore dimensions and complexity of the shape and then easily remoulded to different specifications. Once done, it can then be fashioned in a different material such as wood or foam, none of which would have been as effective during the design stage.

The most effective modelling medium however, has to be card and paper. They both have a myriad of uses and their properties can be altered easily, by, for example, folding or bending to suit many challenging situations. They can be used to make templates, models of artefacts and systems or to construct environments.

As each particular modelling medium has its own advantages and disadvantages, it is sometimes useful to mix various ones together, making use of particular properties. Why not build a frame using construction kits and then put on a 'skin' using paper or card or perhaps construct an object using wooden dowelling and then use modelling clay as joints? The possibilities are almost endless.

Modelling enables ideas to be put into a realistic three-dimensional context. Many young children have difficulty in drawing or seeing things in a three-dimensional perspective and modelling removes this perceptual problem. Children are able to *see* their designs in the shape they had intended.

A model is often the end product of the designing and making process. It may be that this is as far as a child can go with his ideas. If, for example, he has redesigned the school from scratch or added extensions to the existing site

using models, the next step would have to be to build it with bricks and mortar!

### The teacher's role in technological activity

One of the most misleading pieces of recent educational jargon is the concept of the 'open-ended' activity. To the uninitiated, it conjures up visions of a classroom free-for-all. However, this phrase is commonly used in technology. In reality there is little in education (and in technology) that is truly open-ended. What causes the confusion in technology is the nature of the design and technological process and its subsequent assessment. Does the teacher assess each shape in the process, in isolation or are they assessed together to gain a holistic perspective?

To achieve in technology, children have to exhibit an ability to identify their own needs and opportunities, to generate their own designs, to plan and make their own artefacts, systems and environments, and to evaluate by themselves. A daunting task for any child.

What is missing from this scenario is the role of the teacher. Does she sit back and watch chaos reign? The teacher's role, at the very least, should be one of support and guidance. In many instances, it is one of instruction, particularly during skill development. If children are involved in an activity that demands that they have to cut something with scissors and they do not have such a skill, then commonsense would tell the teacher that such a skill would have to be taught *before* the children attempt such work.

Knowing what skills will be needed, before a class of enthusiasts gets going on a technological activity, calls for forward planning. It is in this pre-activity planning that teachers influence what the children actually have to do. The technological jargon is called adding *constraints*. These constraints shape the activity, and narrow down its possibilities before the children even begin.

The skill in planning comes in finding the balance between constraints and allowing the creative instincts of the children to function properly. For example, perhaps during a topic concerned with endangered animals, the teacher may want the children to design and make a model zoo. Left as an open-ended task, the children will likely ask for a whole range of materials – wood, card, paper, straw and so on. However, the teacher may want the children to work only in card because there is little wood left in the stores at that time of year. Therefore, the constraint can be built into the problem by asking the children to: 'Design and make a model zoo using card only'. The activity can be further constrained by controlling the amount of card available.

Free choice of materials and equipment may be an unnecessary distraction in terms of technological activity. If children are working on mechanisms, construction kits would perhaps suit their needs best, in order to achieve a functioning finished product. Why use valuable time cutting and shaping card or cotton bobbins and trying to make gear wheels that never seem to mesh together properly? If the activity demands such work, then fine, let the children perform, if not, such work will act as a distraction, causing frustration and anxiety as well as eating up valuable class time!

All the way through their design and technology work, children can be given constraints. This is no different from similar work in the real world. If a word processor breaks down, the letters have to be written by hand or posting delayed until it is fixed. Manufacturing industry attempts to maximise output using minimal materials, and with minimum wastage. This is one aspect of efficiency; the others concern saving time and money. If it is put to the children in these terms the constraint will appear less like a dictat and more of a stimulation of real life, while keeping the ownership of the activity apparently in the hands of the child (see Figure 5).

## Forward planning

One of the major concerns teachers have about planning for work within technology is whether to carry out skill development work first and then enter into designing and making or to set the task in motion and deliver brief skill input sessions as and when they are necessary. On this count, there are no hard and fast rules. Forward planning may account for many likely

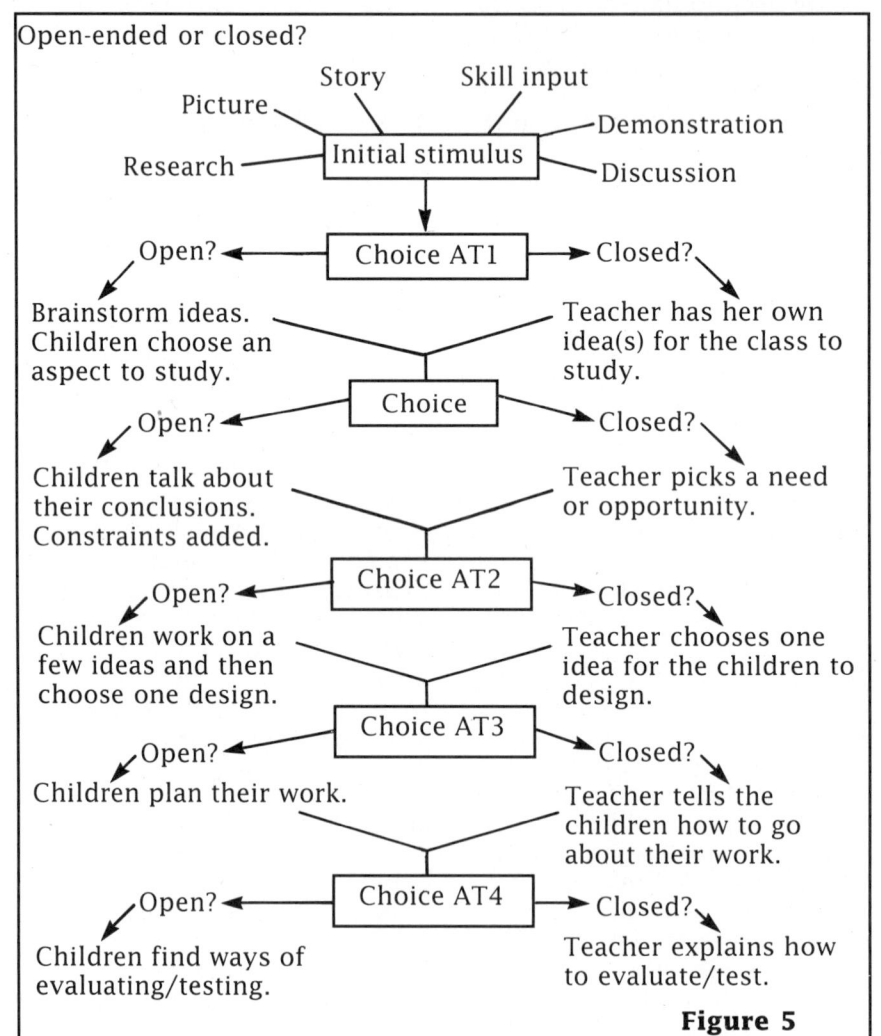

**Figure 5**

problems, but there will always be occasions when the unforeseen happens and these have to be dealt with *in situ*.

If a problem does arise that was unforeseen then the action of the teacher to the situation is also crucial. A mere question on the teacher's part might stimulate a successful response from the child. There is no need to give the answer straight away without giving the child and others in the class an opportunity to try and solve the problem for themselves first.

If time does not allow for such deliberations, or if the children find the problems too difficult, then you can offer advice. Such advice can be couched in vague terms or be aimed more directly at the problem, depending on the nature of the problem. Finally, if the problem is still proving to be too awkward, then a direct instruction may have to be given.

The key point here is to encourage the children to think things out for themselves. This will usually stimulate further activity and help create ownership of the activity. Children who have been spoon-fed within the classroom often exhibit difficulty in coming to terms with having to make their own decisions. Equally, teachers who do not let their pupils exhibit creative talents often have difficulty in coming to terms with teaching technology.

## Technology methodology

If a class is generally disruptive or perhaps a small number of children within a group cause problems, teaching technology may seem inappropriate. However, often the teaching of technology is such, that pupils of an active nature tend to enjoy it. Design and technology is a strict discipline and for children to succeed, they have to give great commitment and make great efforts for long periods of time. The child who has imagination and a more freewheeling style is often a good prospect for technology.

Figure 6 shows the essential ingredients of any technology course over a cycle of about two to three years. The programmes of study relating to technology have been

| Skills | Concepts |
|---|---|
| working with materials and equipment | knowledge of materials and equipment |
| exploring and investigating | energy |
| imaging and generating | economic awareness |
| modelling and communicating | aesthetics |
| organising and planning | systems |
| evaluating | structures and forces |
| | mechanisms |
| | health and safety |
| | socio/environmental |

**Figure 6**

subdivided into skills and concepts. The skills relate to those needed to identify and carry out designs. The concepts relate to the knowledge needed to manufacture artefacts, systems and environments. Knowledge is also needed about what materials can and cannot do. There are elements of science (forces, energy and so on) and the skills of the craftsperson too, but also other skills and concepts present that are perhaps less apparent to the untrained eye (organisational skills, communication skills and so on). Many of these skills and concepts the lay person might associate with technology (for example mechanisms, structures, modelling and so on). But there are many other equally important skills and concepts that might not have such obvious association (such as energy and its control, exploring and investigating aesthetics, organising and planning and so on). It is important to stress that all the skills and concepts listed get together throughout the technology cycle. This is why technology is so different from other subjects; it crosses and links up the art/science boundaries and the practical/academic boundary.

Working within the subject area of technology will help children to develop all these skills. They will tackle new skills in an active, exciting and motivating way, so much so that they are likely to be taken on board almost incidentally. The oldest method of learning is by *doing* and technology is learning by doing.

As you begin to teach technology there will be a fair amount of teacher involvement and intervention, and the amount of time allocated to the work will be limited. The task will not be highly complex (in respect of sub-tasks and variables) and the quality of the work will not be so high (see Figure 7).

As each child progresses, the quality and finish of her work will improve. Activities within technological work such as research and planning will become more detailed and fewer constraints will need to be added. This will mean, in turn, more variables for the child to consider which will increase the demands on curriculum time, although teacher input is likely to be less pronounced.

By the end of the primary phase an average child should be able to work independently on parts of his technology project. Any completed artefact, system or environment should show a degree of quality and finish. The aim in terms of progression is for children to produce a high quality, well-researched product, taking many hours (15/20) to complete. (However, pupils are unlikely to reach this stage until their mid teens.)

## About this book

Any design and technology activity will take place within a certain context and five of these contexts have been highlighted in this book, as themes for topics.
- home
- school
- recreation
- community
- business and industry

The intention is to present the children with themes to work through within contexts that they are familiar with, such as the home, school and recreation and to progress into working in less familiar contexts, such as community and business and industry. However, there are occasions when work associated with, say the home may not be as familiar to a child as, say, business and industry experiences. For example, a child in the early years is likely to be less aware of the need to conserve energy in the home

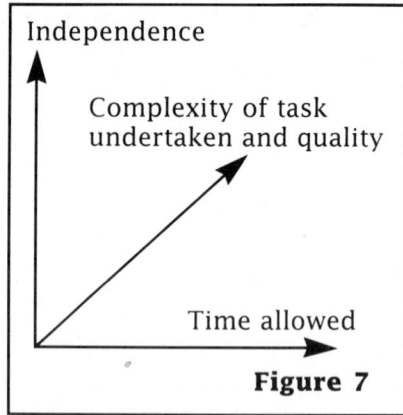

**Figure 7**

than she is about comparing the costs of comparable toys or sweets.

It is also true that there is a certain amount of overlap between contexts. The example just cited of conservation of energy in the home *could* be construed as being in the context of 'home'; but equally, it could be construed as having a 'business' context if, for example, the emphasis were on energy efficiency related to cost.

The answer to the problem of 'which context' is one of emphasis. By guiding children to develop and research work one way or another, you will influence which context takes precedent if there is an overlap. Try, for instance, contextualising the following:
- a school fête to raise money for charity;
- a game to help a deaf person speak;
- clearing litter from the school grounds;
- baking a cake for a friend's birthday.

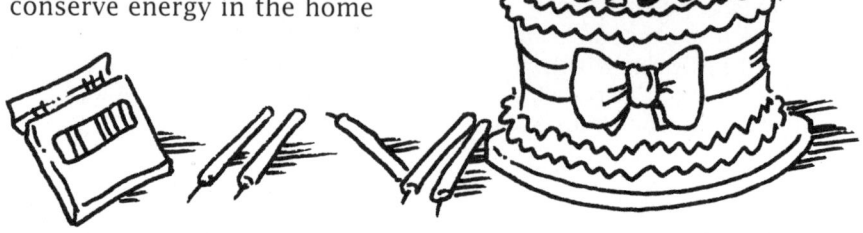

# CHAPTER 1

# Food

In primary schools food is often under used as a technological resource. This may be because there is frequently a lack of home economic facilities in schools, although most schools do have or can borrow the basic equipment for example a microwave, camping stove, portable electric hob, or have access to the school kitchen under supervision, the activities in this chapter, will only require basic items of crockery and cutlery in the main.

Another possible reason for schools not utilising home economics, is because of health and safety concerns. Working with food demands high standards of hygiene and personal cleanliness. The children must clean their hands and clean up properly after working with food, so that work surfaces are kept clean. They should wear aprons and take care to keep long hair tied back. This is not just good practice but also of great relevance to their personal and social development in terms of health and hygiene.

The safety angle from an equipment viewpoint is less of a problem, as long as sharp cutting instruments and heat or electricity are not used. Where hot equipment (such as when melting chocolate) or electrical equipment (for example food mixers) are used, careful supervision by the teacher is vital. The cleaning and storage of such equipment is also of importance. Have available bowls of warm soapy water to wash both surfaces and utensils. Utensils also need careful drying, especially knives or blades. All electrical equipment, which must not be immersed in water should be stored out of children's reach when not in use.

The progression and continuity of activities in this chapter comes in terms of how the food is used. It starts with activities where the emphasis is on children experiencing foodstuffs and raising awareness/skills. Later activities involve a more careful study of the working properties of food, building on the earlier activities.

Food 15

# ACTIVITIES

## Home: making a side salad

### Age range
Five to seven.

Many children will be familiar with side salads and dips, which are often served at parties either at their own homes or when visiting friends or relatives.

The activities in this section are intended to get the children to design and make a side salad or salad mix. It is not so important that they produce high quality food, but that they have the experience and develop the skills of working with food.

## 1. Sampling ready-made side salads

### Group size
Individuals.

### Objective
To raise awareness of the ingredients that make up a side salad.

### What you need
Different kinds of side salads (for example, coleslaw, waldorf salad, and pickle), spoons, saucers (one for each mixture).

### What to do
Ask the the children to look at each different type of side salad in turn, and consider its colour, texture, appearance and so on. In technology terms, it is important that they comment on the appearance such as how the food is cut – for example, coleslaw is cut in strips, pickle is cut in chunks and so on. Following on from this, if it is appropriate for each child, they can taste the mixes, commenting again on which ones they like or dislike and providing reasons for this if possible.

Ask the children to record their comments on paper. You may need to help some children by acting as scribe.

## 2. Sauces and dressings

### Group size
Individuals.

### Objective
To raise awareness of the differences between different types of sauces.

### What you need
Different kinds of sauce, for example, mayonnaise, ketchup, brown sauce, thousand island dressing; spoons, saucers (one for each sauce).

16 Chapter 1

## What to do
Put a small quantity of each sauce on separate saucers and lay them out for the children to observe and taste (if appropriate). Ask the children to record their comments. It is important that only very small amounts of each sauce are tasted because, on their own, many sauces are quite sickly.

Build up a language bank of words which the children use to describe appearance and taste. If this bank is located nearby, for example on a blackboard or on sugar paper written large enough for all to see, they can use the spellings when they are recording their comments. Words such as 'tangy', 'nice', 'tasty', 'horrid' may emerge, and will give the children an interesting and valid 'prompt' to description. Emphasise to the children the importance of not only saying what they like and dislike, but also *why*.

## 3. Gathering information

### Group size
The whole class or large groups.

### Objective
To help children develop ideas about what ingredients they might use when making their own side salad.

### What you need
Chalkboard.

### What to do
Brainstorming is a forum to which most children enjoy contributing. Use the children's experiences of mixes such as pickle and coleslaw and sauces such as mayonnaise and ketchup (from Activities 1 and 2) and ask them how each *one* is different. Help them to reach the conclusion that the mixes are simply sauces with other ingredients added. This can then lead into a group discussion about how sauces might be made into mixes, which sauces might be used, what could be added and how they would be prepared and so on.

Encourage the children to come up with ideas of their *own* during discussion and as the chair of this discussion you should direct the children's ideas so that they continue to consider the question. However, it is important to accept *all* reasonable answers even if they are not strictly to the point. Once the discussion reaches a natural conclusion, the ideas can be reviewed to eliminate the more impractical suggestions. By doing this the children will still 'own' the emergent ideas, even though you may have contributed a great deal.

## 4. Preparation of ingredients: cutting skills

### Group size
Pairs or small groups.

### Objective
To develop skills in cutting vegetables and fruit.

### What you need
Grater, knives with at least one suitable for chopping/cutting hard vegetables such as carrots, raw vegetables and fruit such as carrots, cauliflower, tomatoes, cabbage and so on (avoid onions), soap, water and towels.

### What to do
For many children the skill of cutting food will be new, although most will have cut their own food at mealtimes. Different vegetables and fruit will provide different problems when cutting and slicing them. Compare, for example, the difficulties of slicing a raw carrot with the problems

Food  17

encountered when cutting tomatoes.

An initial discussion is a useful way to encourage the children to think about the different properties of various vegetables and how they affect cutting techniques. This may be done as a whole class activity, with individual children offering and answering questions such as 'How is a carrot different from cabbage?' and 'How is lettuce similar to cauliflower?' You should then demonstrate and provide the necessary instruction, for example:
- make sure apron is on, hands are clean and working surface is clean;
- wash vegetables;
- place on a chopping board/surface and hold firmly;
- cut using the blade point as a pivot.

These cutting skills can be demonstrated to the class as a whole and then you can supervise small groups as they practice these skills. They should consider all the different techniques available, such as grating, slicing, chopping into chunks, shredding and so on.

## 5. Brainstorming: establishing the need

### Group size
The whole class or large groups.

### Objective
To identify needs and opportunities for using a side salad.

### What you need
No special requirements.

### What to do
The main feature that distinguishes technology and design from traditional craft is that artefacts, systems and environments are made for a reason, not just in order to develop skills. The reason for making is designated as a *need* or an *opportunity* and it influences what is being made.

A group or class discussion about where they might find a use for a salad dip or side salad will help in giving a wide variety of choice. Start by asking the children where they use such mixes, for example, pickle may be used on sandwiches, coleslaws with salads and so on. In terms of organising the making of such mixes, it might be useful for the class to agree (or for you to decide) how they are going to use them, following such a discussion. An interesting angle might be to create a situation where they can be used. Perhaps as part of a buffet for a visitor, or for lunch to help make the dinners more interesting.

## 6. Design proposal

### Group size
Individuals.

### Objective
To begin the process of designing the side salad.

### What you need
No special requirements.

### What to do
Having worked through the previous activities, the children now have to think about how they are going to make their own salads. What

sauce will they use? What vegetables? How will they cut the vegetables? How will they mix them? These questions can be asked specifically, in order to help the children to focus their ideas on what is needed and will encourage them to make decisions. The children should record their answers on paper and in this way they will have drawn up a design proposal.

They should identify the equipment they need and decide how many of it they require. It is at this stage that you can impose some constraints, perhaps restricting the choice of sauces and vegetables to two or three to save on cost and organisation. Other constraints could be imposed on the quantities of sauce and vegetables used, perhaps restricting it to two spoonfuls of sauce and three of vegetable.

## 7. Detailed planning for making

### Group size
Individuals.

### Objective
To plan how to make their side salads.

### What you need
Paper, pencils, photocopiable page 166.

### What to do
Having designed their side salads and planned the quantities of ingredients they require, the children should work out the sequence in which they will work. They can use photocopiable page 166 to help them plan the order by cutting out the activities and sticking them down in the order they will need to do them. This process will produce a recipe for their design and should be acknowledged as such.

## 8. Executing the plan

### Group size
Individuals.

### Objective
To make a side salad.

### What you need
Sauces, vegetables, spoons, cups/containers, knives, grater, for each group.

### What to do
The children will have to follow their plans and their design proposals in order to make their side salads. They should be encouraged to follow hygienic and safe working practices so that once they have made their salads they can taste their creations.

Having tasted, they need to consider whether it needs improving. Perhaps they should add a little more sauce if the taste is bland or a little more vegetable if the sauce is too strong in flavour or too runny? They could try adding a different vegetable to enhance the flavour. Once they have made their side salads, the children can store them safely, in readiness for the need for which they were made.

They should finish this activity by cleaning and tidying away all the equipment they used.

## 9. Is it tasty?

### Group size
Pairs, small groups or the whole class.

### Objective
To evaluate the side salads.

### What you need
Teaspoons or other small spoons.

### What to do
Having made their side salads the children need to evaluate them. Do they like the look and taste? What do they like or dislike about them? If they have made enough, others might be allowed to taste them and comment on the appearance. Ask the children to talk about and describe what they have done in order to reinforce sequences and procedures. If they have made them for someone else, what did *that* person think of them? How well did they go with the sandwich, the buffet or salad? There is no real need for the children to write their responses, although a picture depicting how the salads were used and a sentence or a word underneath the pictures would be appropriate.

## Extension
For older or more able children there are many variables which can be introduced. For instance, the number and quantity of sauces and vegetables can be varied. (Remember, however, that this may add to the cost of the activity!) Perhaps two sauces can be mixed and three types of vegetable added. Spices and seasoning could be added, such as salt, pepper, mint and so on. Having made their side salads, the children could carry out more extensive market research to find out people's response to their creations.

# School: a packed lunch for a school outing

### Age range
Six to eight.

This section is intended to help raise children's awareness of factors that affect choice when designing and making. In the case of the following activities the choice is determined by cost, the type of material available, particular needs and, perhaps most interestingly, consumer opinion.

The context for this activity is 'school' and the need, which has been presented for the children, is a 'packed lunch for a school outing'. Having stated the need does not detract from the work being the 'childrens'. They can easily seek new and exciting opportunities for making within this stated need.

## 1. Scene setting

### Group size
The whole class.

### Objective
To create a context for a technological activity.

### What you need
Story books such as *Bunnikin's Picnic Party* (Ladybird, 1940), and the well-known stories of 'Goldilocks and the Three Bears', and the 'Teddybears Picnic' would also be helpful.

## 2. What's in a packed lunch?

### Group size
The whole class (initially) and then small groups.

### Objective
To brainstorm the likely contents of a typical packed lunch.

### What you need
Chalkboard or flipchart, paper, pencils, scissors, adhesive, crayons or felt-tipped pens.

### What to do
As many young children bring packed lunches to school daily they will already be familiar with the contents. Gather the class together and ask for suggestions about what might be included in a packed lunch. Jot all the children's ideas down on the chalkboard or flipchart, including the ridiculous. The children are unlikely to use collective nouns, such as fruit and sandwiches, but are more likely to suggest individual items such as bananas, apples, pears, jam sandwiches, cheese sandwiches and so on. Therefore, an interesting task would be for you to ask the children to group the various items into sets, such as fruit and sandwiches. If the collective nouns have already been written on the board, the children can search for them and make lists under each title. If writing is difficult for all or a number of the children then they can draw pictures of the various items under the collective nouns. Ask them to include their own choices and indicate them in some way.

### What to do
As with a lot of work with younger children, it is often helpful to create a scenario for educational activity. The teacher needs to set out the reason for having a packed lunch, for example 'for a teddy bear' or 'for the school trip'. This might be discussed with the class, or more likely, it will be decided in advance by the teacher. The context can be real or imaginary and working within the context of creating a packed lunch for a school outing may lead to a specially engineered trip, for example a picnic or a walk to visit woodland, a farm or just the local park. If this is not feasible because of, for example financial constraints, the lack of local amenities or because of any disabilities which the children may have, then perhaps a book will provide a useful beginning. To an extent, the nature of the 'trip' will dictate what is included in the packed lunch. For example, a packed lunch for a long walk might well be different from a lunch prepared for a picnic in the local park.

It is also necessary to take into account for whom the packed lunch is intended. A packed lunch prepared for an animal in a story will be quite different from that prepared for six- to seven-year-olds.

Food allergies and preferences will also need to be considered. What goes into the packed lunch will ultimately be guided by you, but this should be done in negotiation with the children. In technological terms this work will be in a 'school' context, but with a shift of emphasis it could easily be moved into the home, community or recreational context.

Food 21

# 3. Preferences

## Group size
Small groups of three or four.

## Objective
To find out children's preferences about what they would like in their packed lunches.

## What you need
Paper, ruler, pencils, a variety of food stuffs, such as bread, butter and margarine, sandwich fillers (sliced meat, cheeses, spreads and so on) fruits, biscuits (chocolate and plain), crisps.

## What to do
When planning to make up a packed lunch it is necessary to discover the preferences of the people who will be eating it.

They might try to imagine what, for example, a bear would prefer, if a story scenario is the choice (for example, Paddington Bear would appreciate marmalade sandwiches!) This exercise could be done by each child on an individual basis, but a survey carried out in this way will be long-winded and time-consuming. It will be easier, and essentially more productive, to allocate tasks to small groups. For example, one group, might work at how the lunch is to be packaged – will they use food wrap, paper, foil or lunch boxes?

The items listed below are some of the major issues which may need to be resolved, although depending on individual classroom circumstances, there may be others:
• brown or white bread;
• margarine or butter;
• the type of sandwich filler (meat or cheese);
• the flavour of crisps (salt and vinegar or plain);
• the sort of fruit (an apple or a banana);
• the type of biscuit (for example, chocolate, plain);
• the flavour and type of drink (orange or blackcurrant, still or fizzy);

Each group should choose an aspect to research. They will need a list of names and will have to mark down on that list what individuals prefer and, if possible, their reasons. Some children may have allergies to certain foods or may have to keep to special diets. By carrying out this research, the children will become aware of the 'needs' of others; this plays a key role in technological activity.

In most cases, preferences will be based purely on opinion and habit. To give the activity a more interesting practical angle, it would be useful to ask the children to actually taste each of the alternatives, before giving their choices. Most of the foods are readily available low-cost items. You could prepare these prior to the lesson, cutting them into small pieces for sampling. Alternatively, the children themselves, could carry out the preparatory work.

If allergies are known beforehand this can be taken into account, with those children being allowed to leave out the foods to which they are sensitive.

# 4. Data recording

## Group size
Small groups of three or four.

## Objective
To store, retrieve and process data relating to children's food preferences.

## What you need
Paper, pencils, a computer with appropriate software.

## What to do
Having explored their preferences within the class the children should be encouraged to store this information on a computer. You may wish to prepare the initial database, entering the children's names and leaving space for them to fill in, allowing enough 'columns' to cover all the variables. If each group is allocated their own time working with the computer then they can, in turn, enter their data.

A number of database packages will also interpret and present the data as percentages, bar charts, or pie charts. However, these packages are not an essential requirement for this work, although the children will need to find out the opinions of the majority, for example, most children prefer butter to margarine, only one person wants blackcurrant drink and so on.

If computer facilities are not available, the children could present their findings in the form of a block graph cutting out and sticking down squares of paper on to graph paper.

# 5. Decisions

## Group size
The whole class, based on previous group work.

## Objective
Using preferences to help decide what will go into a packed lunch.

## What you need
Pencils, paper.

## What to do
Once collated, the children can begin to analyse the information they have discovered about preferences. How will this affect what they decide to include in the packed lunch? Some decisions will be easy, others more difficult, but it will be up to you to focus the children's attention on the various issues. For example, most children may prefer white bread. This may mean that they all have white bread, but, on the other hand, it may also be possible to accommodate individual preferences.

Ask the children what other factor might influence their choices? Try to encourage them to think about healthier options, the price of ingredients and the time it takes to prepare the food.

An interesting situation may arise if there is one child who will not conform to the majority. For example, she may be the only one who does not want to drink orange juice. The others may press her to have orange, but it may be that she cannot drink orange juice for medical reasons. The other children will have to accept this and thereby begin to understand that choices often depend upon people's individual needs. It may be that a few in the class are vegetarian or have cultural influences that dictate what they can and cannot eat.

Once overall agreement has been achieved, with one or two

variations, the children can record the items they will include in their packed lunch. This might be drawn on a computer using a graphics package or they can draw pictures and stick them on to a large cut out of a sandwich box.

## 6. Making skills

### Group size
Individuals leading to the whole class.

### Objective
To learn the skills needed to prepare sandwiches.

### What you need
Margarine or butter, presliced bread, knives, plates, sandwich fillings (such as cheese, peanut butter and so on) soap, water, towel.

### What to do
Superficially, making sandwiches appears to be a relatively easy task, but for many young children who have never had such an experience, the task may be more problematic. They will have to:
• spread the butter or margarine;
• decide upon the amounts of butter or margarine to be used;
• decide upon the amount of filler to put on the bread;
• cut the bread into halves or quarters.

Ask the children to make a sandwich for themselves. They should use a readily available filler (such as jam or spread), to make the task slightly easier. Explain to them that they will not be allowed to eat it straight away. Once the sandwiches have been prepared they must be left on display until everyone has had a go at making one. Then, as a class, you can look at each sandwich in turn, commenting on such things as: how much butter and filler was used; whether the bread kept its shape or whether it was torn during spreading and how the sandwich was cut. Once the critical evaluation has been completed, the children can eat their sandwiches.

It is important to stress points of hygiene when making food which will be eaten. The children must always wash their hands before and after handling food and the surfaces and their equipment must be clean.

Finally, the children can record what they did on a storyboard, sequencing each activity.

## 7. Getting organised

### Group size
The whole class and small groups.

### Objective
To gather the ingredients for a packed lunch and raise awareness of factors affecting choice.

### What you need
Paper, pencils, money.

### What to do
Before ingredients are obtained, the children will have to be made aware of *when* they are going on their trip or when the imaginary trip is taking place. This can form part of an initial, whole class discussion or it can be dictated by the teacher and the class informed.

There will need to be an initial cash outlay to fund the exercise, or donations such as bread, butter and fillings, could be brought into school from home. The class may consider holding a raffle to raise funds to pay for the ingredients, or they may agree to share the total cost between them.

Divide the children into small groups of three or four and assign each group a section of the class packed lunch to work on. For example, some groups may have fruit as a category and, looking at preferences, may find they will need ten apples, five bananas and six oranges, or another group may have to calculate how many slices of bread they will need. Each group should make out a shopping list. For some this will be an easy task, for others not so. They may need to find out how many slices of bread are in a loaf, or whether there are any bananas available, and if not, what will they do?

The next stage is to visit a local supermarket or store. From the money available, each group can be allocated a certain amount of cash. The children should then work in their groups to collect the items on their shopping lists. Encourage them to think about the cost and quality of the food; for example, it is better to buy slightly more expensive fresh fruit, than bruised or damaged ones. The intention is to raise children's awareness of factors which affect choices.

## 8. Assembling the packed lunches

### Group size
Individuals.

### Objective
To finalise the design proposal and to prepare the packed lunch.

### What you need
The food and packaging bought in Activity 7 above.

### What to do
All the food should be laid out on separate tables, for example one for fruit, another for meat, a third for bread and so on, so that the children can move from one 'station' to another. Before they begin to collect together the ingredients for each packed lunch, the children should be encouraged to write down once again, what their own individual packed lunch will consist of. If they have forgotten, then the lists compiled in Activity 5 can be placed in a prominent place. These lists or drawings would constitute the final design proposal, but ask them to write and quantify why they chose each particular item. For example, 'I chose a banana because it is not too messy to eat' or 'I chose cheese because I am vegetarian'. This sort of final proposal can also be designed as a labelled picture. If the children have been asked to think about packaging as well, then this will also have to be shown on their proposal.

Once this proposal is complete the children will visit each table in turn, to collect the ingredients they need in order to make up their lunches. Making the sandwiches will be fairly time consuming and allowance for this will need to be built into the lesson plan. It may be a good idea to limit the number of children allowed at the sandwich table at any one time. Other groups might collect their packaging, fruit, biscuits and so on, at the same time. If the proposal is written prior to preparation in the same lesson then this could be the first port of call, thereby staggering the numbers. As the children work through, get them to describe what they are doing and why.

## 9. Comments

### Group size
The whole class and individuals.

### Objective
To evaluate the success of the lunch.

### What you need
Pencils, paper.

### What to do
By this stage the packed lunch will have been prepared, taken out and consumed. On returning to the classroom the children should be encouraged to discuss how well their packed lunch served the original need. This can be done initially by a whole class discussion.
• How much did the children like their packed lunch?
• What was good about it?
• What did they not like about it?
• If they had to make another packed lunch what would they do differently?

There are many areas which the children may decide that they would do differently on another occasion. Perhaps the drinks leaked, or the food went soggy, or melted in the bags/boxes because they became too warm? Perhaps there wasn't enough food to satisfy their hunger or perhaps they had too much? Did their lunch turn out to be as good as they thought it would? Ask them to comment on the activity as a whole. Were there problems? If so what? How might they solve these problems in the future?

All this can be discussed as a whole class. Then each child can write an 'evaluation' of his own lunch, possibly accompanied by a drawing.

# Business: making and selling cakes

### Age range
Seven to nine.

The need for children to develop economic awareness is now widely recognised, and has applications across the curriculum. Linking schools with industry can often be very productive, enabling children to gain some appreciation of the 'market' and how it affects the product and pricing. The activities in this section are intended to simulate the 'market place', where children will compete against each other in teams to make and sell their products.

The children will be shown how to make cakes. Then they will have an opportunity to redesign, make, advertise and sell their products. The context here is very definitely business.

## 1. Making cakes

### Group size
Pairs or small groups.

### Objective
To build up skills in making chocolate cereal cakes.

### What you need
For 50 to 60 cakes: 250g box of breakfast cereal (cornflakes, krispies, oats and so on), 250g bar of cooking chocolate, paper cake cases, large bowls, tablespoons, saucepans, scales, electric or gas rings, cookery books.

## What to do
The design and technology process, in this instance, is initiated by making. Explain to the children how to make chocolate cereal cakes using the following recipe:
• Pour 50g of cereal into a large bowl.
• Melt 50g of chocolate in a glass bowl over a pan of hot water. (SAFETY!)
• Pour the melted chocolate over the cereal and mix together thoroughly.
• Put a tablespoon of the mixture into the paper cake cases and leave them to set.

It is important, that each child is given the chance to make cakes as they will need to draw on this experience in later activities in this section. However, for safety sake the following guidelines should be used:
• only one or two children should cook at a time, and they must be supervised;
• make sure there are insulated handles on the equipment;
• be extra careful when using hobs or boiling water; ideally an adult should pour any hot water.

Once they have made the chocolate cereal cakes, the children can write out what they did, in the format of a recipe in a cookery book, possibly with the inclusion of pictures. You can provide them with recipe books so that the children can see how recipes are written out. The children can then eat their cakes and write a sentence or two, at the end of their recipe, describing how they tasted.

## 2. In business

### Group size
The whole class.

### Objective
To introduce the concept of manufacturing as a business process.

### What you need
Paper, pencils.

### What to do
Explain to the children that by making their cakes, they have experienced the basic manufacturing process.

Discuss how businesses are run and the different roles that each person plays within them. Start with the children's own experiences and knowledge. What sort of things can they think of that are made in factories? Who makes them? Introduce the idea that people actually make the items. If the workers make the product what do they think the managers do? Introduce the idea of a person overseeing production, rather than necessarily making the items.

Explain to the children that the manager has to look after the finances. She may have to buy in raw materials to make the product, look at how well the product is made and decide what needs changing and improving. The manager may also have the final say on how the item is priced. Alternatively, this may be a collective decision made by the whole group.

Ask the children what they think a salesperson does and introduce the ideas of advertising, promoting and marketing. In order for people to buy a product they need to be aware of it. How can this be done?

This is a very simplistic view of manufacturing, having identified only three major people in a workforce. However, as a starting point and in order to raise children's awareness of the world of business systems, it is more than adequate.

Ask the children to write a little about who they would like to be in a manufacturing business and why.

Food

## 3. Quality control

### Group size
Individuals.

### Objective
To develop evaluation skill through role play.

### What you need
Paper, scissors, coloured crayons.

### What to do
To help the children develop their role-play skills they need to have some idea of what quality control involves. Without necessarily using the term 'quality control', they should be encouraged to comment critically on objects that they make but emphasising what is good about the item.

In this activity, the children are to make simple concertina-shaped figures and shapes from paper. Before they make them they need to be told that each attempt is going to be judged using the following criteria:
- how attractive it looks;
- how well it is made;
- how much improvement is needed to make it better.

They should fold the paper in half and then in half again on the same axis. If you are using fairly large paper, then it can be folded again. The children can draw a figure or shape on the front, making sure that part of the outline adjoins the folds. They can then cut out the shape and unfold it to reveal a chain of shapes. Encourage the children to colour and decorate their figures or shapes to make them look attractive.

Only allow the children to have one attempt at making their chains, and once they have all made one they should set them out together. The children can then be judges and assess all the chains except their own, awarding marks out of ten for each shape. Remind the children of the criteria you spoke of before they began to make their chains. Once all the marks have been given they can be totted up and the winner announced.

Encourage the children to talk about how they judged the chains using the criteria, and ask them to provide specific examples. This will help to reinforce their evaluatory skills.

## 4. Advertising

### Group size
Individuals.

### Objective
To develop an awareness of advertising and sales in business.

### What you need
A4 paper or equivalent; variety of fruit; knife to cut the fruit; examples of advertisements and glossy packaging.

### What to do
Using examples of advertising, such as packaging and posters, as an initial stimulus, ask the children to look at the ways in which companies attract people to their products. The children are likely to think of things such as bright colours, large writing and big pictures, but they should also be encouraged to think about the more subtle sales ploys that are used, for example, placing adverts at eye level and in prominent places. The children can also be guided towards looking at one product against another to find out how

aesthetics can influence what is bought.

Follow up this initial discussion by setting out the fruit and asking the children to choose one from those available. Let them taste the fruit, describe what it looks and tastes like, and ask them to design a poster or display to promote the sales of their chosen fruit. You may like to help the children by writing the words that the children used to describe their chosen fruit on the board. They can then choose and correctly spell the words that they require.

The final displays can be evaluated by the whole class. Remind them to look out for innovative ideas, the use of colour and language, and ways that their attention was caught.

## 5. Opportunities

### Group size
The whole class and then small groups of four to five.

### Objective
To identify opportunities for developing chocolate cereal cakes.

### What you need
Paper, pencils.

### What to do
Gather the children together and discuss the chocolate cereal cakes that they made in Activity 1. How do the children think these can be altered in order to encourage people in the school to buy them? The children may come up with ideas such as: adding nuts, raisins or hundreds and thousands; putting a cherry or sweet on top of each cake or perhaps just dusting them with icing sugar. The children will probably begin to realise that the way the chocolate cereal cakes are presented and advertised will affect sales.

Group the children into four teams of four or five and give each child a clearly defined role within the team. Each group will need a manager, a sales and advertising person, and of course workers. The children can decide whether to combine, share or keep rigidly to their job roles, but their first task is to work out who will do what. You may want to have some influence over this, acting as arbitrator, or allocating particular roles in order to develop the social communicative skills, of particular children. For example, you might want to ask the shy child to be the manager or alternatively, the class leader, may be told to be a worker to avoid them bullying or dominating the activity.

## 6. Planning

### Group size
Small groups.

### Objective
To develop ideas about making and organising working procedures.

### What you need
No special requirements.

### What to do
The first task of the group, having decided upon their

roles, will be to come to a decision about how they will alter the chocolate cereal cakes. Having had some initial ideas as a class in the previous activity, each group should narrow their choices down to two or three ideas. They can then set about researching which method they will finally choose. They may conduct a tasting session to see which topping or decoration tastes the best and they may explore the cost of items. Do cherries cost more than raisins? How many Smarties are going to be added? How will this affect the overall cost? It is important to allow the children as much freedom of choice at this stage as possible; giving them the opportunity to develop and refine their own ideas.

Finally, the children will have to record the outcomes of their research together with any decisions that they made in the light of the research. For example, they may have found that few of them like nuts and therefore decided not to use them.

## 7. Refining ideas

### Group size
Small groups of four to five.

### Objective
To refine ideas and draw up a design proposal.

### What you need
Paper, pencils.

### What to do
The range of ideas which the children came up with in Activity 6 can now be narrowed down further by introducing the concept of working within a budget. Tell the children that they have a fixed budget to work with, say 100 units. You can then act as their supplier, setting out that X grams of cereal will cost Y units and so on. If the children have thought of a wide range of ingredients then you should make the more absurd ones very costly so that the children have to think hard before they choose to buy them.

The next task will be for the children to cost out how many chocolate cereal cakes they can make with their 100 units. Each group should then decide on a price at which to sell their product. They must work as a team, but the manager should have the final say if they cannot come to an agreement.

They might also choose (or you might decide for them) what the profit will be used for, for example charity, school funds, prizes and so on.

Once these factors have been discussed, the group should be able to draw up a design proposal, itemising what they will need to make their product and the reasons for their choices in each case.

## 8. Plans

### Group size
Small groups of four or five.

### Objective
To plan out the mini-enterprise task.

### What you need
Pencils, paper.

### What to do
Before the children set about making their design, they will have to identify who is going to do what. Ask them to list the jobs that need doing; if required give them some assistance. The list will include:
• weighing out the cereal;
• weighing out the chocolate;
• counting out additional ingredients;

- melting the chocolate;
- mixing the ingredients;
- placing the ingredients in paper cases;
- decorating the cakes;
- designing a poster and/or display to advertise their product;

They will also have to plan:
- tidying up;
- manning the stall;
- selling the product;
- totting up the profits.

The allocation of jobs must be agreed upon by the whole group and the results written down. If you like you could ask the children to sign contracts!

Finally, add the last constraint. Give the children a set time in which to complete their work. An hour should be sufficient time in which to make the cakes, but you may need extra time to design a poster or display and tidy up. The children should work out how long they think each task will take and write it up in the form of a storyboard or as a sequence of activities.

## 9. Cake making

### Group size
Small groups of four or five.

### Objective
To make the product following a design plan.

### What you need
Ingredients and utensils to make chocolate cereal cakes (see page 26); additional ingredients, such as icing sugar, Smarties, raisins and so on; large sheets of paper, felt-tipped pens and crayons.

### What to do
The children should follow the instructions they have set out in their design proposals (see Activity 7) and planning schedules (see Activity 8). As they work they will meet problems and they should be encouraged to solve these for themselves. In this way the lesson is likely to be highly motivated and productive.

The children should be encouraged to avoid wastage of materials. This can be aided by charging them for spillages and so on, showing how wastage affects the quantity of items that can be made.

Also as the children work emphasise the need to check the quality of the product. If necessary you could allow the 'manager' to carry out quality control.

Once made the children can sell the cakes. They will have to decide, as a class or in their group:
- how much to charge for the cakes;
- where to sell them;
- when to sell them;
- how to display and advertise them.

## 10. Questions

### Group size
Individuals.

### Objective
To evaluate the mini-enterprise scheme.

### What you need
Pencils, paper.

### What to do
Having made and sold their product; the children need to evaluate the whole process. You can help them to do this by giving them a series of questions such as:
- How well did they work as a team?
- How well did their chocolate cereal cakes sell?
- Did they meet their sales targets?
- How might their teams work better in the future?
- How could they have improved the sales of their product?
- Did they encounter any competition when selling their product?

Food

# Recreation: balancing a diet

## Age range
Eight to ten.

Healthy eating is perhaps the most important issue in food education. Contrary to popular belief, healthy eating is not just a matter of eating less fat or eating more vegetables. Healthy eating is about achieving a balance in the food that we eat, suited to the needs of our own bodies. Some people need higher amounts of carbohydrate in their food, others may have an allergy to certain kinds of fruit.

The context for these activities is recreation – eating for enjoyment, but with the important message of 'healthy eating' running through all their work.

This section will help children to begin to look at their diets and endeavour to achieve a better balance in the food that they eat.

## 1. Favourite meals

### Group size
Individuals.

### Objective
To design a meal.

### What you need
Pencils, paper, paint, crayons, felt-tipped pens, possibly modelling clay.

### What to do
Give the children the freedom to draw, paint, colour, cut out pictures of, write about or design on a computer their favourite meals. This may consist of a one-course, fast-food special, or it might comprise a three- or four-course menu. However the meal is conveyed – as a picture or sequence of items as per a menu – the children should include as much detail as possible from gravy and custard to after-dinner mints. For each item they should provide a reason why they have chosen it.

The children could also design menus, use modelling clay or Plasticine to simulate a three-dimensional version of the meal. However, it must be stressed that this design task is only a stimulus for further activity rather than an end in itself.

## 2. Balance

### Group size
The whole class initially and then individuals.

### Objective
To introduce the idea of a balanced diet.

### What you need
No special requirements.

### What to do
Start by asking the children what they think the word 'balance' means and develop this into a general discussion about balance. Having established the language, draw the children's attention to the phrase 'an unbalanced meal'. What does it mean? Does it mean too much of one food and not enough of another? Ask the children to say which of the following meals are balanced:
• a plate of chips;
• a bowl of rice;
• a side salad;

- a cream bun;
- a samosa;
- a doner kebab.

In fact none of them are balanced even though some contain more than one item.

The word 'variety' should be introduced and explained to the children. For example, a plate full of chips does not provide variety, nor does an apple on its own. Variety means having a staple food such as potatoes, supplemented with vegetables and/or fruit, together with protein (meat, fish and so on). The children should also think about variety in terms of temperature, colour and texture. Ask them to think of meals that do provide variety. The children should be able to conclude that a balanced meal is made up from a number of parts, mains (proteins – meat, fish, nuts, soya and so on), filler (staple foods like potato, rice, pasta and yams), fruit and vegetables and a drink.

## 3. Components

### Group size
Individuals.

### Objective
To develop the concept of a balanced meal.

### What you need
Coloured pencils or felt-tipped pens, photocopiable page 167.

### What to do
Having discovered that balanced meals are made from four components the children need to practise identifying what constitutes mains, filler, fruit and vegetable, and drinks. 'Mains' are principally meat, fish and poultry or for vegetarians, soya or an equivalent, in other words the protein part of the meal. 'Fillers' are principally carbohydrates and will include things such as potatoes, bread, rice, pasta and so on. Fruit and vegetables, and drinks as categories are self explanatory.

Using photocopiable page 167, the children should colour each item on the plate: mains should be coloured red, fillers yellow, fruit and vegetables green and drink blue. The children can also apply their knowledge to other meals. Can they recognise the categories in the meals they designed in Activity 1? Using the colour code technique they can easily identify what is present or perhaps, more importantly, what is missing in these meals. Can they think of items to add or take away to make these meals more balanced?

## 4. Developing ideas

### Group size
Small groups of three or four.

### Objective
To research where balanced diets can be developed.

### What you need
Videos, articles in papers, magazines and books about food and diets.

### What to do
There are many opportunities to develop ideas about balanced diets, ranging from home (their own diets, the family diet or a relative's diet) to their local community (diets for the elderly and ethnic

groups) and the broader community (famine). In groups of three or four let the children brainstorm likely opportunities, then narrow them down to one or two that are most favourable to present to the whole class.

Possibly take the opportunity to look at the concept of malnutrition as opposed to starvation and famine. For example, rice on its own staves off hunger, but provides little in the way of nutrition. Perhaps focus on fast foods, for example, MacDonalds and local cafes and how such outlets could provide a better balance to the foods that they sell. It is likely that such a choice of context is not too far away from many children's favourite meal!

## 5. Fast food

### Group size
Small groups of three or four.

### Objective
To gather data concerning what fast food outlets sell.

### What you need
Pencils, paper, database facility.

### What to do
In any high street in the country, there is likely to be at least one fast food outlet of one type or another. A class visit to the high street with pencil and paper at the ready should generate lots of data about what they sell. The more outlets that can be visited, the better the perspective the children will gain.

Making a video of fast food outlets in the local street showing menus, advertisements and so on, would help the children to write down the information while remaining in the classroom. Tell them to list what the customer is given if, for example, he orders a 'cheeseburger with fries' or 'todays special'. Ask each group to focus on one of these meals.

Once back in school the work can be collated and analysed. This can be done using a computer and the children can organise their group's data and either present it in pictorial form or as a table of results. You could suggest they use the headings: mains, filler and so on.

They could also draw each meal, colour code it and perhaps produce the data as headed lists. This exercise can be repeated and data can be added to as the children explore different sources.

Once complete, the data needs to be looked at in groups and then as a class. What do fast foods contain most of? What do they lack?

## 6. Designs

### Group size
Individuals.

### Objective
To develop design ideas based on previous research.

### What you need
Pencils, paper.

### What to do
Having analysed fast food menus, the children should be more aware of the items that make up most fast food meals – principally mains and fillers. Ask the children to suggest how foods like a 'big burger with fries' can be made into a more balanced meal. They might think of having less chips and adding other vegetables such as a side salad or peas. Perhaps an apple or orange could be given away free with every meal?

Let the children evolve their own ideas, focusing on one of the many menus they have collected. They should explain how the meal is unbalanced and how it could be made more balanced by adding and taking away items.

## 7. Opinions

### Group size
Individuals.

### Objective
To research what others think about their modifications and to refine ideas.

### What you need
The design ideas developed in the previous activity.

### What to do
Having developed a clear idea about the changes each child would like to make, the next step is for the children to find out how realistic their changes would be. Would people buy their 'balanced meal'? If not, why not? What do the owners of the fast food restaurants think about the children's ideas? What other factors will affect whether people will buy/eat their proposed fast food?

There are many opportunities for the children to refine their ideas. Added interest can be provided if they present their initial ideas to an expert, such as the owner of a local café. If this is not

possible, then you can take on this role, raising the issues indicated above. Fellow pupils in class or around the school are also a good body on which to carry out market research. Even better would be to ask a cross-section of people 'in the street'. (If the latter was done it would have to be done under strict supervision.) Ask the children to devise their own questionnaire, perhaps producing it using a computer. It is important that they ask the 'right' questions and they will probably need some guidance.

Examples of 'good' questions include:
• Would you eat a burger and chips with any vegetable or only one type of vegetable? Name the vegetable.
• Would you eat an apple if given free with a burger meal? (YES/NO)

An example of a 'bad' question would be: 'Do you like burger and chips?' This type of question does not reveal any information about their design idea.

Finally, the children can use all their research to refine their individual ideas and produce a design proposal of their own.

## 8. Modelling

### Group size
Individuals.

### Objective
To make a three-dimensional model of a balanced meal.

### What you need
Modelling materials such as modelling clay, Plasticine, papier-mâché and so on.

### What to do
The children can work from their design proposals from the previous activity to create their meals. To actually manufacture a balanced meal using real food may not be feasible (if contacts are made during earlier activities then such possibilities may ensue), so this activity allows the children to manufacture a model of their balanced meal and display it either on paper plates or real plates. They may have had similar experiences in Activity 1, but the key difference here is in the extent of planning and preparation, building on initial skills.

There is no need to use a medium that is alien to the children, unless you intend to teach them a new skill. To save time, a more familiar medium can be chosen. Choosing familiar materials means that you can stress that you want the children's products to be of high quality in terms of accuracy, appearance and finish. Modelling clay is perhaps the easiest medium for children to work with. This can be shaped, fired or just left to dry and the children can experiment with different ways of painting and decorating to produce quality representation. Cocktail sticks attached to labels and added to the finished model, will give a better feel to the model showing how the children have thought about what has gone into their meal in terms of nutrition. Again, if the opportunity arises, 'experts' can be invited to view the finished models. Ask the children to design their own display, showing *all* their research and development work.

Food

## 9. Success?

### Group size
The whole class and individuals.

### Objective
To evaluate the designs.

### What you need
Pencils, paper.

### What to do
Evaluation in technology terms is concerned with how ideas develop, how decisions were made, and the processes undertaken. For example, ask the children to look at the problems they had in obtaining information. Did they obtain enough information initially? How well did the questionnaires work? How successful were they at getting in touch with the 'experts'? Could they have gone about their work in a different way and been more successful?

Finally, ask them to look at their final designs and make suggestions about how they met the needs which were first identified and then how they met the *needs* of the 'fast food' outlets.

# Community: food and health poster

### Age range
Nine to twelve

The activities in this section lead the children ultimately to design and make a poster about food and health. The context is the community, so the poster might be aimed at the local community or it could be about broader issues such as famine relief and therefore be aimed at a wider community. With the focus being on the community the children must concentrate their efforts to find needs and opportunities within the community to which they can assign the task of designing a poster. At this age level the children should be given as much freedom to direct the tasks as possible.

## 1. Famine

### Group size
The whole class.

### Objective
To raise the children's awareness of famine.

### What you need
Reference books about famine, word-processing facilities.

### What to do
Begin by discussing with the children what they understand by the word 'famine'. Which countries are most at risk? Why are they most at risk? What can be done to prevent famine? Encourage the children to seek answers to these questions, and others generated in the discussion.

Once they have built up a working knowledge of the issues involved, the children can then investigate other people's feelings on the subject. Ask them to devise a questionnaire designed to find out what people think about the key issues. This may be done as a group activity in twos or threes or as individuals. The questionnaires can then be put on a word processor and printed out for use.

Add the constraint of having to question a cross-section of the community, and introduce the idea of 'sampling' as a method. For example, one group of children may sample people over 40 years of age, another may ask teenagers, another may ask infant children and so on. If the work is shared across the class the data can be pooled for collective use.

To collect this data the children will have to go out into the 'street'. Choose a likely spot, perhaps in a precinct. Keep the children close, within sight, and take volunteers or extra staff for supervision. The children will need a clipboard or a book to lean on. Encourage them to be polite to the people they want to interview.

## 2. Habits

### Group size
Individuals.

### Objective
To gather data about people's eating habits.

### What you need
Pencils, paper, word processor.

### What to do
Ask the children to construct their own questionnaire consisting of about, ten questions, to find out what people eat, things that they like, dislike; things eaten most often; their favourite things and so on. You can advise the children if there is a need to modify their questions on the word processor before they save them on to disc and print them out. Add the constraint that they must sample a certain number of people or give them a specific age range to question.

Once the children have completed the questioning process they can collate the responses.

## 3. Analysis

### Group size
Individuals.

### Objective
To analyse the data from questionnaires and surveys.

### What you need
Computer with database facilities.

### What to do
Once the children have collated the responses from their questionnaires about eating habits or attitudes towards famine and famine relief, they can transfer this information on to a database. This database can be constructed by you or the children depending on the time available. For work on eating habits headings should include age, sex and then foods eaten, favourite foods and so on. For famine relief, headings might include 'Do people care?' and 'What images do they notice or not notice?' and so on.

From this information the children should be able to gain an insight into whether people have good or bad eating habits or whether the images used to portray famine have an impact, and to see whether any trends are apparent, such as 'too much fat/carbohydrate', 'too little fruit/vegetables' or 'young people do not notice the posters'. If the information gathered is not conclusive and difficult to see then you can point out the issues to the children. It is likely that many trends will be apparent, so that the children will have to make choices about what to design a poster for, for example, 'We have found out that young people take no notice of posters about famine therefore we are going to *design and make* a poster about famine so that young people will take notice'.

Having decided what they are going to design the children can work on a design brief.

## 4. Layouts

### Group size
Pairs and small groups.

### Objective
To investigate poster layouts.

### What you need
Various posters, advertisements, magazine front covers and so on.

### What to do
As an initial stimulus to designing the poster show the whole class examples of different types of posters and advertisements, drawing their attention to particular features, such as using large pictures, colour, the size of lettering, the number of words and so on. This is only intended to serve as a guide for the children and they can be given samples of posters from which to draw their own conclusions.

This work could be extended further by looking at posters around the school, in the street, in the health centre and so on. The children should begin to realise that it is not only the style of a poster that is important, but also how many are seen and the impact they have.

Once the children have finished this research they will have a sound basis for deciding what essential features their posters will have.

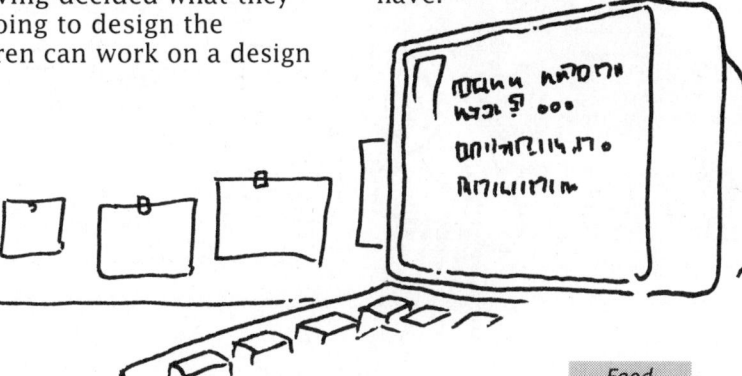

## 5. Proposals

### Group size
Individuals.

### Objective
To write a design proposal for a poster.

### What you need
Paper, pencils.

### What to do
Having carried out the initial investigations with respect to needs and opportunities in Activities 1 to 4, the children will have identified opportunities for designing a poster aimed at a particular sector of the community; for example: 'Old people do not eat enough fresh fruit' or 'Teenagers don't seem to care about famine'. Each child must now decide at whom she is aiming her poster. This will affect what the poster will contain, and the language and the images used.

Ask each child to make three or four rough sketches of layouts and design variations and from these sketches choose one design. This final sketch will act as their design proposal. Ask them to write about the ideas they rejected and why. It might also be possible for them to design their various layouts using a computer program.

## 6. Pictograms

### Group size
Individuals.

### Objective
To plan out and make the posters.

### What you need
Large sheets of paper, scissors, felt-tipped pens, crayons or paints, stencils.

### What to do
The design proposals that the children wrote out in the last activity must now be transcribed into the real thing. Ask the children to make a list of everything they will need to make their posters. They should organise this equipment as best they can on or around their tables before they start. What size will their posters be? What colours will they use? What medium will they use? You can add constraints by limiting the paper size and mediums to be used.

It is important that the children draw out their designs roughly in pencil before they paint, colour or stick as the work should be of high quality. Drawing a flow chart or pictogram showing the order they are going to work would be a useful task.

## 7. Evaluation

### Group size
Individuals or the whole class.

### Objective
To evaluate the posters.

### What you need
No special requirements.

### What to do
Now that the children's posters have been designed and made, it is important that the children test them. Does the poster work? Does it have impact? Do the people it is aimed at take notice of it? Does it put the message across? Ask the children to establish a list of criteria, perhaps in the form of a survey or questionnaire, to see how effective their designs are. This will provide fairly objective information. On the basis of this evidence, they should be encouraged to say how they might modify their designs.

One variable not covered by this work is the actual placing of the posters. Can they be seen at a distance? Can they be seen if they are surrounded by other posters? After this initial assessment the children may want to modify their posters.

# CHAPTER 2

## Textiles

Of all craft materials, textiles are perhaps the most familiar to the primary teacher. There has long been a tradition in primary schools of working with textiles – from embroidery to weaving, from tie and dye to batik. It would be a waste not to utilise these already acquired skills and talents. Perhaps, in textile craft, we have the best example of how technology differs from traditional craftwork. In the five sections in this chapter the craft skills required are likely to be familiar to most primary teachers. The range is from making simple flip-flop slippers for themselves to making 'model' school uniforms through to puppet shows, embroidery and patchwork blankets for people in need. However, it is the way in which 'the craft' is packaged and delivered to the pupils that is 'new'. The children will have to research and develop their ideas within a manufacturing situation.

Textiles

# ACTIVITIES

## Home: flip-flop slippers

### Age range
Five to eight.

As with many activities in the early years, these activities revolve around a role-play situation. Although the context of the earlier activities in this section is very much 'business' and manufacture, the real design and make context is targeted at 'the home' the people in it and the rules within it.

There are many skills introduced here, including the use of computers, research, cutting and so on, but it is interesting to note that traditional CDT jargon, such as joining, shaping and assembling, is applied to a textile medium without losing any of its intended meaning along the way. The main manufacturing aim of these activities is to make slippers from textile material.

## 1. Shoe shops

### Group size
Small groups of four or five.

### Objective
To set up a role-play situation.

### What you need
Shoes of various sizes and styles, boxes, shelves.

### What to do
Before the children set up the shoe shop ask them to think about where they buy their shoes. How are the shoes set out? Are they organised in colours or sizes? Are they separated into boys shoes and girls shoes? What happens when they visit a shoe shop? Do they have their feet measured? How are they measured? What sizes of shoes do they wear? This preliminary discussion serves to raise the children's awareness of shoes and shoe shops and to ascertain how much previous knowledge they bring to the activity.

Tell the children that they are going to set up a shoe shop in the classroom. Where would be the best place to put it (if, indeed, there is to be a choice)? How will they set out the shoes so that people can see them? Why will people need to see them? Use large upturned boxes covered with sugar paper or crêpe paper as shelves. Allocate each group a particular job. One group could set out and arrange the shelves/display. Another might set out the shoes in some sort of order. Another group can make a shoe gauge or equivalent, perhaps from construction kits. Other groups can draw and colour pictures of shoes and write literature to advertise and promote the shop and its contents.

Once the children have set up the shop they can begin a structured play exercise where they act as shop-keepers and customers, trying on and buying shoes. Ask the children who are playing customers to say why they have chosen one type of shoe in preference to another. Bring out issues such as style, colour, fashion, cultural needs and so on.

## 2. Shoe design

### Group size
Individuals and the whole class.

### Objective
To look at shoe construction.

### What you need
Pencils, paper, photocopiable page 168.

### What to do
Take one shoe from the shop and talk about how shoes are made, the names of the parts and how they are joined together. If it is possible, try to visit a shoe manufacturer or cobbler as this will help to broaden their experience.

Give each child a copy of photocopiable page 168 and ask them to colour the sole black, the heel red and the upper green. These are the important parts of a shoe which the children should be able to identify. Can they draw their favourite shoes and label the parts?

Having identified these parts the children can look at how they are joined together. Soles and heels may be glued on to the upper or nailed on using tacks. The upper parts are stitched together. Ask them to look carefully, perhaps using a hand lens or magnifying glass, at the stitching and point out the different parts that make up the upper.

## 3. Collecting data

### Group size
Pairs.

### Objective
To measure feet and record data.

### What you need
Rulers, pencils, paper, measuring tape.

### What to do
Children are likely to be familiar with their own shoe sizes, but if not, they may be able to discover what it is by checking for the number printed in or on the soles of their shoes. Do all the children in the class have the same size? If not, why not? Are all the children's feet different widths as well?

The concept of foot size is applied to length and width, so the children need to be introduced to these terms and know how to recognise them. Ask them to work in pairs and draw around one of their partner's feet. Then, using this outline, they can measure the length and width of their own feet. If they have never used a ruler or tape-measure before, they will need to be shown them from where on the measure to start recording.

The data obtained can be collated and shown as a bar chart or alternatively, the children can record their data on a computer as part of a draw program, or collectively on a database storage and retrieval program. Ask them what they notice about the data. Is one size predominant? Do girls have larger feet than the boys?

## 4. Searching for uses

### Group size
The whole class and then individuals.

### Objective
To identify opportunities for making flip-flop slippers.

## What you need
Pencils, paper, flip-flop shoes.

## What to do
The children have looked at shoes, how they are made and how they are sold. They know how to measure feet. Now introduce the idea that they are going to make a pair of shoes themselves. Show them the flip-flop shoe, and ask them to describe it in terms of construction. Tell them to point out the sole, upper and heel and to find out how it is joined and from what materials it is made.

Having examined the shoe's construction ask the children to think in what way such flip-flop shoes might be useful. At home are they allowed to walk through the house with their outdoor shoes on? If not, why not? What about wet feet when they have a shower or bath?

Introducing such ideas will stimulate discussions and generate many ideas. Let them write a brief statement, about why and for whom they would make a pair of shoes; for example: 'I am going to make shoes for my sister, because she is always being moaned at for bringing dirt into the house on her shoes!' They may want to represent this as a picture instead of writing it, but either way it can be used as a design brief.

# 5. Research and development

## Group size
Individuals.

## Objective
To research foot sizes and other needs.

## What you need
Pencils, paper, rulers, tracing paper, card.

## What to do
The children will have to carry out some research at home to find out the length and width of the person's foot for whom they are making flip-flops. Ask them to find out what colours that person likes and which materials they would or would not wear. Once they have found out all this information the children need to write it down or draw it so that they will be able to use it later on. Emphasise the importance of drawing around both feet and, in class, question them as to whether both feet were the same size. It is likely that there will be some variation in size, but most significantly you should point out the difference between left and right feet. How can they recognise a left foot from a right foot?

Show the children how to use tracing paper to transfer their drawings to card and make a template. Card is the best medium to use for a template as it is more rigid than paper and thereby easier to draw around, particularly when young children are working.

# 6. Making a mock-up

## Group size
Individuals.

## Objective
To refine the design brief.

## What you need
Card, pencils, scissors, staples, pins.

## What to do
Before the children embark upon making their shoes it would be useful for them to make a mock-up of the flip-flop first. They can use their templates as guides and cut strips of card to act as the bridge across the foot. The children should make the strips of card longer than the measurement they took for the width of the feet so that the person's feet will be able to slide in and out of the shoes easily. They can staple these strips to the sole and take them home so that they can be tested for size.

Also ask the children to think of at least five ideas for

varying the shape and design of the strips, for example, they could use two thinner bands or have a band with a scalloped edge. They should draw these on paper so that when they take the mock-up home they can also ask the consumer which they prefer and why.

Once armed with all this information the children can refine their ideas about size and design before they start to make their flip-flop shoes.

## 7. Which materials to use?

### Group size
Small groups of three or four.

### Objective
To research from what material to make the shoes.

### What you need
Scissors, various materials such as paper, card, felt, plastic, fabric and so on.

### What to do
Depending on the time and resources available let the children explore the different properties of a variety of materials. They will have to explore a variety of properties.
• Do they tear easily?
• Are they rigid or floppy?
• What happens if they get wet?

Let them research each property in turn, perhaps with each group choosing to look at one property or one type of material. They should record their results and these can be looked at as a class. Ask the children to decide which materials they would not use, giving their reasons why; for example, paper tears easily, and cotton is too floppy. They may need considerable guidance in this, depending on the variety of materials available. It is important that you only put out those materials that the children can actually manufacture from. It is pointless putting out leather if there is not enough to go round!

The final choice should be based on reasoning – 'this one because it is the strongest' or 'because it is the best colour' or 'it's the easiest to work with, especially cutting and sticking'.

## 8. Joining materials

### Group size
Small groups of three to four.

### Objective
To develop skills in joining materials.

### What you need
Needle, thread, sticky tape, adhesive, stapler, photocopiable page 169.

### What to do
Ask the children to think of as many ways of joining materials as they can. Using the choices of material that were made in the previous activity, ask them to explore each method of joining (or those methods you wish them to choose from). If sewing is chosen, the children may need a little instruction first so that they can succeed in stitching pieces together.

They will need to join the pieces together and then test the join by trying to pull them apart. Which method is the strongest? The children should record their results and analyse them, choosing which method works best with their chosen material.

The children will now have completed their research. Ask them to draw a design proposal based on their research, using photocopiable page 169 as a guide. Whatever they write on their proposals they will have to convert into manufacture.

## 9. Making to size

### Group size
Individuals.

### Objective
To make their flip-flop shoes.

### What you need
Materials (see Activity 7), scissors, fixing materials (see previous activity), chalk.

### What to do
The children will have all the necessary information and skills needed to make their flip-flop shoes by this stage. The first stage in the manufacturing process will be to select their material. Make sure that you cut the material into suitably sized pieces beforehand so that wastage is minimised. Show the children how to mark around their templates on the material using pen, pencil or chalk (for felt) and mark out the strips for the bridges. Once marked out these pieces can be cut out so that they are ready for assembly. If the materials are fairly stiff or thick the children may need some help doing this. The children can then join the pieces together as their proposals: again help may be required to achieve this.

As they are working ask them to explain what they are doing and why. Encourage them to focus on cutting and drawing so that they maintain a high quality and degree of accuracy at all times.

**NB:** if sharp fabric scissors are used, these must be strictly supervised to avoid accidents.

## 10. Do they fit?

### Group size
The whole class and individuals.

### Objective
To evaluate the finished product.

### What you need
Pencils, paper.

### What to do
The first evaluatory task will be for each child or a selected few to talk about what they have done, how they have made the shoe, problems they encountered and so on. They should be encouraged to look at each others work and say what they like or dislike about it. This can be done as a whole class activity.

The next stage will be for the children to take their shoes home and try them out. Do they fit? Does the person like them? Are there any problems? Do they do the job required?

When the children return to school they can record this information either as a piece of writing or as a drawing.

# School: school uniforms

### Age range
Seven to nine.

One of the most common misconceptions in technology is the idea of 'modelling'. To most this means using construction kits to 'make' models of something, following a fixed set of instructions. However, modelling is much more than this. Models are principally 'working ideas' used while generating and developing ideas. The activities in this section use two aspects of modelling: computer modelling and the development of a model as an 'end product'.

Not all schools have a uniform if this is the case then the following activities can easily be adapted to suit, for example, the brownies uniform, the PE kit or even the uniform worn by the staff in places like MacDonalds!

# 1. What's wrong with our uniform?

## Group size
Small groups of three or four.

## Objective
To evaluate uniform in school.

## What you need
Pencils, paper, word-processing and database facility.

## What to do
Explain to the children that they are going to conduct a survey to find out people's views on school uniform. If your school has no uniform then the survey can be aimed at finding out whether the pupils would like a school uniform or not. This same survey might be carried out on teachers and/or parents as the target group. If the school already has a uniform the emphasis of the questions will be on change. To encourage their usage of the computer, ask the children to think of five questions they might ask to find out people's views about school uniforms. Add the constraint that the answers must be simple, for example:
• Would you want a school uniform? Y/N.
• If we had a uniform what colour(s) would you like? Red/blue/green.
• Would you want a school tie? Y/N.
• Would you want a school badge? Y/N.
   Or if there is already a uniform:
• Do you like the present school uniform? Y/N.
• What would you change?
– Colour? Y/N. To what?
– Remove blazer? Y/N.

Try to get the children to think of their own questions and only supplement them if they appear to be struggling. They can use a word-processing package on the computer to write and print out their questionnaires. These can then be photocopied and left with people to complete and be collected later.

Tell the children to sample a maximum of about 20 people – too many or too few will cause statistical problems. The results can then be analysed and ideas for designing a new uniform or making changes to a uniform can be drawn from them. It may be possible for you to generate a database with headings such as 'Uniform Y/N', 'Colour?', 'Tie? Y/N' and so on. Then groups of children can enter the data as they collect it, putting it under the appropriate column.

# 2. Modifying the uniform

## Group size
Small groups of three or four.

## Objective
To identify possible modifications and/or new opportunities to design and make.

## What you need
Pencils, paper.

## What to do
Having studied the results of the survey the children can assess whether there appears to be a need for change. For example, the survey may reveal that people prefer one colour to the one that exists already. A change may be something as simple as a change of colour or as profound as having a uniform where none previously existed. The children must utilise their creative aspects. The survey will provide a stimulus for ideas, and for further research if necessary. Its results need not be adhered to exactly, so long as its influence is apparent in the children's work.

Ask the children to look also at style and fashion ideas that are popular and compare these to the results of the survey. For example, they might want to introduce baseball caps as compulsory uniform or a summer outfit based around Bermuda shorts and T-shirts.

Again, the possibilities are endless, but the children may need to be encouraged to look 'further' than what they first perceive as being the 'correct' answer, in other words, the answer they think the teacher would like to have. As it is only a 'model' that they are working towards, there is no real need to restrict their creative talents.

## 3. Computer – aided designs

### Group size
Pairs.

### Objective
To generate computer aided designs of possible school uniforms.

### What you need
A computer with a 'draw' or 'paint' facility.

### What to do
Most school computers have a draw and paint facility. After a demonstration showing the children how to control the screen and what goes on it, they should be encouraged to use the results of their data analysis to come up with some ideas about changes to the school uniform.

The advantage of working with computer graphics is that the colouring facility provides instant success, and the bright colours have an instant impact. The main drawback is likely to be the printing facilities, with colour pictures printing out in black and white and shades of grey. The only real way to overcome this is for the children to paint the colours they see on screen on to the print-outs.

If the children have lots of ideas for changes to a uniform ask each group to focus on one idea. For example, one group may work exclusively on school ties, while another may work on a school badge, and a different group on school sports wear. You may have to provide some constraints, for example, everyone may have to agree on which colours have to be used, but there will be ample scope for individual flair within each chosen area. The pupils can then be brought together to evaluate other designs, offering their own opinions about what could be or might be (or should be) done.

## 4. Asking opinions

### Group size
Small groups of three or four.

### Objective
To gauge opinion about computer-aided design.

### What you need
Word processor with desk top publishing facility.

### What to do
Having generated a number of computer-aided designs the next step will be for the children to find out what other people think of their designs and perhaps choose one as their favourite. Again, using a word-processing facility, they should think up and print out a number of questions to ask certain target groups; for example:
• Which designs do you prefer? A, B, C or D?
• Do you like the colour? Y/N.
• Do you like the style? Y/N.

They should try to keep their questions brief and aim to sample about 20 to 25 people in total. Once the information has been collected they can again analyse the results. For example, they might find that 20 out of 25 people preferred design 'D', or 16 out of 25 people liked the style. Where the evidence is conclusive the children should be encouraged to take those ideas on board.

Some pupils will need advice about what the results are telling them and initially you can help them by getting them to add up the number of 'Yes' and 'No' answers or the equivalent. The problem comes, however, where the evidence is inconclusive – if ten people say 'yes' and ten say 'no'. If time is available, ask the children to sample a few more people in order to tip the scales one way or another, or to use their own instincts to come up with a decision.

## 5. Studying dimensions

### Group size
Pairs.

### Objective
To draw up a final design proposal.

### What you need
A computer with a computer-aided design facility.

### What to do
Using the information they gathered in the previous activity, the children can now work exclusively on one design. Ask them to keep their other ideas as research and development work.

The next stage of their design proposal will be to consider the dimensions, lengths and widths of each part of their proposed clothing. This can be done on screen, after they have had the opportunity to develop the skills required. It is likely that what is displayed on screen will not print out exactly the same size on paper. Anyway, these measurements need not be too precise; rather the process is intended to raise awareness of drawing to scale.

It may also be possible for the children to suggest likely materials for manufacture of the garment but this is not really the main issue, and might confuse their activity in terms of designing.

Once they have printed out the illustration of their final piece of clothing they will have to paint and label it, providing reasons for using the parts shown. As a separate exercise ask them to write a few sentences about how they explored their ideas, which ideas they have not chosen and why, as well as those they have chosen with their reasons for choosing them. Finally, ask them to write a couple of sentences about how realistic their design proposal is.
• Could it be made?
• Could they make it?
• If they made it what skills would they need?
• Do they need those skills?

Ask them to comment on how using a computer to draw, compares with drawing pictures using pencils and paper.

## 6. Templates

### Group size
Pairs.

### Objective
To introduce the use of a template and to plan work.

### What you need
Card, scissors, paper, pencils, photocopiable pages 170.

### What to do
In this activity the intention is for the children to generate their design proposals into models, using a card manikin. The children should use the template on photocopiable page 170 to make their manikins. They will need to be shown how to fix paper cut-out models of their designs on to these card manikins. This is done by leaving tabs at various points on the outline as they draw. These tabs can then be folded over the card template to hold the garment in place.

Let them experiment with this technique before they plan their manufacturing sequence.

It may be necessary for you to put a list of things that the children will need to do on the board, but perhaps in a jumbled order for them to reorganise. The list will be something like this:
• Make a list of equipment needed.
• Collect the template and other equipment on the list.
• Draw the design to scale and proportion so that it doesn't look too big or too small for the template.
• Put tabs on the design drawing.
• Print out the design.
• Colour the design in.
• Cut out the design.
• Put the design cut-outs on the template.

Textiles

## 7. Making the designs

### Group size
Individuals or pairs.

### Objective
To make their design using paper and the card templates.

### What you need
Scissors, pencils, rulers, felt-tipped pens or crayons.

### What to do
Having planned and organised their work the children can now make their designs from paper. They should be encouraged to aim for high quality in their work which means that they should try to draw and measure accurately, cutting out neatly and colouring within the lines.

Although not obviously apparent, the hand tools used here are as appropriate to craft-based manufacture as any. All craftspeople have to be able to measure out and mark accurately, cut out accurately and finish their work properly. In this respect, 'paper' is an ideal starting medium for developing all these skills. However, an alternative to working with paper might be to use white cloth and this can be painted, drawn on and dyed. Also working with real fabric makes the exercise more realistic, but will cause problems when colouring and fixing on to the template. Material flaps will not be as easy to attach to a template as paper ones and they may have to be pinned.

It is also important when working with materials to see that they are stored safely and maintained properly. The children should be encouraged to put things away tidily – pencils in blocks or trays, scissors in boxes or hung up and so on. Ask them to look at their equipment before they use it. Pencils should be sharp, so too should the scissors. Rulers should be straight and clearly marked for measuring.

## 8. How well did it go?

### Group size
Individuals.

### Objective
To evaluate the finished project through presentation.

### What you need
Pencils, paper.

### What to do
Having completed the design and manufacturing process the children should evaluate all aspects of their work – the processes used, the computer-aided design program, the word processor, the skills they learned and used, and any problems they faced and how they solved them.

The children should display their work so that the rest of the class can view it and write up what they did and how they came up with their ideas and made their decisions. This information can form the basis of a short talk or presentation, to the rest of the class, the headteacher or the whole school, perhaps during assembly. As part of such a presentation they should highlight the fact that knowing what other people thought of their ideas played a significant part in the process.

This process can be continued by leaving a blank piece of paper with each design or a few questions for people to answer. This information will generate more ideas for modifications. It can be pointed out that designs for clothing are constantly changing to suit changing needs and fashions.

# Recreation: glove puppet show

## Age range
Eight to ten.

The principal context for technologists in this section is recreation. This does not mean that the activities are intended to be used just for 'fun'. It means that the needs and opportunities that are being sought are based within a recreational context. Other aspects of the activities in this section are the introduction of 'sewing' as a skill and the development of a presentational show as a finished product. Essentially, the children will work as a team to produce the show, but will work individually on designing and making their own puppets.

## 1. Puppet show ideas

### Group size
The whole class and small groups.

### Objective
To brainstorm ideas for a puppet show.

### What you need
Pencils, paper.

### What to do
Tell the children that they are going to perform a puppet show, and that they are going to make the puppets for the show. Ask them to think of all the things that they will need to find out in order to do both tasks. Ask them to think of at least five items they will have to research before they make the puppets and put on the show. Some children may need some guidance to help them in the form of questions; for example:
• Who will the show be for?
• What will the show be about?
• Why are they doing the show (for entertainment; for educational reasons; perhaps to teach about safety)?
• What sort of puppet, or puppet features do they have in mind?
• What are other puppet shows like?
• What skills will be needed?

Undoubtedly the list is endless, but with these few questions and some of their own they will have enough guidance to begin their investigations.

You can structure what and when they investigate, by itemising a number of the most important questions, say the best five, and giving small groups an allotted time to research them. Doing it this way reduces demands on limited resources. Alternatively, encourage each of the children to research one question. This can be done by negotiation within the teams, each child being allocated a task to investigate and research further.

## 2. Compiling a database

### Group size
Small groups of three or four.

### Objective
To devise ways of gathering information.

### What you need
Computer with database and word-processing facilities; pencils and paper.

### What to do
Each child will now have a specific job to do and it is up to her to think of a way(s) to investigate her chosen area. For example, if a child decides to research other puppet shows, she may need access to books and/or puppeteers so

Textiles

that she can find out further details about puppetry. Another child may choose to carry out a survey of a particular target group (perhaps younger pupils, or his own peer group) asking what they would like to see in a puppet show.

If a computer with word-processing and database facilities is made available the children can plan and write out their questions, then record the details on disc for future reference. Other children in the group, may begin to sketch and draw possible puppet features, looking at existing puppets for ideas.

## 3. Research and development

### Group size
Individuals and small groups.

### Objective
To begin their research and develop ideas.

### What you need
Pencils, paper, computer with database and word-processing facilities.

### What to do
Having decided on what to research and how to gather that data, the children must now set about 'doing'. However, before they get going, check that each child knows what she is trying to achieve – a quick glance at a list of questions that they have prepared should suffice.

Give the children a fixed amount of time in which to gather data, for example, a block of time in each day, say 20 minutes, or an hour during one week. Alternatively, they may be allocated one whole block, say a morning. Time checks will be valuable to hurry the plodders and to help extend those who tend to rush to much. Once their time is up encourage them to analyse the information generated.

Talk to the children about the importance of obtaining reliable and representative information. If they have only asked five people in a survey is this really enough? They should try to survey a minimum of 20 people as this will give them lots of data to analyse and will make any patterns, links and trends more apparent. Ask the children to store this data (on disc if it is relevant to do so) and if they need to, carry out any further research.

Children researching puppet shows will need to look in books or perhaps contact a local puppeteer and interview him. Historically, there are lots of types of show to choose from, for example, Punch and Judy and shadow puppet theatre. Stories such as 'Pinnochio' are also good starting points for getting ideas and so are television shows such as *Thunderbirds*. When watching or reading these stories the children should look at which characters are good and bad; the design of the puppets, storylines and background scenery.

## 4. Looking for patterns

### Group size
Individuals and small groups.

### Objective
To analyse data gathered.

### What you need
Ring binder, results from the previous activity.

### What to do
Having spent time assimilating data, the next step is for the children to analyse it, looking for patterns, links and ideas. To structure this activity ask each child to explain what he has researched and what he has found out from this research. This can be done as a whole class exercise, with each child being given a couple of minutes to present their findings.

Having focused the children's attention on their work they should be encouraged to look further into it, this time working as a team. Ask them to come up with an idea for each of the following questions:
• What is the puppet show going to be about?
• Who is the puppet show for?
• How many characters will there be?
• What characteristics will each puppet have?

The questions identified in Activity 1 may be used again but this time the children have to justify their choices, so ask them why they have chosen these particular ideas. It is important that they begin to realise that choices and decisions need to be based on something more than *ad hoc* guesswork – even if it is simply 'because I/we like that character best'.

Finally, ask each child to list ideas that they rejected and give their reasons why they rejected them. The purpose for doing this is so that they will have time to reflect and review their decisions, examining them from other angles.

All the work and details from Activities 1 to 4 should

be kept together in a file to show how the children's ideas developed.

## 5. Sewing skills

### Group size
Individuals.

### Objective
To develop sewing skills.

### What you need
Needles, thread, buttons, cotton, fabric, examples of sock puppets.

### What to do
By this stage some children will already have a clear idea of what they want their puppet to be like; others will have no idea. However, it is likely that the children's ideas will be quite complex and therefore, difficult to manufacture. At this point you should add the constraint that all the puppets will have to be sock puppets.

Show the children one or two examples of sock puppets to demonstrate the possibilities of such a puppet. However, before the children can start to design and make such a puppet, they will need to know how to sew. Knowing how to sew on buttons is perhaps the most important skill for the children to learn, although other items can be stitched on as well. If you decide against sewing on hair, eyebrows, tongues and so on choose a light coloured sock and let the children draw on it.

Once the children have had sufficient time to practise sewing, they can be encouraged to use this skill in their ideas for the development of a puppet character.

**NB:** it is important to stress to the children that needles are dangerous and must be handled with care and stored away safely afterwards.

## 6. Developing a design

### Group size
Individuals and small groups.

### Objective
To generate a design proposal for a puppet.

### What you need
A computer with a graphics facility, paper, coloured felt-tipped pens and crayons.

### What to do
The children should have, by now, a good idea of what their puppet show is going to be about and at whom it will be targeted. They should therefore begin to think about this when developing their sock puppets. Although they are producing their puppets individually the children will be working in teams to produce the puppet show and therefore they will have to consult with their partners as they develop their ideas. To begin with, ask them to think of a few faces. They can draw these on paper or use a computer to sketch the pictures. They can then print them out and colour them in. Tell them to look at the body proportions of humans and animals, and then show them how cartoons and caricatures exaggerate certain features.

Once the children have explored these concepts they can try modelling their ideas on actual socks. They can stick features to the sock with sticky tape, using card or paper shapes to represent the features. By modelling in this way before making the puppets they will be able to develop ideas as they work.

Once they have finished their models they can produce a design proposal to show how

Textiles

they are going to construct the actual puppet, what it will look like, the equipment and resources they will need and the time they think it will take to make.

## 7. Planning the show

### Group size
Small groups of three or four.

### Objective
To plan the puppet show.

### What you need
Paper, pencils.

### What to do
The children will now almost be at the stage of making their puppets and putting on the show. However, they will need to plan:

- what their set is going to look like;
- whether there will be a script;
- who is going to say what;
- whether there will be any props.

If there is going to be a script the children will have to write down:
- what each character will say;
- when and in what order these speeches appear;
- the actions that accompany the speech.

Alternatively to avoid the tedium of writing scripts the children might *ad lib*, using the basis of a story as their own starting point. There is no real need to produce high quality props and sets, unless you have lots of time available. Tell the children that they can make props from paper, card, construction kits and junk material. However, they will need to be organised and set out a plan for making all these additions as well as their puppets. How much time do they think they will need to make all these things? They can work together in small groups or apportion tasks.

At the end of this planning session the children should have produced:
- a picture(s) of their stage set;
- a script;
- a list of resources needed.

## 8. Making the show

### Group size
Individuals and small groups.

### Objective
To set about making a puppet show.

### What you need
Card, colours, socks, needle and thread, buttons, felt, various pieces of extra fabric.

### What to do
Having sorted out who is doing what, the equipment and resources that they need and the time available, the children will be ready to begin the manufacturing process. This can be done as a class activity or in small groups, setting aside a work area.

It must be stressed to the children that they must not waste materials by cutting out from the centre and ruining whole pieces of card and other material. You can help to avoid this by giving out limited resources and telling the children to work within these constraints.

It is also important that the children follow their design proposals closely and assessment should be based on how closely they follow their own proposals.

It is likely that the children will not have covered every detail in their design proposals and if any unforeseen problems arise you should let them try to solve them on their own, unless their is a serious safety risk or a chance of gross misuse of materials. In this situation, you should provide guidance before instruction.

Once complete, all their work should be finished properly and all equipment should be cleared and tidied away.

## 9. The performance

### Group size
Small groups of three or four.

### Objective
To carry out and evaluate puppets and the puppet show.

### What you need
Puppets and props from the previous activity; pencils, paper.

### What to do
The groups of children will now have to put on their puppet shows for their chosen target groups. Once the shows are over, tell them to ask their audiences what they liked or disliked about the shows, the puppets, the sets, the stories and so on. Can they think of any ways they might improve on it? The children should write down what their audiences say or present them with questionnaires. You could also video the shows so that evaluation can take place at a later date.

This gathering of evaluatory material will then form the basis of a larger evaluation task, which will include a preview of how the children developed their ideas, where the problems were, how they might tackle the task differently if they were to do it again and so on.

They must also review the decision making process used to come up with their final puppet and show.
• Was the design proposal used closely?
• Were changes made?
• If so, why were they made?
• Did others dictate/domineer or were decisions arrived at amicably?
• Why was one material used in preference to another?

They may choose to present this information as a handwritten or word-processed piece of work.

# Business: embroidered designs

### Age range
Nine to twelve.

The context for the activities in this section is business. They are intended to simulate the development of an artefact (a tapestry) and assess its viability as a 'marketable product'.

Embroidery work is a traditional craft that has had a long association with primary education and the first activity is a typical 'craft type' exercise aimed at developing basic manufacturing skills. It is also important to note that *all* aspects of the children's work, from their initial ideas through to evaluation should be kept by the children as part of the activity. This in itself will aid evaluation and also provide a framework for assessment.

## 1. How to embroider

### Group size
Individuals.

### Objective
To develop skills in embroidery.

### What you need
Needles, canvas, various colours of relevant thread, examples of tapestry work.

### What to do
Start this project work by showing the children what a tapestry looks like. Show them the canvas and how the holes are placed symmetrically, ready to sew the thread through. Ask them how the thread might be stopped from going straight through the holes; this will establish the idea of knotting the thread at one end. Showing them a variety of embroidered tapestries from simple linear shapes to more complicated 'tapestry' pictures will introduce the scope available to them once they have mastered the basic techniques.

To introduce the children to the basic techniques ask them to work on rectangles of small pieces of canvas, creating a simple border using a basic running stitch, and adding a slightly more complicated pattern in the central region.

Introduce the basic cross-stitc, if you have time, as it is a good stitch to use when creating more complex tapestry pictures.

Finally, show the children how to 'finish off' a piece of work by threading their needles behind the stitches. At all times encourage accuracy and quality of presentation.

Stress the fact that children should take great care when using needles and they should store them safely. Encourage them to avoid wastage, using threads completely and not throwing away 'mistakes'. Encourage persistence and perseverance.

Once they have completed their samplers, ask the children to produce a storyboard account of how to embroider. This will be useful in later work.

## 2. Looking for markets

### Group size
Individuals or small groups.

### Objective
To evaluate how embroidered goods are used.

### What you need
Catalogues and magazines.

### What to do
Having been introduced to embroidery and examples of tapestry work, the next stage is to ask the children how these might be used. Tell them that they are going to form a business either in small groups or as individuals, which will design and make embroidered materials for sale to the public. However, before they begin, they must identify likely markets for their product.

- Who would buy it?
- Why would they buy it?
- What function would the tapestry perform?

As an initial stimulus the children can brainstorm as a class how such tapestries may be used or are already used. With this information they can then set about researching their possible markets. You can help them by supplying a few questions.

- What are embroidered items used for at present?
- What new uses can they think of?
- Where are they going to get their data from?

To find answers to the last question, they should look at catalogues and magazines and perhaps go on a visit into town to see which types of shop sell embroidered materials and what those materials are used for. They might also be directed to look at cultural influences, and visit a local museum to research how embroidery has been used historically.

## 3. Setting up a database

### Group size
Pairs and small groups.

### Objective
To build up a database of information.

### What you need
A computer with database facilities.

### What to do
The children will have gathered a wide variety of data from the previous activity, including, pictorial evidence, prices of goods, lists of products and materials used. This initial research may well have resulted in them having to rethink their initial research. For example, they may have found little data about ranges of products, but they may have discovered that a variety of different materials have been used. Ask them to create a database, of their results. These results should be appropriately titled, with groups and lists of data correctly headed.

As their research develops, new lists may be needed or old ones may become obsolete. The children may have to return to existing data to review it and refine it as their ideas change and develop. They should be encouraged to look closely at the data, initially recording everything, but as time progresses they should select only the data that is relevant to their own work.

## 4. Testing materials

### Group size
Pairs and small groups.

### Objective
To research properties of different materials.

### What you need
A selection of different material such as cotton, nylon, wool, leather, plastic and so on; various different types of thread and canvas, kettle, water, photocopiable page 171.

### What to do
The children will have, by this stage, looked at likely markets, surveyed existing products and evaluated patterns and styles. Ask them to investigate the different properties of various materials. To do this they can carry out the following tests:
• What happens when hot items are placed on the material? (This can be done using boiling water in a plastic cup or a metal pan, but care must be taken to ensure safe working procedures here!)
• What happens when the material is soaked in water? Does it get weaker?
• When the material dries does it twist and buckle or lose its shape?
• Does the material stain?
• Is the material washable or not?

The children should use this information to build up a picture of which materials are available to them and what the limitations of each material is. They can record their results on the worksheet on photocopiable page 171. Also on this sheet are questions that will help them to interpret the data. Again, this is likely to influence their ideas and possibly generate new angles for research.

## 5. Computer-aided design

### Group size
Individuals.

Textiles 55

## *Objective*
To develop a design proposal using computer-aided design.

## *What you need*
A computer with a graphics facility, coloured pencils or felt-tipped pens, paper.

## *What to do*
Having carried out all their research the children should have a number of ideas in mind for what their business will make and sell. They can now look at what they are going to design. Will it be a floral picture, a random pattern, a symmetrical design, or perhaps a more complicated tapestry such as a picture of a footballer, a ballet dancer or horse? Ask the children to generate two or three possible designs using a computer or paper and pencils. Having done this, tell them to alter aspects of their designs such as the shade or other features.

The children should then devise a simple questionnaire to find out which design the 'market' prefers. They should question a minimum of about 30 to 40 people to obtain an acceptable sample. Armed with this information the children will be able to refine their ideas and move towards generating a design proposal.

# 6. Coming up with a design

## *Group size*
Individuals.

## *Objective*
To generate a design proposal.

## *What you need*
Paper, pencils, crayons

## *What to do*
The children should now be in a position to generate a design proposal. Ask them to do this in the form of a picture with labels. The labels should indicate, the materials that will be used (type of canvas, thread and so on) and the colours and the design. If each item is numbered, then the children can write out their reasons for their choices on a separate piece of paper. For example, they may have chosen red as a background because it was the most popular choice for their survey. Perhaps they have chosen wool thread because it washes better than other fibres, or not chosen nylon because they are making a teapot mat and nylon would melt.

As a class, discuss the criteria that affected choices; for example:
• The use of embroidered artefact will be....
• The market identified is... because....
• The equipment to be used is....
• ...has been chosen because....

It is important that the children understand the term 'market'. It is also important that the progress of all their ideas has been recorded as they have developed so that when final choices are made they can be justified.

# 7. Drawing a storyboard

## *Group size*
Individuals.

## *Objective*
To plan what they intend to do as a storyboard or flow-chart.

## *What you need*
Paper, pencils.

## *What to do*
As the children's ideas have developed you will have influenced the resources which they intend to use; for example, leather strips may have been too costly or only canvas with large holes and embroidery thread were available.

Ask the children to write a plan of what they are going to do. They can do this in the form of a storyboard if time is available, or as a flow chart, or as a combination of both techniques. They should also write out a list of resources they will need. This can be checked by you so that disappointments can be avoided when the children come to manufacture the items. For each stage in the plan ask them to estimate a possible time factor. This may be as short as a minute or as long as a couple of hours.

Finally, ask them to highlight areas in the plan where they feel that safety or hazards are an issue.

## 8. Making for the markets

### Group size
Individuals.

### Objective
To make their embroidered designs.

### What you need
Canvas, embroidery threads (plus other materials listed in Activity 7) needles, scissors.

### What to do
The children should place their design proposals in front of them when making their designs. As they work, encourage them to take account of safe working practice and pay attention to detail. They should be encouraged to finish their work properly and tidy up each time they complete a stage.

This manufacturing process is likely to take the children a while to finish. Ask them to note down the actual time they take as this will be useful when they come to evaluate their working procedures. If problems occur while they work ask them to solve these themselves as far as it is safe for them to do so. For example, they may run short of one type of thread; what will they do? Will they use a different colour? Start again with a new colour? Leave it blank till later? You should help them to formulate their own decisions through guidance, unless of course the problem they are faced with causes severe concern and distress, in question, in which case you should intervene.

## 9. Making judgements

### Group size
Individuals.

### Objective
To evaluate the finished artefacts and working procedures.

### What you need
Pencils, paper.

### What to do
Once complete the children should evaluate what they have made. Encourage them to lay down some criteria so that they can begin to understand the concept of assessment. A brief brainstorming session should supply a range of criteria for them to choose from, for example, appearance (How does the piece look in terms of style and colour?) and making (Was the artefact easy to make?). Remind them that the intention of the whole project was to look for an embroidered product that might sell in the shops. So how does their product match up to the ideas they laid down as they searched for new opportunities (Activities 2, 3, and 4) and as they generated a design proposal (Activities 5 and 6)? What working time was needed to make one? How long do they think they would need to make more than one?

Give the children an arbitrary cost on their time per hour, for example £1.00, and ask them to add this to the cost of the canvas per square metre and thread per packet. From this data they should be able to work out the outline cost of each item. How much would they need to charge for the item if they wanted to 'break even'? What would they need to charge to make a profit?

Ask the children to evaluate their working procedures. If they were going to produce large amounts of these embroidered items, how might the work be made more efficient? Depending on the age and ability of the children one or more of these evaluatory ideas could be utilised.

# Community: patchwork blanket

## Age range
Nine to twelve.

Making a patchwork blanket involves knitting small squares and sewing them together to make a large blanket. The activities in this section utilise this simple craft technique, but in a technological context – that of developing an artefact for someone in need in the community. Although the craft skills may appear simple, the research and development work is quite demanding, and in keeping with children of this age.

## 1. Patchwork ideas

### Group size
The whole class and small groups.

### Objective
To brainstorm ideas about who might need a patchwork quilt.

### What you need
Pencils, paper, a patchwork blanket.

### What to do
It would be useful if you could begin this activity showing the children an example of a patchwork blanket. Show them how the blanket is made up from small knitted squares which have been sewn together to make a larger unit. Explain to them that this idea is often used as way of providing something people need. Why do they think that people might need the blankets? In small groups the children can brainstorm a few ideas about the type of people who might have a use for such a blanket. All over the world there are people who may be cold and hungry. The children can work in their groups to make a list of a few of these and then work as a class to pool their ideas.

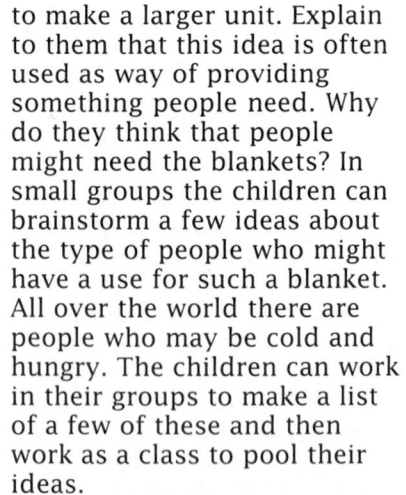

It is likely that many ideas will overlap. This in itself is no real problem and you can take this opportunity to narrow the focus. Quite often an incident reported on the news at the time of doing this activity will prompt a concentrated response, again this is not a problem, indeed it helps to give a real 'edge' to their work, fuelling motivation.

## 2. Search for needs and opportunities

### Group size
Pairs and small groups.

### Objective
To research possible needs and opportunities.

### What you need
Access to research materials such as books, encyclopaedias, magazines and newspapers.

### What to do
Depending on the ideas that were brainstormed in the previous activity the children will need to research in more detail, one or a number of

possible avenues for development. Their list is likely to include old people, the homeless, people in disaster areas such as those where an earthquake has taken place and so on. They may also know that in hot desert regions, the temperature falls dramatically at night and this vast change in temperature can cause severe physical trauma. Introduce the word 'hypothermia' as an avenue for possible research.

Ask each group to research a few ideas, with each person in the group taking a different area to explore. An alternative may be for each group to choose or be given a topic to find out about. Tell them to collect articles and find out from books about the people they are researching; the environment they live in (this may be a squalid inner city area or a remote region high up in the mountains). Geographical texts such as an atlas, or even a street map may be of use to them here. If news items on television are available, utilise these as well as newspapers.

The children need to collect as much data as possible and build up a composite picture of a group of people – their needs (including protection from the cold), their living environment, their lifestyle, their problems and so on. Once this information has been gathered ask them to make a presentation to the rest of the class, including pictures and a written speech of about three to four minutes. This will help to focus the children's ideas. After each presentation allow the rest of the class to comment and ask questions in order to help develop ideas further.

## 3. Insulation

### Group size
Individuals and pairs.

### Objective
To research properties of materials.

### What you need
Different fabrics such as wool, cotton, polyester, nylon and so on; beakers or cups with lids, kettle, water, thermometers.

### What to do
To help the children develop their ideas further, ask them to investigate the insulation properties of various fabrics. If they have not done any previous work concerning conduction and insulation of heat, they will need some initial instruction – introducing various terms and the concept of heat 'travel'.

The investigation might be devised by the children if they are at an appropriate stage in their scientific development. If not it can be turned into an instructional exercise. Ask the children to boil up some water and pour a fixed amount into a heat-proof beaker or cup. (It is important that this part of the exercise is supervised closely.) The beaker can then be insulated with one of the fabrics and a lid of thick card placed on each beaker, making sure that there is a hole in it for the thermometer. Tell them to measure the temperature every minute for ten minutes and then show the results as a graph. If the children cannot draw graphs just get them to take the temperature after one minute and then after ten minutes, and work out the difference between the two temperatures. This can then be shown as a bar chart.

The important aspect here is the results and their analysis.
• Which fabric gave the lowest temperature drop?
• Which one the highest?
• Which is the best insulator of heat?
• Which is the worst?
• Which one will be most appropriate as a blanket?

Having tested the fabrics for insulating qualities the children should be encouraged to investigate other properties, such as wear and tear, weight, comfort and so on.

## 4. Style and appearance

### Group size
Individuals, pairs and small groups.

### Objective
To generate ideas about the style and shape of artefacts.

### What you need
Pencils, paper, a computer with a graphics facility.

### What to do
Before they generate a design proposal the children will also have to think about what their artefact will look like. It has been assumed up until now that they will be making a blanket. Now they can be allowed to open up the perspective a little – what will they do if there isn't enough material to make a blanket? Such a scenario should stimulate a number of alternatives such as making scarves, shawls, wraps, foot warmers, leggings and so on. What will be appropriate for one group of people may not be appropriate for another. Ask the children to discuss the possibilities and weigh up the advantages and disadvantages of each item in terms of one particular target group. The factors which they may have to take into consideration will include:
• how much material they have;
• the amount of the body that will be covered;
• the amount of body that has to be covered;
• the weight of the artefact;
• the time needed to make it

All these criteria will be relevant to their ideas and this stimuli may help them to narrow down the focus a little. Remember to make sure that they record all their ideas and ask them to look at cultural influences, colour preferences, style and so on. Can these be included in their designs?

## 5. Knitting and sewing

### Group size
Individuals.

### Objective
Skill development in knitting and sewing.

### What you need
Wool, knitting needles, thread, sewing needles, other fabrics.

### What to do
The children will have conducted a lot of research by the time they reach this activity. They now need to develop their craft skills in order to manufacture a good quality product. Depending on their skills, this may be done at this stage, or it is more likely to run in tandem with their research. They will have to be shown how to knit – garter stitch will be quite sufficient. They will also need to know how to finish a piece and what to do if they miss or drop a stitch.

Ask them to knit a piece of knitting 10cm × 10cm and time

how long they have taken to do this. This will help them to estimate how long the actual manufacturing process will take them. Ask them to estimate how much wool they will need for each square.
• Is this wool available?
• Will they have to buy it?
• If not, where will it come from?

Old jumble and torn pullovers are a good source for wool, but if this is used as the source of material, the children will have to calculate how much time unpicking and rerolling will add to the overall manufacturing time.

As the children build up their skills in working with such fabrics they should be encouraged to note down all their ideas and options, and how they affect their design.

## 6. Making choices

### Group size
Individuals.

### Objective
To generate a design proposal.

### What you need
Pencils, paper.

### What to do
So far the children will have come up with ideas, dismissed ideas, made choices and expressed preferences. They now need to pool all this information into *one* design proposal. This proposal will have to include:
• who they are going to design and make for;
• what they are going to make (blanket, scarf, and so on);
• what materials and equipment they will need;
• where they are going to obtain these items from;
• an outline/plan of what they intend to do with respect to manufacture.

For each element they should justify why they have made their choices in preference to others. For example, they may choose to make a scarf because it is quick to make, or because they do not think there will be enough materials available to make anything bigger. They may have decided to use materials of particular colours because they are in keeping with the cultural designs of their target group or because they do not show the dirt or perhaps they think an elderly person will see the blanket more easily if it is brightly coloured!

## 7. Procedures and plans

### Group size
Individuals.

### Objective
To plan what they intend to make and the procedure they will use.

### What you need
Pencils, paper.

### What to do
Before the children set about making their objects, they need to formulate a work plan. This can be done on an individual basis, but is more likely to be done in conjunction with you. A certain amount of time will probably already be allocated during the school day or week for technological activity and the nature of manufacturing in this case is such that the work can be easily left and picked up again. However, it does demand large pockets of time once the work is underway.

Ask the children to identify the main stages in the making process and to put them in order as a plan, flow diagram or storyboard. The list is likely to include:
• gather materials (make sure they have a list);
• unpick wool from old jumpers;
• knit 'x' number of 10cm × 10cm squares (each square should take 'y' minutes/hours).

It might be that a number of children have had the same idea and want to work as a

Textiles  61

team to ensure their artefact is finished. If this is the case they should list this, combining their expertise as they plan. It is interesting to note that in this particular manufacturing process individual expertise can be assessed easily within a group activity.

## 8. Making squares

### Group size
Individuals or small groups.

### Objective
To make their composite artefact.

### What you need
Materials the children have listed in Activity 6.

### What to do
The children can now begin to make their artefacts. It is important to note that actual manufacture is likely to take as much time as all the other activities put together, putting the technology process in perspective. If each child produces a square and these squares are pooled to satisfy one or other designs, then this needs to be noted as it may be necessary to do this at the latter end of the exercise when time is running out. It is likely some children will work faster and more efficiently than others, these will probably achieve on an individual basis. Others may only partly achieve, so their efforts may have to be combined. The children could also finish their work off at home with the help of parents, friends and so on, or they may decide to change their designs to make a smaller item if time is running out. All these are justified so long as the reasons for doing so are recorded.

## 9. Evaluating

### Group size
Individuals.

### Objective
To evaluate the product and procedures.

### What you need
Pencils, paper.

### What to do
Once the time that was allocated has run out the artefacts will be made or partly made and the children will need to evaluate what they have made and the procedures undertaken. As a class ask them to talk about and list the procedures they have gone through, starting with their initial research.

This evaluation may be packaged by telling the children that they have to plan a charity event to make blankets, say in a local community centre or church hall.
• Why would they work in this way?
• How might they improve on and/or make more efficient the procedures they went through? For example, would they try to make blankets or scarves or what?
• How would they obtain the materials and resources?
• What plans would they use for the volunteers to work from?
• How much time would they allow?

The children should try to justify their choices based on their own experiences.

# CHAPTER 3

# Wood

Of all the materials available to the craftsperson in the primary school, wood is perhaps the least familiar, although over recent years there has been a much greater emphasis on wood as a 'technological' material, for example in the construction of bridges and other structures. The Jinks method of construction using corner strengtheners as joints is based almost exclusively in wood and many primary technology suppliers sell what are basically woodworking tool kits, containing saws, hammers, pliers and so on. However, all this does very little to help teachers who are insecure or unfamiliar with working in wood.

This chapter looks at wood as a technological medium, developing skills and concepts in working wood, for example, joining, shaping, assembling and cutting. The tasks encountered will not be unfamiliar to most teachers and will be well within their own sphere of competence. The detailed technical skills of working with wood and other resistant materials really takes off in the secondary sector, but what is provided here is principally an experience of and an introduction to working with wood.

As with all the other chapters, the craft skills are encapsulated in a broader technological activity, providing a focus and a relevance to the work in hand. The final feature of this chapter is the inclusion of structures and forces as a parallel concept to woodworking skills.

Wood 63

# ACTIVITIES

## Home: key-ring / hook design

### Age range
Five to seven.

The principal objective of the activities in this section is for the children to design and make a key-ring or coat-hook using wood as the principle medium. The key skills that are developed are using a hammer and a hand drill. With children of this age, the work is geared towards experimental activity, but will provide skill development in the use of specific tools and will also introduce the idea that there are different types of tools which all have different working properties.

## 1. Working with wood

### Group size
Pairs or small groups.

### Objective
To introduce some woodworking tools and how to use them.

### What you need
Junior hammer, panel-pins, soft wood and various wood off-cuts such as pine.

### What to do
This activity is concerned with skill development and the children can begin it by identifying various tools and materials. Initially, you should give them three types of wood to look at (soft, hard, balsa), some panel-pins and a small, junior hammer.

The principal problem usually encountered by young children is the actual manipulation of tools especially the hammer. Therefore, don't give them a large hammer to use, as it is likely to be too broad in the handle and too heavy for them to strike a nail with any degree of accuracy or co-ordination. Instead choose hammers that are small and easily handled.

Most children will start to use the hammer by holding it near the head and they should be encouraged to hold it further down the shaft so that they can use the weight of the head more efficiently, allowing the nail to be struck with more force. It is also likely that the children will miss the nail a lot at first until they gain confidence and experience. As each child has a go at hammering a nail into one of the pieces of wood, challenge them to hammer it as straight as they can without it bending or twisting. This can be extended to asking them to hammer in the nail using the least number of blows.

Holding the nail steady at the start of hammering is yet another aspect of this skill development and no doubt there will be a few sore thumbs! The nail should be held between the forefinger and thumb, and tapped gently until it grips in the wood, the digits can then be removed and the nail struck with greater force (but accurately!)

Ask the children to turn their efforts into making usable objects; they can pretend to make an artefact or find a use for what they have already constructed.

**NB:** this work needs to take place on an activity or proper workbench to avoid damaging desks.

## 2. Looking at wood

### Group size
Pairs or small groups.

### Objective
To raise awareness of different types of wood and their properties.

### What you need
Junior hammer, panel-pins, softwood and hardwood off-cuts such as beech, oak, ash (hard) and pine, balsa (soft).

### What to do
Ask the children to build on the skills of using a hammer and hammering by investigating how easy or hard it is to hit nails into different types of wood. The two basic types of wood are hardwood and softwood (avoid fibreboard or other composite wood materials such as chipboard) and the children should be given the opportunity to investigate at least one type of hardwood and one type of softwood. If the pieces of wood are of equal size and shape this will also be of value as the children can investigate properties such as weight, density, whether they float or sink in water and so on. If it is not possible to work with wood of equal size and shape then get them to compare the appearance of each. Are they dark or light? Is one wood darker than the other? Introduce the idea of the grain of wood and show them the lines that run along the wood. Is the grain the same for all types of wood? If not, how is it different?

Having studied the wood the children can try hammering panel-pins into each different type. Which type of wood do they find the easiest and the hardest to use? Ask the children to record their findings and then, as an extension to this work, they can investigate other pieces of wood using a nail and hammer. Remember to encourage them only to use the woodworking area and to observe *strict* safety rules when using a hammer and nails. Foolish behaviour must be pointed out and punished.

## 3. Drilling wood

### Group size
Pairs or small groups.

### Objective
To build up skills in drilling and using screws.

### What you need
Hand drill, wood screws, screwdriver, pieces of softwood.

### What to do
The children will not need to know at this stage how to attach a drill bit to the drill using a chuck key, but this can be shown to them.

Demonstrate how a hand drill is used, pointing out how the drill must be kept straight and the wood placed in a vice to keep it steady. Demonstrate how the wood will spin if it is not put in a vice.

Once the children have been shown what to do, they can practise drilling using a hand drill. Encourage them, after a little exploratory work, to make patterns in the wood. Sometimes drilling straight

# 4. Using woodwork skills

## Group size
The whole class, then individuals.

## Objective
To identify opportunities for using woodworking skills.

## What you need
Pencils, paper.

## What to do
By this stage the children will have gained some knowledge about the properties of wood. They should now begin to think in terms of what it can be used for. Show them a piece of wood with a nail hammered into it so that half of it is left out of the wood. Ask them what it might be used for and write down their ideas on the board. It is likely that most of their ideas will be on the theme of keyholders and coathooks. If not, then feasible alternatives can be taken on board, but make sure that the work needed to make these objects would be simple enough for the children to achieve.

Ask the children to talk and write about what they might make and why. For example, they might discuss how their parents can never find their keys or how their nightclothes need to be hung up in their bedrooms, or they may want to hang up the headphones from their personal stereos so that they do not get broken.

After this initial stimulus, there should be lots of ideas listed and recorded and you can encourage the children to think about which is the best one for making. You should

through and at other times just making holes. This can be developed into an aesthetic exercise, with the children making patterns and shapes in the surface of the wood and then colouring and painting them. Alternatively, if they are given pre-cut cubes of wood, they can make and decorate dice.

Having developed a degree of skill in drilling holes into softwood, ask the children to screw screws into the pre-drilled holes. They might try putting screws straight into the wood, but it is likely that young children will have difficulty doing this as the screwdriver will have to be pushed and twisted while screwing. If however, the children put the screws into pre-drilled holes, they need to use less force in order to achieve success. Point out to them that the pre-drilled hole has to match the size of the screw as too large a hole will mean that the screw will not grip and will fall out.

You may want to continue with this skill practice by letting the children try drilling into hardwood or ask them to speculate whether using hardwood would be easier or more difficult to work with.

direct them towards ideas that are easily made involving only the skills they have developed so far.

## 5. Investigating hooks and hangers

### Group size
Pairs or small groups.

### Objective
To evaluate existing hangers.

### What you need
Various hangers and hooks, pencils, paper.

### What to do
The children will need to develop their ideas from the previous activity further. Ask them to bring in a variety of wooden hangers and hooks from home these may be kitchen utensil hangers, key-rings, towel rails and so on. Let them look at each in turn and ask them to find out how the wood has been worked. Where has it been drilled? Have screws or nails or something else such as hooks been attached to the wood? The likelihood is that holes have been pre-drilled so that screws will fit through and the hanger attached to the wall, door or unit. The hooks are probably screw in hooks.

Tell the children to draw one or two of these hangers and label the parts they have identified such as hooks, holes for screws and so on. Ask them to look at what has been done to the wood to make it look good? It may have been painted or varnished or decorated with patterns.

The children should also discuss what they like or dislike about some of these hangers, for example: 'it's too big' or 'it's the wrong colour'.

## 6. Designing a hanger

### Group size
Individuals.

### Objective
To design their own hangers.

### What you need
Pencils, paper, coloured crayons or felt-tipped pens.

### What to do
The children can now try to design their own hangers. First of all ask them to say what the drawing they are going to do will be of, for example, 'I am going to make a key-ring for my mum'. Then encourage them to say *why* they are going to make it, for example, 'because my mum can never find her keys'. This will focus the children's attentions on what purpose they are designing for.

To help them to design properly tell them to include on their pictures things like: the shape of the hook; where the holes will be drilled; where it will be fixed to the wall and so on. They should also include how they will decorate it and with what colours. To avoid complications, tell them that they will use a rectangular piece of wood, about 15cm × 5cm × 2cm. This can then be pre-cut in quantity before the children make their designs. It may be possible for them to state whether they want a long piece or a short piece and whether they want softwood or hardwood. If they are given a choice with these latter two, then they should be encouraged to give reasons for their choices.

Wood

## 7. Planning for making

**Group size**
Individuals.

**Objective**
To plan what they are going to make.

**What you need**
Pencils, paper, photocopiable page 172.

**What to do**
Before the children set about making their items, ask them to plan and sequence what they are going to do. This can be left as an open exercise for them to write or draw the sequence of activities, or you can discuss various stages with the whole class and ask them to put them in sequence. The latter allows for more teacher control, while still giving the children a say in the work plan.

If the children draw up their own work plans then you will have to scan through them and fill in any gaps before the children commence work. The order of work is likely to be something like:
- mark and drill holes where screws are to be fitted;
- mark and make smaller holes where the hooks will go;
- hammer in the nails, or screw in the screws or hooks;
- paint the hanger using the design in the picture you draw.

Keep the sequence of activities short so that the children can work to it and make good use of it. It may also be of value to let them list the equipment – they can use photocopiable page 172 to help them do this.

## 8. Making your hanger

**Group size**
Individuals.

**Objective**
To make their designs.

**What you need**
Hand drill(s), hammer(s), panel-pins, small nails, wood screws, hooks, rectangular pieces of softwood 15cm × 5cm, paints, brushes.

**What to do**
The children should make sure that they have their design proposals in front of them. Emphasise to them the need for safe and proper use of equipment when they are working. Depending on available resources it is likely that only three or four children will be able to work on their own design at any one time and they may still have to share and wait for tools if they are short in supply. However, the logistics of working around a small workbench will dictate the final numbers.

Each child should work until they have reached the point where they have drilled their holes and added the hooks. The decorating can be done as a different task elsewhere in the room or on a separate occasion. The paints will need to be quite thick because water-based paints are likely to soak into the wood. Oil-based paints may be more useful, although they cost more.

At all times the children should work safely, and should be taught to clear away, clean up and care for all the equipment they have used.

## 9. Did it work?

**Group size**
Individuals.

**Objective**
To evaluate their product and the processes used.

**What you need**
Pencils, paper.

**What to do**
Having made their product, the children should test it. They will then be able to comment

on what they have made. Does it work as they expected? Do they like what they have made? What do they like about it? What do they like best about it? Ask them to talk about what they have done how they made the hanger, the tools they used, the process they undertook and so on. This evaluation process can be left as a discussion or the children can transfer some of their ideas on to paper in the form of a drawing or a written exercise. Ask them to compare what they have made in their design proposal. Does it look the same? Has it turned out as well as they expected?

# Recreation: assault course activity

## Age range
Six to eight.

In the activities in this section the children will design and make a model assault course using balsa wood. Some activities will also cover skill development work, such as cutting and joining the wood, and studying structures, particularly relating shape to strength and stability. The starting point for activity will be an open-ended design using construction kits. Many mistakes will be made, but this will serve to focus the children's attention on the key issues involved.

## 1. An assault course

### Group size
Pairs or small groups.

### Objective
To make a model of an imaginary assault course.

### What you need
Construction kits such as LEGO, Meccano or Stickle Bricks.

### What to do
Tell the children that they are going to make a model of an assault course. Give them only the briefest of introductions to help them. This might be in the form of, for example, a discussion about the features of an army assault course, television programmes such as *The Krypton Factor*, climbing frames and fun centres in local parks and so on.

After this introduction the children can make their designs using construction kits. When they have finished ask them to describe how it works. You can then have a class discussion about each design in turn. Is it strong? Would it be safe to climb on? How might it be made to look better or safer? Point out key features such as triangular shapes, the use of cross-beams to improve strength and so on.

This practical activity need not take very long as it is only intended to be a stimulus for other activities. If construction kits are in short supply, then straws and Plasticine or even strips of card and sticky tape will suffice. In some ways these may be better to use because they will highlight problems of construction such as strength and stability, that construction kits are designed to avoid. The distinct advantage of construction kits is their ease of use and therefore, children with manipulative co-ordination problems may find them easier to use than card or straws.

## 2. Studying structures

### Group size
Pairs or small groups.

### Objective
To evaluate existing structures.

### What you need
Pencils, paper, pictures of various structures.

### What to do
The children should now be given the opportunity to evaluate other structures. Show them pictures of structures such as scaffolding, climbing frames, fairground rides and so on. What shapes can the children see in the structures? Are the structures wider at the bottom than at the top? What do they like about the structures? What do they not like about them?

The key points that the children should realise are:
• triangles and squares are the most evident shapes;
• tall towers tend to be wider at the bottom than at the top;
• cross-beams are used all the way up.

## 3. Investigating structures

### Group size
Pairs or small groups.

### Objective
To investigate why structures are made in the way they are.

### What you need
Paper tubes, straws, sticky tape, scissors, photocopiable page 173.

### What to do
Having looked at and recognised certain patterns and features in certain framework structures, the next step is for the children to ask why these structures have these features. Why is the Eiffel Tower wider at the bottom than at the top? Why does scaffolding have cross-beams? These questions will form the basis of a number of investigations into structural shape, stability and the forces on them.

Using photocopiable page 173 the children can carry out a number of tests using structures made from straws. The first test uses one straw and the children need to find out whether it stands up. Can they get it to stand up? Is it stable? How easily does it fall over?

The next test uses four straws attached at the top with sticky tape. The same questions should be applied to this structure as were to the single straw. However, this structure should be much more stable, but if a force is applied from the top, the 'legs' will splay out and the structure will collapse.

The third structure has all four legs fixed together at the base. This will be the strongest structure, capable of supporting the greatest force.

Using straws or paper rolled into tubes, the children can make a model of an existing structures such as the Eiffel Tower, an electricity pylon or Blackpool Tower. These models can then be tested as the previous structures were to see how well they resist the forces applied to them.

The children should record and store the data from these

tests to be used later on. They should now be able to conclude that objects that are wider at the bottom are more stable and that cross-beams add rigidity and increase the strength of a frame.

## 4. Cutting and sticking

### Group size
Individuals, pairs or small groups.

### Objective
To provide skill development in cutting and gluing balsa-wood.

### What you need
Balsa-wood pieces (1cm × 1cm square strips), wood adhesive, junior hack-saws, rulers, pencils, photocopiable page 174.

### What to do
Making objects from pre-cut materials is one thing, getting children to measure, mark out and cut their own material to size is another. Tell the children that they are going to make a simple cube using 1cm × 1cm square strips of balsa-wood. This means that each child or group will have to cut 12 small lengths of about 10cm from one or two large strips of wood. Prior to cutting, however, they will need to measure out the length of the long piece of wood and divide it into 12.

The children can use the instructions on photocopiable page 174 to assemble the cube. What will have to be pointed out is that although a 10cm cube is being made, all the individual pieces are in fact less than 10cm in length. Why do they think this is?

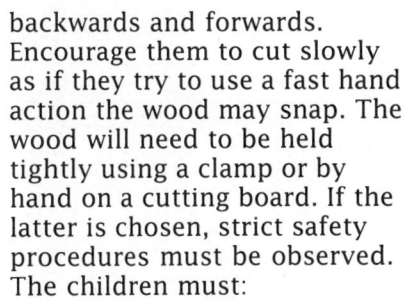

The children should be shown how to cut the wood using long gentle strokes backwards and forwards. Encourage them to cut slowly as if they try to use a fast hand action the wood may snap. The wood will need to be held tightly using a clamp or by hand on a cutting board. If the latter is chosen, strict safety procedures must be observed. The children must:
- hold the wood firmly;
- hold the wood well away from where they are cutting;
- cut at a shallow angle;
- make slow sawing movements;
- concentrate the whole time.

A slow methodical motion when cutting will reduce the likelihood of accidents. Encourage them to follow the lines they have drawn on the wood as they cut.

Ask the children to write down the sequence they went through to make their cubes. Finally, the cubes can be painted.

## 5. Using frame structures

### Group size
Individuals.

### Objective
To identify new needs or opportunities for using frame structures.

### What you need
Pencils, paper.

### What to do
Having built their own structures in the previous activity, the children should discuss how they might use this experience to design 'fun' frames for people. Talk about the types of structures they might design such as climbing frames and activity frames.

Who might they design them for? Young children? Elderly people? Handicapped people? Ask them to think about activity structures that already exist. Can they be improved upon, added to or made simpler to suit new needs?

The children should write their ideas down in the form of a few short sentences and then list at least three ideas which they might like to make. They should also add a sentence to explain why they think they should make one each. Also they may want to sketch out these initial ideas.

## 6. What frames do others like?

### Group size
Individuals or small groups.

### Objective
To find out people's needs and opinions through a survey.

### What you need
Word processor with printing facility.

### What to do
Tell the children that they should find out what other people like or dislike about their initial ideas for 'fun' frames by compiling a questionnaire. The questions they are likely to ask will include things like 'what is your favourite type of climbing frame or assault course activity?' This can be left as an open-ended question or perhaps the children can draw a few examples for their interviewees to choose from. They might ask about where people think such a frame should be put, for example, in school, on the park, a local supermarket for children to play on while their parents shop and so on.

Encourage the children to think of at least five relevant questions. (You should check these questions to make sure that they make sense!) Direct the children to aim their questions at their chosen target groups – young children, the handicapped, elderly people and so on.

Ask them to prepare their questionnaire using a word processor. They may need help when setting out the questions to ensure that they leave enough space for the answers, add lines, draw any tick boxes and so on. They must then survey at least 20 people in that target group. Tell them about data protection and the fact that they need not ask for people's names.

## 7. Looking at your survey results

### Group survey
Individuals.

### Objective
To analyse data and generate a design.

### What you need
Pencils, paper.

### What to do
Having carried out a survey to find out other people's opinions, the children will need to analyse the data. They may find this difficult without help, but encourage them to look for ideas by themselves before you begin to help. To encourage the children to look at the data systematically, ask them to look at their first question. What do most people say? This is where objective 'closed' type questions are most helpful because they can be analysed in terms of a simple count up, for example, 19 people say they like it, one person says he does not.

From this exploration each child can be asked to think about the following ideas before she begins to work on her final design proposal.
• Who is the frame being built for and why are you making it?
• How will the frame be made stable?
• How will the frame be made strong?

Using these three simple questions, the children can design an activity frame. Ask them to label the parts and possibly state their reasons for using each bit. This constitutes an annotated diagram. At this stage it is not so important that they mark on the correct dimensions, but if the children are able, they can be encouraged to think about size. Also encourage them to think about how good the frame will look; for example, if it is intended to be located in a woodland setting, they may choose to build it out of logs.

## 8. Planning and making

### Group size
Individuals.

### Objective
To plan and make their frame using balsa.

### What you need
Balsa-wood strips (1cm), junior hack-saws, wood adhesive, rulers, pencils, paper.

### What to do
Before the children set about making their designs from the previous activity, ask them to list the tools and equipment they will need. Give each child a fixed length of balsa and tell them that they will only be allowed to use this one piece (initially). Encourage them to think about how many pieces they will need and therefore how many shorter pieces they will be able to get out of one length.

Even though many designs will be rectangular rather than cubic, or angled and very likely quite complicated, the realisation that they do not have a limitless supply of material will give the children good cause for thought. You may even like to ask them whether they think they are going to have enough wood to make their designs. If the answer is 'no', then ask them to think about how they are going to get around the problem if they can't have any more wood. Will they make the model smaller or simplify it? This may necessitate them going back to the drawing board.

Ask the children to tell you how they are going to set about building their frames, remembering that they will need to allow time for adhesive to dry and so on. Once all ideas are in place they can set about making their design. Encourage them to measure lengths before they cut them and to follow their design proposals as closely as they can. Rough measurements based on visual judgements will, however, suffice; for example, looking for lengths that will be similar, if one length is likely to be longer or shorter than those already glued.

## 9. Evaluating your frame

### Group size
Individuals.

### What you need
Pencils, paper.

### What to do
Having made their design, the children must now evaluate their work. Principally, ask them to compare their models with their design proposals. Do they match? If they are different, how are they different? Why are they different?

Next the children can evaluate their construction. Does it look good? How might it be made to look better? Why was it made in the first place? What needs were to be satisfied? Does it still meet those needs? If not, does it come close to meeting those needs? Is it stable? Is it strong? If not, how can it be made more stable and/or stronger? Possibly, get the children to think about the problems in turn and say whether (and how) they solved them.

Finally, they can evaluate how successful their activities were *overall*. If the work has not been painted, get them to comment on how this may alter their model.

## School: weatherboard design

### Age range
Seven to nine.

The project set out in this section is to design and make a weatherboard. The opportunities for such a design may exist within particular classrooms or in key areas such as the hall, reception area, nursery area and so on. The skills needed for the design are principally cutting skills using a jigsaw. If such a saw is not available then a tenon-saw will suffice.

## 1. Brainstorming

### Group size
Individuals.

### Objective
To brainstorm areas where a weatherboard would be useful.

### What you need
Pencils, paper.

### What to do
Tell the children that they are going to make a weatherboard out of wood. Ask them to think what information might be conveyed on a weatherboard – for example, whether it is cloudy, sunny, raining, snowing, thundering and lightning, foggy. Perhaps temperatures and the date, may also be included.

The children can then think about where such data might be useful. They might think of the nursery or infant class, or it could form part of their own science studies concerning the environment, or it may be useful in the school reception areas so that dinner assistants and teachers can be warned about the weather so that they can make decisions about playtimes. An initial tour of the school might help the children develop their initial ideas about the location of a weatherboard.

Having introduced the prospect of designing and making a weatherboard, the children can then list what they think it might have on it and also the places where it might be put and the reasons why it might be put there.

## 2. Researching weather information

### Group size
Pairs or small groups.

### Objective
To research weather information services.

### What you need
Books, encyclopedias, a computer with database facilities.

## What to do

Encourage the children to bring in weather information from various sources such as newspapers, magazines, holiday brochures and so on. Ask them to study and list the data given in each report. Does this match up with the information they thought ought to be given on their weatherboard? Perhaps more significantly they can identify any information that is given in the reports that they did not list for their weatherboard. Ask them to monitor weather and weather reports over a period of time, for example, one week or one month, again checking what data is given and how it is displayed. Many Teletext information services give data such as this as well.

The children can set up a database on a computer and record events as they occur using specific headings such as sun, rain/snow, wind speed, amount of cloud and so on.

They can also look at how weather is currently recorded and has been in the past; for example, items such as weather cocks, wind vanes, and weather stations and most recently satellite information. Which is most reliable?

Having recorded evidence and details from various sources, encourage the children to write about what they have found out. They may want to refine their initial ideas about what items or features should be included on the weatherboard, for example, they may need to show clouds and temperature but not wind speeds and so on, hopefully with some justifications.

## 3. Where will the weatherboard go?

### Group size
Pairs and small groups.

### Objective
To discuss the positioning of the weatherboard with people who might be interested.

### What you need
Pencils, paper, a word processor.

### What to do
By this stage children will have some ideas of what they want to include on the weatherboard. Ask them to itemise these points. Also their initial survey about the school will have led them to think of likely sites for the weatherboard. However, they now need to focus on the actual site. Where do they want to site the board? Why do they want to put it there? Who are the people most likely to make use of it? Ask them to answer these questions before they attempt the next step, which is to discuss their ideas with the people they have targeted as potential users of the weatherboard. To do this, they must write down a few questions that might help them in their design. Do they need a weatherboard? How would it be useful to them? What might they want to see on it? What design features should it have?

Ask the children to design a questionnaire, enter this into a computer and print it out, leaving spaces for people to fill in their answers. The questionnaire can then be left with the relevant target groups or completed 'in the field'.

Once filled in, the children can analyse the data and write a few sentences about the ideas that the survey has given them. What should be emphasised or developed from this piece of work, is the need for the weatherboard to look good as well as to be functional. This means that the children will have to think very hard about their use of colour, shapes and the overall design.

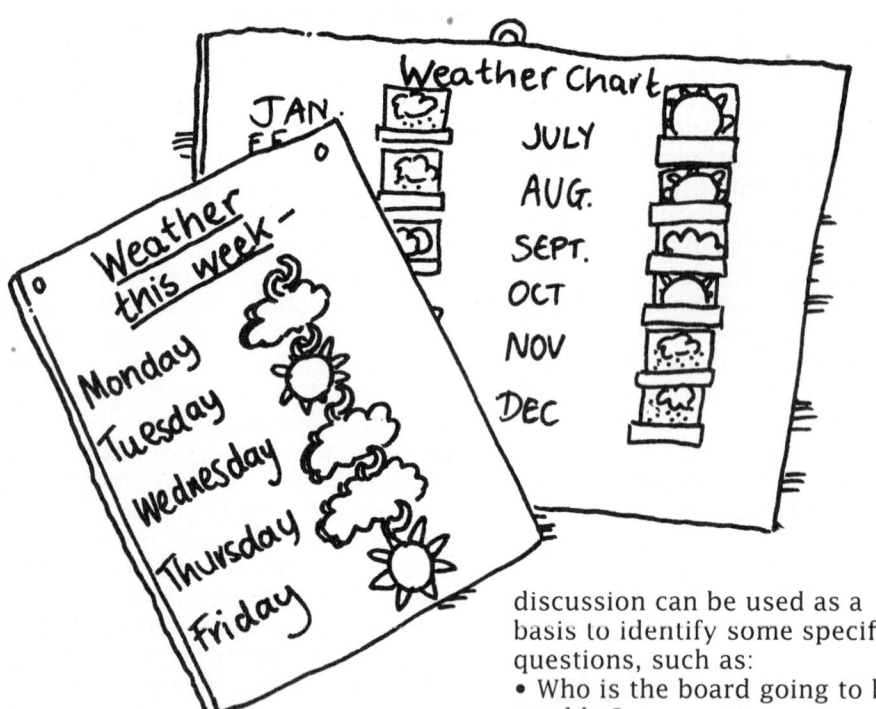

## 4. Picking out parts of the design

### Group size
Individuals.

### Objective
To identify parts of the design and develop ideas.

### What you need
Paper, pencils.

### What to do
Discuss with the class what they think might be included on their weatherboard in light of their research. This discussion can be used as a basis to identify some specific questions, such as:
• Who is the board going to be used by?
• Where will the board be placed?
• What symbols will be placed on the board?
• What other data will be placed on the board?
• How will the information be fixed to the board?
• Where will each piece of information be placed?
• How big will the board need to be?

This list of questions constitutes a design analysis. The children can use their answers to draw up a rough design specification. The answers to some of these questions may be fixed; for example, you may decide that the board is to be of a specific size and shape. They may be told that the information is going to be hooked on nails or slotted in to place. Again this removes one more variable, but even having directed them, there are still enough opportunities for manoeuvre within such constraints.

## 5. Making a mock-up

### Group size
Individuals.

### Objective
To create a mock-up of their ideas.

### What you need
Paper, card, scissors, coloured crayons or felt-tipped pens, adhesive.

### What to do
Using the specifications they have decided on and the constraints imposed in the previous activity, each child can use paper to make a mock-up of their design ideas to see what it will look like. Try to encourage them to be as accurate as they can and to aim to produce work of good quality. This may mean colouring in carefully, using stencils for lettering or numbers, cutting out shapes smoothly, and possibly measuring widths and lengths so that they fit properly.

Give each child paper or card pre-cut to the right size for the baseboard. The children will then be able to place items on the board using a non-permanent adhesive stick. This way they can explore spaces and assess how each item looks in relation to the others. To help them, give them a few questions to think about:
• Do their designs look good? What do other people think of them?
• Can the information be seen at a distance or do you need to be close up to see it?
• Do people understand what is on the board?

The children may also think up their own questions in the course of this modelling.

On the basis of this simple construction the children should be able to refine their ideas even more. They should be reminded of aesthetics, blend, shapes, symmetry, balance and so on. They should also consider how well their design will fit into the environment in which it will be sited. Will it look good? Will it be seen easily? Let the children record the decisions they make and the reasons behind them.

## 6. Drawing a design

### Group size
Individuals.

### Objective
To generate a design proposal.

### What you need
Paper, pencils.

### What to do
On the basis of their research, the children should be able to generate a design proposal, drawing on all their ideas to date. Ask them to draw their final proposal, if possible to scale, or at least in proportion. This proposal should give information about the layout of information and other features such as where holes will have to be drilled. They will also need to provide sketches of each symbol showing its colour.

These design proposals will be used when the children come to plan and make their weatherboards so they need to be quite thorough. The drawing should be done using pencils and rulers and any details can be handwritten. Once completed, these proposals may also be used by the children to give a presentation to the class and discuss their final proposals with the people for whom it is being designed.

## 7. Working out a schedule

### Group size
Individuals.

### Objective
To write a schedule of work and compile an equipment list.

### What you need
Pencils, paper.

### What to do
Using the design proposal from the previous activity as their check, the children need to plan how they are going to carry out the work of making a weatherboard and what materials they are going to need. Ask each child to list everything she might need including paints, brushes, wood and so on. If the children get stuck, help them by suggesting items in a diffuse way, for example, how are they going to cut the wood or how will they drill the holes? You will probably already have all or most of the equipment to hand, but in terms of the children's own organisational development, the exercise is a valid one.

The method of writing a schedule can be approached in a number or ways. One way is to allow the children to write down, on their own, what they will do and transform this into a sequential flow chart. Another way is to have a class discussion outlining what will need to be done. This can be written on the board. If the various stages are not placed in order, then the children can still work out their own schedule.

Each method has its own merits depending on, for example, the time available,

Wood

the children's ability and so on. If each design is different there will probably be a number of stages that will overlap; and it will then be up to the children themselves to add to the list and produce a flow chart.

Ask the children to give an indication of how long they think each stage will take and to point out any possible safety hazards.

## 8. Making the weatherboard

### Group size
Individuals.

### Objective
To make their weatherboards.

### What you need
Hammer, nails, jigsaw, tenon-saw, sandpaper, pencils, paints, brushes, wood or card.

### What to do
The children can now set about making their designs. (It has been assumed that they will have had previous skill development work in sawing wood with a tenon-saw and/or coping saw, sanding wood, painting wood and using a hammer and nails.) Before any wood is cut, it needs to be marked out properly so that the children will know where to cut and avoid wastage. Make sure they use the saws properly and hold the wood in a vice or on a cutting board when they saw. The jigsaw is quite a specialist tool and may not be appropriate for some children as the wood will have to be turned in the vice so that the appropriate angles can be cut.

Once the children have cut out the baseboard and symbols from the wood they will have to sand all the rough edges until they are smooth. They can then be painted and left to dry. Holes can be drilled in the wood using a hand drill. The children should mark out where the holes are going to go before they drill and hold the wood in a clamp or vice when they drill.

If problems occur during the manufacturing process, the children can improvise; for example, if they cannot use a jigsaw then they may have to cut only straight lines using a tenon-saw. This will alter design shapes, but allows them to complete their work.

## 9. Evaluating the weatherboard

### Group size
Individuals.

### Objective
To evaluate the completed object and the processes of planning and making.

### What you need
Pencils, paper.

### What to do
Having completed their manufacture in the previous activity, the children can put the pieces together, making sure that all the parts fit together as designed. If they don't, then the children will have to alter one or two shapes so that they do fit.

Once completed they can take their products and show them to the people for whom they were intended. The children should ask them specific questions, for example: do they like it? Is there anything missing? Is the work of a good enough quality to be put on display? On the basis of such questions they can then decide whether they have satisfied the needs they identified earlier in this project.

Ask them to comment briefly on how they set about tackling the work. How did they find out about parts of their design? What choices did they have to make? About which parts did they not have a choice? How might they make the work easier next time? What particular features stood out and/or how might they advise other children who are tackling similar exercises?

# Community: earthquakes and structures

### Age range
Eight to ten.

The activities in this section are centred around the community, but the community in a more global sense. Therefore, the children will probably be working in a relatively unfamiliar context.

The technological activities focus on studies related to *structures*. Therefore, the children will have to find needs and opportunities for designing and making structures in areas of the world where earthquakes are a major hazard.

## 1. Investigating earthquakes

### Group size
Individuals.

### Objective
To make an initial study of earthquakes and to identify geographical areas.

### What you need
An atlas, maps, books about earthquakes, a computer with data base and data logging facilities.

### What to do
How are earthquakes caused and which areas in the world are most susceptible to earthquakes? Such earth movements are often featured on television and in the press. If a recent quake has occurred then this can be used as a focus for these activities. If there hasn't been an earthquake recently, then there is plenty of resource material which relates to earthquakes.

Having made an initial study of localities and how earthquakes come about, it would be useful for the children to measure and talk about earth tremors in general. The children could make and set up a home-made seismometer to measure ground movements in their locality. Building work (particularly piledriving) and heavy traffic will often cause movements and thereby be a ready source of data showing vibrations on and across the earth's surface.

If the school has data logging devices, then this can be used to record 'in the field' using a vela. Once back in the classroom the children can compile the information into graphs and draw some conclusions.

On completion of this work, ask the children to write briefly about how earthquakes are caused and what problems they create with respect to structures such buildings, roads, bridges and so on.

## 2. What would you do in an earthquake?

### Group size
Small groups.

### Objective
To role play and discuss what happens during an earthquake.

### What you need
Objects specified by the children such as a microphone, reporter's hat and coat, bricks and so on.

### What to do
Ask the children to work in small groups to write a short sketch about what it must be like to be in an earthquake disaster. As a stimulus, you could bring newspaper articles, but a general discussion at the start of this activity about what takes place will probably suffice.

The children might want to talk about high-rise flats collapsing and crumbling, or bridges and dams falling down. Remind them to think about the facilities such as water, gas and electricity which would be lost if they had an earthquake in their area. Which buildings do they think would be safest to be in during an earthquake, and which would not be safe? The children might want to create their own designs or 'safe-house' which will not crumble or if it does collapse, will not cause very much damage.

The sketch need not be very long, three to four minutes will be ample time. They might want to structure their sketches so that they resemble a television news report with a reporter explaining what is happening and then interviewing people about how they are coping with the situation.

After the children have performed their sketches they should write a short piece about or draw pictures showing ways for solving some of the problems caused by earthquakes.

## 3. How do others design for 'quakes'?

### Group size
Pairs or small groups.

### Objective
To look at structural design in different cultures.

### What you need
Books relating to building design, photocopiable page 175.

### What to do
One of the most destructive things that occur during earthquakes is the collapse of buildings, crushing those within and outside.

Earthquakes also often occur in parts of the world which are densely populated with people living and working in high-rise buildings. Use newspaper features, photographs and articles to help the children to realise that architects are faced with two conflicting criteria when designing buildings – people need places to live and, in areas of dense population, high-rise buildings solve this problem, but they cannot withstand earth tremors.

Encourage the children to look at how other buildings might be affected in an earthquake, for example, a bungalow and a typical red-brick terrace house. What would be the advantages and disadvantages of thin (possibly paper) walls compared with brick or stone? To help the children with this discussion and research, ask them to look at the buildings shown on photocopiable page 175.

To conclude this activity the children should identify which of the possibilities they think are best, together with the reasons for their choices.

## 4. Shapes and strength

### Group size
Pairs or small groups.

### Objective
To research various structural shapes with respect to strength.

### What you need
Thin card, paper, adhesive or sticky tape, weights, construction kits.

## What to do

Show the children how to fold and shape paper or thin card so that they end up with tubular, triangular and rectangular three-dimensional shapes.

Tell the children that they are to design a fair test using slotted masses to find out what shape is strongest, when on its end (like a pillar) and when on its side.

They should write up their results and conclude which is the strongest and the weakest shape. Generally speaking, the tube usually makes the strongest pillar and the triangle the second best. When weights are placed on the shapes when they are on their sides there is little difference between the three, but there is a significant difference between the amount of weight the pillar can bear in this position and when upright.

Ask the children to discuss building shapes. Do buildings tend to be circular or rectangular shape? Why do most tend to be built as rectangles or cubes? Do the children think that a circular building or a triangular one would be any more stable than the traditional rectangular shapes? Ask them to use construction kits to devise tests to try and find out. These buildings can be placed on a board and moved from side to side to simulate an earthquake. Which design withstands the movement and which collapse?

Encourage the children to repeat there tests a few times to ensure that the data are accurate. They can then record their conclusions and write a short piece about the ideas these tests give them in terms of structural design.

## 5. Looking at arches

### Group size
Pairs or small groups.

### Objective
To look at arches as supports.

### What you need
Card, paper, slotted crosses, photocopiable page 176.

### What to do
Tell the children that they are now going to look at and study beam support. Make sure that they realise that a beam is a long straight piece of material supported at both ends, for example, a bridge or a wide floor.

Ask the children to place a piece of paper across vertical pillars to represent a beam. They should record how it lies, for example, whether it sags in the middle or loses its shape. Encourage them to make an arch from card and lay it underneath the beam to see how well it acts as a support. If the arch is placed between the two pillars this will allow it to stand without being glued.

They can then investigate other ways of strengthening the beam such as making cross-ply beams by placing two beams across each other at 90° or by corrugating the beams. Show them how by putting triangles at the corners of the beams and the uprights this also helps to reduce buckling and bending, and thereby increase strength.

Discuss internal and external forces with the children. Internal forces are the forces inside the structure – the forces that keep it in shape, rigid and strong. External forces might be things like wind, other objects that the structure supports or objects that it collides with. If the internal force is greater than the external force then the building remains stable. If the external force is greater than the internal force then the building will begin to lose shape, buckle and eventually collapse. The worksheet on photocopiable page 176 will help the children when carrying out this work.

Finally, ask the children to record any ideas they have gained from this work. Which support is best or the strongest and which is most appropriate for holding books, walking on, spanning a bridge or gap for example?

## 6. Pulling ideas together

### Group size
Individuals.

### Objective
To generate a design proposal.

### What you need
Pencils, paper.

### What to do
Having carried out their research into structures and earthquakes, the children should use this information to design a structure to withstand earth tremors. This should be considered as the *need*. They should decide what sort of building they are going to design, for example, a hospital, house or another building. They must draw a plan showing the design of the building and the materials they are likely to use. Ask them to focus on the building's overall shape, for example, whether it will be tall, short, big, small, rectangular, triangular and so on. Each decision must be clearly identified on the plan together with the reasons for the choice; for example, the building will be triangular because this is the most stable structure. Will it have floors? If so, how many? How will these be designed, supported and strengthened – by corrugation, with arches? They should also give an indication of materials they would use to build it from, again with justifications for each decision made. This annotated proposal can now be used to help the children plan and make.

Once they have completed their plans, ask them to review the details. Are there any decisions still to make? Have they thought about the dimensions, the roof, shape and design? They will also need to list the resources they will require to make the model. Tell them they can use balsawood and other easily accessible craft materials such as paper, card, adhesive and so on. They should avoid the use of specialist materials such as hardwood. Let them add to or edit their proposals once they know what materials are available to them.

## 7. Planning for making

### Group size
Individuals and small groups.

### Objective
To plan how they are going to manufacture their models.

### What you need
Pencils, paper.

### What to do
Assuming that the children already have some knowledge of how to work with wood, ask each group to work out how much of each piece of equipment they will need. Each group can be told approximately how much or how many of each material and tool is available and they must then negotiate, as a group, what their individual needs are. Encourage the children to think about minimising waste so that all of them take only as much material as they really need.

The next step is for the children to plan what they are going to do, and possibly who in the group will do what. You should tell them how much time they will be allowed to complete their models – for example, one hour a week on Tuesday afternoon for the next five weeks. Using this constraint, they must work out how much time they will spend on each item in a flow chart.

Alternatively, it might be easier for them to work out what activities they will do for each hour that is available. Suggest to them that they might share the work, in terms of who does what and when – for example, one child may get the materials, another may tidy up and someone else may cut out from the materials given. This apportioning of tasks is a good opportunity for the children to learn about working together, albeit on a fairly minor scale.

## 8. Constructing an earthquake shelter

### Group size
Individuals.

### Objective
To make their models.

### What you need
Balsa-wood, other easily available craft materials, tenon-saws, pencils, rulers, sandpaper, adhesive.

### What to do
Having completed the design proposal and plan each child can now set about making his model. Remind them that they should measure accurately, marking out *before* they cut. Encourage them to make the best use of the materials they have chosen because, you should tell them, 'there are no others available' (even if there are). This will make them think hard about avoiding wastage when marking out their designs on card or balsa-wood. Get them to follow their plan and their design proposal carefully.

Some children will have a good concept of size and will have already worked out the various dimensions of their models, others will have not put measurements on their proposals. In order to achieve a quality finish, measurements are very necessary, but if for ability reasons such efforts are inappropriate, ask them to think in terms of small rather than large, as this will help to avoid unnecessary wastage. They can do this by marking out and cutting the largest part first. The rest will all be smaller. The consequences of working from smallest first go without saying!

The reason for most problems which occur during making is likely to be that the children have not measured, or not measured out accurately. Another problem is likely to be in terms of assembling and fixing the pieces together. Children invariably leave little time for adhesive to set. They must allow adhesive to set on one piece of the design before they can add any others. This will slow down and no doubt affect their work schedule, hence they may have to re-evaluate their schedules as they proceed to ensure that work is completed on time! If this means modifying the design, then they will have to weigh up the advantages and disadvantages of each course of action.

## 9. Does the structure satisfy the needs?

### Group size
Individuals.

### Objective
To evaluate work and working procedures.

### What you need
Pencils, paper.

### What to do
Once the children have completed their work, they can

Wood

evaluate their designs. Do they meet the needs of an earthquake zone? Are they strong and stable? What about how they look? They may be functional, but there's no need for them to be an eyesore! Did the children take aesthetics into account as they designed and made their models? If not, how might they make their design more attractive or fit in better with its likely surroundings?

Ask the children to write a short piece about the way their designs developed from early ideas to the finished models. What problems did they encounter? What choices did they have to make? Why did they make one decision in preference to another? How did they solve the problems they had? Was the work completed? Was it completed on time? How might the designing and making process be made more *efficient*? Did they have *all* the skills to make and draw? Was their work finished properly?

Finally, the children can make small models from Plasticine or other modelling materials of humans or other items so that people looking at the models will gain an overall perspective of their models in proportion to humans.

# Business: cottage industry

### Age range
Ten to twelve.

The principal idea behind this final series of activities is to use the context of business and industry within which the children can develop skills of using wood together with associated tools and equipment. The basic skills are those of shaping the wood and this skill is quite specialist, using a surform and/or sandpaper rather than a chisel and mallet. The idea is to use the natural features of wood such as the grain, knots and so on, and to enhance them to produce artefacts that are of sufficient quality to be sold.

## 1. Looking at the detail on wood

### Group size
Individuals.

### Objective
To look at wood and enhance its features.

### What you need
Small pieces of softwood, various wood stains and varnishes, small paintbrushes, thinners, paper, pencils.

### What to do
Provide each child with one small piece of wood and let them examine it from all sides and angles. Point out the grain of the wood and the lines that run along (or across) it. Can they see any knots in the wood? If so, what happens to the grain around the knots?

Ask the children to decide which side of the wood they like best and tell them to draw what that side looks like. They can then use their imagination to create features out of the knots and the grain. Depending on the wood they are using, this may be quite easy or difficult. Maybe a knot looks like an old, grotesque face, or maybe the aerodynamic shape of an animal or car. Ask them to add to the lines and whirls on their drawing in order to enhance this feature.

The children can mark these features on the wood using a dark brown or black paint. Once this paint has dried, tell them to put a thin coat of varnish on the wood to seal it. (This must be done in a well-ventilated room as the odours from varnish can be harmful.) The brushes used will have to be put in thinners straight after they have been used to avoid their being spoiled.

Once the varnished wood has dried, the children will be able to see how the varnish brings out and enhances the details of the wood grain and other features. Ask them to write about what they have learned.

Varnishing is described as a finish for wood. Encourage the children to use this wood and perhaps explore the different types of varnishes and stains which can be used and the effects that it is possible to achieve.

**NB:** thinners should only be used in a well ventilated room and only in small quantities. Keep thinners well away from any naked flames and make sure the children wash their hands thoroughly after use. Any spillages must be covered with sand.

## 2. Shaping wood

### Group size
Individuals.

### Objective
To explore shaping and detailing wood.

### What you need
Softwood, mitre-boards, hand drills, tenon-saws, surforms, sandpaper.

### What to do
Give the children some initial instructions on how to use the equipment and then let them explore; for example, they could use the mitre-boards to cut 45° angles across the edges of the wood or practise using the surform to plane off along the grain, or one side.

Make sure that the children secure the wood using a vice. Do not use planes as they have very sharp blades and are specialist tools. The surform provides less of a danger and provides good practice for eventually using a plane. The shavings that are created can themselves be used later and you can discuss with the children how they might use them (to make hair, beards, eyebrows and so on). Other features such as eyes, nostrils and perhaps a mouth with teeth can all be created using a hand drill. Remember that any piece of wood being drilled must be clamped firmly to avoid movement.

Finally, allow the children to use sandpaper to smooth off rough surfaces. A rough sandpaper will scratch wood, a fine sandpaper will remove rough edges with little scratching. Again, this is a skill that in reality takes time to develop. However, the objective here is not to look for quality turning skills, making intricate rounded artefacts and so on, but for the children to get a feel for the material and begin to understand how to use and appreciate wood's natural features.

Ask the children to record what they have done and the ideas that they have had while using the wood and equipment.

## 3. Investigating small businesses

### Group size
Pairs or small groups.

### Objective
To evaluate cottage industry ideas.

### What you need
Pencils, paper, a computer with database facilities, a variety of objects which people bring as gifts from holidays.

### What to do
Begin this activity by talking with the children about the types of presents people bring

back from holiday – ornaments made from shells, decorated stones and slate and so on. Ask the children to bring in a variety of these objects from home and tell them that they are going to research a number of these artefacts to see how they have been made. These details will be stored on a database created by the children and therefore they will have to think about the headings, titles and layout that they will use; for example, they might simply put 'Object 1, 2' and so on and list the features of each. Alternatively, after an initial observation the children might decide to choose specific headings such as eyes, felt, wobbly, hair, fabric, string and so on.

The idea of collecting this information is to build up the children's knowledge of strategies adopted by 'cottage industries' in order to create saleable items. For example, some items may have to be made by simply fitting a clock into a hole or recess in a stone, shell or piece of slate.

Ask the children to write down whether the material used has been painted and/or enamelled, or varnished. As they explore different items, new data will have to be added to the database.

Finally, they must analyse the data to look for patterns and trends.

## 4. Talking about your favourite artefact

### Group size
Individuals.

### Objective
To make a short presentation relating to an artefact.

### What you need
Objects from the previous activity, pencils, paper.

### What to do
Tell the children to make a presentation of their favourite artefacts from the previous activity. They should talk about:
• where it has come from;
• what it has been made from;
• the techniques that have been used to enhance its features;
• who made it;
• why it was made (to earn a living, and so on);
• why they like it;
• other factors about the artefact such as cost, whether using the materials damages the environment and so on.

This data can be used to establish criteria later on and the work used should be kept for later reference.

## 5. Setting up your own business

### Group size
Small groups of three or four.

### Objective
To work in groups to create a 'cottage industry'.

### What you need
Pencils, paper.

### What to do
By this age the children will probably have gained a degree of expertise in working with wood – shaping it, painting it and generally enhancing the material. They will also have researched 'cottage industries'. Therefore, they should be able to, in their groups, generate and develop their own 'cottage industries' using wood as the main material. To help them formulate ideas, ask them to answer the following questions:
• Who are they going to sell to?
• What is going to be their market – for example, young people, adults, elderly people, specialist groups such as enthusiasts and/or ethnic minority groups?
• Will their artefacts have identifiable features on each item, for example, the same kind of varnish, stain, eyes, hair and so on?
• Why are they selling and making the items – for

example, to make a profit, to raise money for a charity?

The children need to discuss each of these questions in turn, as a group, and try to think of initial ideas and opinions based on reasoned argument. This can be monitored by asking each group to present their conclusions to the rest of the class, together with their ideas about how they might continue – for example, by:
- conducting a survey of likely target groups;
- making one or two sample artefacts to see whether they will sell;
- identifying resources needed and a reliable source of materials.

All ideas should be written down and recorded with justification for each choice.

## 6. Research opportunities

### Group size
Small groups of three or four.

### Objective
To research needs and opportunities for designing and making.

### What you need
A computer with word-processing facilities.

### What to do
Ask the children to investigate likely markets for the products of their 'cottage industries'. They may want to conduct a survey of a cross-section of the local community to gauge response, but to do this they will need to make one or two mock-up items for people to see and comment on. This will have to be accompanied by a survey or questionnaire which they can draft out using a word processor.

The children should survey a cross-section initially and therefore, their questionnaire will need to include sections on age, sex, and interests of the people. They can also include one or two open questions relating to the product, for example, what do you like about the product and what would need to be changed before you would buy something like this? The children should try to interview a representative sample of about fifty or more people and discuss with them why a large sample is needed.

They should record the results of their surveys together with details of any decisions they made or conclusions they reached as a consequence, and the reasons why they have come to these particular conclusions. On the basis of this evidence, opportunities for making should now be clear in their minds and the children should aim their product at a particular target group of people.

## 7. Coming up with a final idea

### Group size
Small groups of three or four.

### Objective
To generate a design proposal.

### What you need
Pencils, paper.

### What to do
Having completed their research, the children should now be in the position to generate a design proposal. This proposal should set out the type of item they are going to make, materials they will need and where they will get the materials and equipment from. At this point add the constraint that they will only be able to use scrap pieces of wood (this can often be obtained free from a local store or senior school or for a nominal price). Other items such as screws, hooks and varnish will probably have to be bought and the children can

find out where these can be purchased.

The children will have to plan a budget, particularly if costs of buying in raw materials are incurred, but you should supply a price ceiling so that they don't plan to buy too much.

Make sure the proposals set out clearly what the children intend to do, and remind them that they will be working as teams rather than individuals. They will have to justify why they have used some ideas and why they have not used others.

Encourage the children to use in their proposals specialist vocabulary such as markets, budgets, stock as much as possible.

## 8. Working out the business details

### Group size
Small groups of three or four.

### Objective
To plan and make their designs.

### What you need
Equipment listed in the children's design proposals; softwood, surforms, hand drills, varnish, paints, brushes, thinners.

### What to do
Let the children discuss and work out the manufacturing process they will need to undertake to ensure a high quality finished item and the best use of their time. To do this they must work out a schedule; they may decide each child will work individually on an artefact designing, making and creating as she sees fit or perhaps they will discuss each piece of wood in turn and decide as a group how it might be developed into an artefact.

They should present their plan as a flow chart, but they may also want to write a more detailed schedule, which takes account of specialist skills. You should provide the children with a realistic time constraint so that they are made aware of time. You may decide that they have until the school fair or local festival to complete the work or you may allocate only one hour a week in class to work on the object. On the basis of this constraint the children will have to adapt and alter their schedules.

Once the schedules have been finished the children can set about manufacturing their product. You can encourage them to observe safe working practices and a high quality of finished products. They may also, after completion, think about pricing and selling their products.

## 9. Establishing criteria

### Group size
Individuals.

### Objective
To evaluate product and procedures.

### What you need
Pencils, paper.

### What to do
Ask the children to establish criteria to assess their work. Did the artefacts sell? Were they sold too cheaply? Were they too expensive? Did the target groups buy them or did others buy them as well? What comments did people make about the artefacts?

The children should also comment on the procedures they used. What worked well? What was their favourite piece of work? What did not work well? How might these aspects be improved on, if they were done again? Did they work well as a team? Did everybody contribute? Did they all have enough to do? How many artefacts did they make in the time allowed? Could they have made more? What would they have to have done to have made more? How would making more have affected their scale of production? This evaluation might be discussed as a class to begin with and then given to them as a written exercise.

# CHAPTER 4

# Environments

Possibilities for design and making environments exist all around us! An environment may be taken as a small area immediate to us in which essentially we live our lives or on the other hand it may be much larger than this radiating outwards to include a town, city or country, eventually encompassing the whole world. The larger environments influence what happens in the smaller environments.

Many teachers believe that, in terms of technology, children should begin by studying the smaller familiar environments such as home and school, and gradually progress to looking at the less familiar, broader environments, such as business and the local community. However, the nature of our modern society is such that many younger children are already very familiar with broader environments. The advent of package holidays and the general ease in which the majority of people can, and do travel makes children's experiences much less predictable than say 20 years ago. Hence, the following sections do not deal with environments as a progression of this type, rather they deal with progression from the familiar to the less familiar in more diffuse terms.

Another problem which occurs when designing environments, is concerned with the materials used and the quality of the product required. Many see technological materials as simply being such things as wood, metal, food or textiles and forget that such materials as photographs, ceramics and even plants, soil and water can all be technological materials! The traditional craft teacher who is used to making 'artefacts' out of wood, may therefore have difficulty equating technology with the manufacture of environments.

The ability literally to shape one's own environment (without having to manufacture in wood, metal and such like) is unavoidably connected with aesthetics and ergonomics (the study of human shape with respect to design), so the traditional views of making for making's sake holds little credence.

Environments  89

# ACTIVITIES

## Recreation: crazy golf

### Age range
Five to seven.

The context for the activities in this section is recreation in the sense that the children are going to design and make their own crazy-golf course. There is a strong 'craft' element throughout these activities in that the children will be making parts of the course from clay.

Crazy golf is an activity virtually all children will have participated in, so the idea of the game and the type of course played on will be very familiar to them.

## 1. Studying a crazy-golf course

### Group size
The whole class.

### Objective
To evaluate a crazy-golf course.

### What you need
Access to a crazy-golf course.

### What to do
To introduce the concept of a crazy-golf course, it is a good idea to organise a visit to one. As part of the fun of the trip the children can sketch one or two of their favourite holes as well as having a game.

On returning to school or during the visit, the children should write about what they liked and disliked about the course or individual holes. Were they all easy? Which one was the hardest? Why was it hard? Encourage them to think about the design, colour, shapes and so on. If the children have kept their own score cards, an evaluation of each hole could also be covered mathematically, perhaps totalling the scores for each hole and then sequencing them in order from the largest number down to the one with the lowest number.

If it is not possible to visit a crazy-golf course, then you could discuss different courses with the class. Perhaps you could set up one or two crazy-golf holes in the classroom to act as a stimulus for ideas. The children could then carry out similar calculations, sequences and evaluations to those carried out in the field.

Encourage the children to talk about why people use crazy-golf courses. Try to introduce concepts such as making money and developing skills as well as enjoyment and fun.

## 2. What is needed on a golf course?

### Group size
Individuals and the whole class.

### Objective
To describe the basic needs of a crazy-golf course.

### What you need
Pencils, paper.

### What to do
Having visited or seen a crazy-golf course, the children can discuss and describe what they

noticed. This should start with the obvious, such as how many holes there were, what equipment they used – golf club, ball, pencil, scorecard – and how the scorecard was set out. Then ask them to think about the designs of the course. Were all the holes static or were there some that moved? Ask the children to talk about how they moved or, if they were static, what the obstacles were like. Were there holes to pass through or blocks to get round? Were the paths sloped or angled? What was used to stop the ball from going on to another hole by mistake? All these questions should stimulate the children's comments and responses.

The children can then move on to describe one specific hole on the course. This may be their favourite hole, the hardest hole or one which they found to be the most fun. They can then draw and write a little about it.

## 3. Generating ideas

### Group size
Pairs and small groups.

### Objective
To begin generating ideas about crazy golf through structured play.

### What you need
A variety of junk material, golf balls, bats.

### What to do
Set the children the task of making their own crazy-golf hole. Remind them of the ones they have spoken, drawn and written about (see Activities 1 and 2) and tell them which materials are available to them (keep these fairly broad). Things such as yoghurt pots will suffice for the hole itself and cardboard tubes can be used as tunnels. If the school has large construction pieces available these will make ideal features and obstacles.

It is likely that the children will make and take apart many designs. This should be encouraged, allowing them to juggle around with many ideas, but at some juncture they will have to choose their best idea or their favourite design and stick with it.

At the design stage it doesn't matter whether the children use cricket bats, rounders bats or even their own hands to hit the balls, although the balls should be golf-ball size. In terms of organisation, you might decide to allow the whole class to work in groups, on the other hand, if you only allow one or two groups to work at any one time it might be easier on the nerves! Such planning depends on the time of year and class size. If the weather is fine the whole activity might take place outside or the gym or hall might be used.

The children's final task will be to evaluate *all* the holes that have been made. This can be done by the children actually trying out all the holes!

## 4. Making pot holes

### Group size
Pairs and small groups.

### Objective
To make clay potting holes for a crazy-golf hole.

### What you need
Clay, modelling tools, boards, paints.

### What to do
This is very much a skill development activity designed to show the children how to

use and work clay. Show them how to throw clay and to fold it so that there are no air pockets. They can then use their fingers and thumbs to make cylindrical shapes or they can make a box shape by joining flat rectangular pieces of clay with water. Let the children explore with the clay, making each shape in turn. (This may take a few sessions to complete.)

Having practised making the shapes the children can make the potting hole in which their golf ball will fall. You can fix the dimensions of this or allow some scope for creativity – some children may want the hole to be narrow making the ball harder to pot or others may want it wider.

Once the pots have been made they can be fired in a kiln or left to dry. Point out to the children how the material changes once it is fired and ask them to describe how it has changed (drier, harder, cannot be shaped easily and so on).

Finally, once their pots have completely dried the children can paint and decorate them.

## 5. Designing

### Group size
Individuals.

### Objective
To design a crazy-golf hole.

### What you need
Pencils, paper, construction kits, modelling clay.

### What to do
Having explored different ideas concerned with crazy golf, ask each child to come up with one original idea for a hole that they would like to make. Tell them that they can make part of their hole from clay, but they will only be given a limited amount of clay to use. Allow them to sketch their ideas on paper and then perhaps model them using construction kits and Plasticine or Play-doh.

As the children work on their designs talk to them so that they are made aware of specific problems. Is the hole large enough for a golf ball? Which part of the design will be made from clay? What will they use to make the other parts? Encourage them to think about surfaces and explain that smooth surfaces will cause the ball to move more quickly while rough surfaces will add grip and slow the ball down.

The children should label their drawings or models to indicate the materials that they will use. Also as part of their design ask the children to write a couple of sentences explaining why they have chosen their design. Is it because this type of hole will be hard to play or the most fun? Have they chosen this design because it is easy to set up and make? There will probably be many reasons or opportunities and in technological terms as long as a valid reason is offered, then the design is justified. Value judgements such as it 'looks good' or it is 'quick to do' are acceptable justifications!

## 6. Planning for making

### Group size
Individuals.

### Objective
To plan what they are going to do and what material they will need to make a crazy-golf hole.

### What you need
No special requirements.

### What to do
Young children are often capable of greater things than we, as adults, think. They learn by watching and copying and in order to do this they must take on board sequences of activities so that they achieve successful outcomes.

In this activity the children will have to write out and draw, perhaps in the form of a storyboard, the sequence of activities they will need to complete to make their clay part of their obstacle. In this way poor writers can use pictures rather than words and can talk through each picture with you while the more able child will be able to provide pictures and writing. The number of pictures can vary from as few as two, to as many as the children like. To help them you may want to suggest that they look back at how they made their clay potting holes in Activity 4. If you do this you can list each stage on the board as the children mention them, leaving them in a jumbled order so that the children have to put them in sequential order themselves.

Such activities are a good introduction to planning and organising key skills in technological activities.

## 7. Making the obstacles

### Group size
Individuals.

### What you need
Clay, board, modelling tools, water.

### What to do
Tell the children that they now have to make the clay parts of the hole that they designed. Remind them that they will have to follow the instructions that they drew up in the previous activity and make sure that each child has a copy of their design proposal in front of them.

Each child should work on her own design, but children can work in groups, sharing equipment and ideas. It is likely that they will meet problems as they work and often these can be resolved by receiving advice from other children. It may also be advisable to have a golf ball available so that they can check that the ball will fit!

Encourage the children to complete their work and to aim to achieve a good quality finish, smoothing off rough edges and so on. They must also be encouraged to tidy up after they have finished, washing tools and equipment and putting the equipment back where it is kept.

## 8. Creating an environment

### Group size
Individuals or small groups.

### Objective
To build an environment around their obstacle(s).

### What you need
Various different types of materials such as junk, construction kits and so on.

### What to do
The children will now have made their obstacles and potting holes from clay. They must now complete the hole by building the environment in which these objects are situated. Much of these ideas will be in their original proposal, but if suitable equipment is not available or is in short supply, the children will have to improvise or modify their original designs. They may want to save on materials by combining one or two obstacles to make a larger hole.

Remind the children that they will need to mark a point somewhere on the surround from which to 'tee off'. Also the golf ball must be able to *drop* into the hole, so their designs will have to take account of this, perhaps using a ramp or working on two levels. However, the children should work as closely to their original design proposals as they can.

Environments

You may decide to assemble all the holes to make a course in the hall or playground. If so, ask the children to decide in which order to place the holes. How much room will they need for the course? Will they need to number the holes? Where will they make the numbers eye-catching? Do they need to use different coloured balls? If so, why? Do they have any golf clubs? If not, what else will do? Who is going to write the scorecards? Who will give out the equipment and collect it? Depending on the time available, the children can do much of this work themselves.

## 9. Trying out the course

### Group size
Individuals and the whole class.

### Objective
To evaluate the crazy-golf course.

### What you need
Golf, course set up ready, pencil, paper.

### What to do
The only way for the children to evaluate their course is to use it. The children can go around the course in pairs and try out each hole in turn. Ask them to record their scores and perhaps record a few comments about each hole on their score sheets. In this way a consensus can be reached about which holes worked and which didn't. Is the course like a real crazy golf course? How is it similar? How is it different?

Once the children have completed the course they can analyse their results. Which hole was the favourite? Which was the hardest?

Ask the children to write a short piece about what they have done and how they designed and made their holes. Were there any problems? This written work can be supplemented with drawings.

# Business: making a shop/café

### Age range
Six to eight.

In this section the children will be directed towards designing and making a shop or café environment in which they will sell items that they have made. Any money that the children raise can be given to charity.

Setting up shops is not a new entity for young children. Most children will have played 'shop', others will have used the business ethic to sell off their old toys, books and games on street corners or by their front doors and most will have visited shops in precincts, malls or in the high street. However, these activities are intended to introduce further detail into these experiences and raise awareness of business and commerce.

## 1. Brainstorming session

### Group size
The whole class, and then small groups.

### Objective
To brainstorm ideas about which type of shops to have in school.

### What you need
Pencils, paper.

### What to do
Tell the children that they are going to design and set up a shop or café in school. The reason for the business is to raise money for charity or school funds; it is usually more motivating for the children if they know what they are raising the money for. This can be decided by you in advance or it may be possible for each group to have a different cause. (If the latter option is chosen then children will have to remain in their working groups from this point onwards.)

Ask the children to identify the type of shop they might like to create. Each group should try to think of at least ten different types of shops and then they can work as a class to produce a class list. The shops must then be grouped in some way, perhaps according to what they sell or the size and style of each shop. This grouping will depend on what ideas the children come up with. As long as they are encouraged to put shops into some sort of *sets*, the titles are less of an issue.

## 2. Word processing

### Group size
Pairs or small groups.

### Objective
To design a questionnaire to use in shops.

### What you need
A computer with a word-processing facility, pencils, paper.

### What to do
Organise a few class visits to a number of retail outlets. However, before the children go on the visits ask them to think of some questions which they might like to ask the proprietors. (You may want to limit the number of questions each child can ask to about five.) Guide them towards asking questions about the types of jobs that the people do and where the shops get their stock from. (The children are likely to need an introduction into the concept of stock control.) Simple questions such as 'What do you sell?' and 'What sort of people buy from your shop?' are also quite legitimate.

Encourage the children to think about the 'design' of the store and to find out why it is organised as it is. This last question will be essential when the children begin to design a business environment for themselves.

Once the questions have been finalised, each group can write these out using a word-processing package – using this the children will be able to check and correct spellings and leave spaces for filling in the answers they are given.

Environments

Finally, they can print out their questionnaires so that they can take them with them when they go on their visit.

## 3. Surveying shops

### Group size
The whole class.

### Objective
To evaluate retail stores and shops.

### What you need
Questionnaires (see previous activity), pencils, paper.

### What to do
It is always advisable to make appointments with the managers of the shops you intend to visit. This adds a constraint, but is likely to result in a better reception than if you just 'turned up'. Another problem which will need to be thought about before the visit is supervision, and it may be that you will need to draft in parents or other teachers to help you on the day.

Alternatively, it may be that groups of children can visit each store in turn. This does have certain logistical problems, but will allow the children to look at a wider range of shops. Let each group take turns in asking their questions to a different retailer. Remember to focus their attention on shop design – walkways, shelf height, storage – and how customers shop, for example, whether they are served or carry baskets and push trolleys that they fill themselves. It will also be useful for the children to look at how items are entered into the till – for example, some shops use overlays on computerised tills, others use bar codes or key in the price.

Ask the manager to explain why one particular method is used in preference to another.

If the children are given any free samples, ask them to keep them safe so that they can be used in a future display.

## 4. Reporting back

### Group size
The whole class and small groups.

### Objective
To describe what has been observed in the field.

### What you need
Pencils, paper.

### What to do
It is important that the children make good use of the data they collected in the previous activity, both their own and other children's. Ask them to comment on what they have found out from the shops they visited and let each group report back to the class.

Encourage them to talk about the working environments they discovered and the layouts of the shops, stores and cafés. Prompt them to talk about who does what in the store and what stock they buy in. It may also be useful at this stage for them to pick one shop and draw a picture of how it was set out.

Following on from this the children can start to look for opportunities for designing and making their own business environment. If they set up a business in school who would be their customers? It might just be the children, or include the staff and parents as well. They would also have to decide when the store would open, for example, playtimes, or after school or on occasions such as parent evenings. The children should start to see that opportunities are wide and varied.

## 5. What will you sell?

### Group size
Pairs or small groups.

### Objective
To develop ideas through modelling.

### What you need
Construction kits, junk material.

### What to do
Before the children begin to develop their ideas any further they will have to decide what their shop is going to sell and therefore what sort of shop it will be – a café, a large retail store selling lots of different things, a small store specialising in one type of product and so on.

Let the children work in pairs or smaller groups to make a model of their chosen shop. At first allow them freedom to explore their own ideas through loose structured play where they can talk to each other, interact and generally develop possibilities. The children will then be ready to structure their ideas further. Point them to their own research, the questionnaires, drawings, observations (see Activities 1–4) and encourage them to develop their *own* ideas not simply to copy in their models what they have seen in real life. Tell them to think about style, practicabilities of movement and the resources needed to create the environment. Also you could give them the challenge of coming up with a *novel* idea to attract customers to their shop.

## 6. Presenting ideas

### Group size
Pairs or small groups.

### Objective
To make a presentation of their ideas.

### What you need
The models made in Activity 5, pencils, paper.

### What to do
Having developed, made and labelled a model of their likely design, ask each pair or group of children to evaluate their efforts by making a short presentation to the rest of the class about their models. Theoretically, they should make such a presentation to their target customers, but this may not be possible. However, in many ways you should be able to assume such a role, asking the relevant questions and so on. If possible try to get one or two of the retail shop managers to attend the presentation. They will be able to help by providing practical ideas and comments.

Following on from the presentation the children should be encouraged to ask their audience for their comments and questions. One child can act as a scribe and jot down people's comments. These notes will be useful later on when the children start to compile their final design proposal.

Give each group one or two scenarios to consider. What if a disabled person wished to visit their store – will they be able to get in easily and look around? Does their design encourage both males and females to visit? Does it encourage young and elderly people to visit? Does it encourage people from *all* cultures?

## 7. Final designs

**Group size**
Pairs or small groups.

**Objective**
To generate a design proposal.

**What you need**
Pencils, paper and models (see Activity 5).

**What to do**
The children should now be ready to generate a final design proposal using the models they constructed in Activity 5. They need to discuss in detail what the shop will sell, who their target customers are likely to be, where they want to set up their shop and at what times they want to open up for business.

They must provide reasons for their choices in the form of simple statements like: 'It looks good' or 'I've got lots of these at home'. The more discerning children, however, may try to identify reasons such as: 'One shop tried this out so I have changed it a little to make it suit our school'.

Also ask the children to state what resources they will need in terms of 'fabric', for example, tables, chairs, desks, shelves, cloth to lay over tables, posters, carpet for walkways, boxes for collecting cash and so on. This list of equipment will help you to consider what is needed by *all* the groups to set up their shops and then you can make appropriate suggestions as to what they can realistically have.

## 8. Business stock

**Group size**
Pairs or small groups.

**Objective**
To organise business stock.

**What you need**
Pencils, paper.

**What to do**
Ask the children to consider the problem of business stock.

Where are they going to get it from? They may be able to get some items of jumble such as books and clothes free, but if they want to sell consumables such as drinks and sweets these will have to be purchased and then resold. The financial outlay for this will probably have to be covered by the school, the PTA or school fund. These ideas are quite common in school, the only difference is that the children themselves will be carrying out the work and not leaving it up to parents and other active adults associated with the school.

As far as possible the children should be allowed to organise their own stock, although you may help by assisting them to construct a circular asking for specific items which can then be distributed through the school's normal communication network.

## 9. Setting up the business

**Group size**
The whole class, and pairs or small groups.

**Objective**
To set up the shops.

**What you need**
Items listed from the children's design proposals plus stock (see Activity 8).

**What to do**
Having organised their stock and found the right place in and around school for the shop, the children will now be ready to set up their businesses. The first job will be to set up their stalls or

shops as indicated in their design proposals. Tell the children that they ought to price items so that they make a profit, but remind them *not* to be too excessive as otherwise no one will buy their goods. Stock which hasn't cost anything can be sold very competitively, but stock which has been bought can only be sold at a small profit.

Encourage the children to pay attention to the layout of their 'shops', making sure that passage ways between each shop or stall are wide enough for people to pass through easily. Are items at eye-level? Are they at eye-level if you are in a wheelchair? The children should also be made aware of the aesthetics of providing a good display which will encourage people to look. A welcoming environment will put people at ease, so that they will buy more or come again.

The children in each group should organise themselves so that everyone has a specific task.

## 10. Did you make a profit?

### Group size
Pairs or small groups.

### Objective
To evaluate their shops.

### What you need
Pencils, paper.

### What to do
Allow a set amount of time for selling, for example, one whole day or every lunch time for a week. Having sold all their goods, the children will be in a position to evaluate their efforts.

- Did they make a profit?
- How much profit did they make?
- Were all the items sold?
- Which items sold best?
- Did any not sell?
- Why did some items sell better than others?
- How many people visited the shop?
- What sort of people visited?
- Were they mainly boys or girls or a wide variety of people?
- How well did they work together?
- Who did what?
- Did they work well as a team, if not, why not?
- How closely did their final design match what they set out to do?
- If they had the chance to do the work again, how would they change it?
- Would they sell a wider variety of items or fewer items?
- Would they have more in the groups or less?
- How did where they were sited influence their shop?

It would again be of value to invite one or two retail managers to visit the shops and pass their comments on to the children. In turn the children could write about what they had originally intended to do and how well their ideas had actually turned out.

## Community: waste land clearance and design

### Age range
Seven to nine.

In both urban and rural environments there are always areas that have been left as waste ground. These are not areas that have been left fallow or ones supporting wildlife that should be left untouched, but areas that have been used and/or abused by people to dump wastes of various kinds. This wasteland may be a stream or pond area, it may be a landfill site or a piece of spare ground. Before children are directed or encouraged to examine such areas, likely sites will have to be vetted in terms of safety. Many apparently harmless wastelands contain hidden hazards, so it is important to research the site thoroughly before allowing the children to visit it. If the site is thought to be too dangerous then stay away. A telephone call to the local environmental health department will be of help in ascertaining likely 'safe' sites.

Throughout this activity safe working procedures must be enforced and adhered to by everyone. Children must wear gloves, strong shoes and old clothing as a matter of course and in certain circumstances will also need goggles. You will also need to think about where the children will be able to change and wash their hands.

## 1. What is biodegradable?

### Group size
Pairs or small groups.

### Objective
To build up knowledge concerning biodegradability.

### What you need
Photocopiable page 177, a variety of materials both organic and inorganic such as fabrics, wool, cotton, nylon, wood, plastic, glass, iron, paper and so on.

### What to do
The main objective of this activity is to familiarise the children with particular properties of objects that are likely to be found on wasteland. Do they rot? Do they absorb water? Do they discolour? There are a number of safety hazards involved in examining actual discarded objects in terms of the growth of fungi and bacteria. It is therefore more practical to carry out a simulation of the process in the classroom.

Children will already be familiar with composts and 'rotten' food, and this can be used to introduce and identify organic materials that biodegrade. Tell the children that materials such as glass, plastic and metals do not rot or do not rot very quickly. They could then carry out investigations using various water types such as tap water, salt water and mild acid such as vinegar or lemon juice, to find out what happens to certain inorganic materials when left in these damp conditions over a time. The children can use the worksheet on photocopiable page 177 to help them test the various objects. The same exercise could be carried out with various types of fabric.

To observe any real result the objects may have to be left in water for a few weeks. After this time, it can be seen that metal (iron) rusts and corrodes, brick tends to become flaky and brittle, glass and plastic may fade slightly but are likely to remain otherwise untarnished, fabrics will have swollen and will shred easily. Food will grow fungus on it and so will grass. Wood may do the same, but it is more likely that it will only swell and discolour if left for a short period of time. From this the children will be able to say what rots and have some idea of the time need for something to rot. It may also be possible to highlight *natural* and *man-made* materials and classify biodegradability according to whether a material is man-made or natural.

## 2. What can be recycled?

### Group size
The whole class and pairs or small groups.

### Objective
To investigate recycling.

### What you need
Pencils, paper, glass, aluminium cans, cardboard, different foodstuffs, different fabrics, photocopiable page 178.

### What to do
Many children will already be familiar with bottle banks, newspaper collections, and compost heaps. Ask them to discuss what materials can be recycled, how they are collected and what they are used for once they are recycled. In the simplest sense glass from bottles is used to make more glass bottles and paper is used to make low quality paper.

Move on to discuss with the children the whole idea of how materials can be recycled. There are lots of ways of recycling which the children may not think of initially such as hand-me-downs, turning jeans into cut-offs, reusing envelopes, making plant pots from yoghurt cartons and using bricks as stepping stones or supports for other structures.

The worksheet on photocopiable page 178 can be used in conjunction with this discussion. The children should use it to list as many ways as they can think of for reusing the objects shown on the sheet. To do this they will need to focus on the reuse of materials and objects for different purposes than they were originally intended.

## 3. Sites for redevelopment

### Group size
The whole class and pairs or small groups.

### Objective
To brainstorm possible areas for development.

### What you need
Pencils, paper, map of local area.

### What to do
It is likely that the children will be able to identify local areas that have been left as waste ground. This may be an area of land in the school itself or part of a garden or a small piece of land close by. Try not to choose an area that is too large as this will cause major problems in terms of time, planning and completing the task. Tell the children that as a class they are going to develop some *local* waste ground. What they will develop it into has not been decided, and therefore, they need to discuss some likely ideas.

If possible, let the children look at a map of the local area. Ask them to find the school, their houses or streets and other familiar landmarks. The children can colour these areas black. They should then identify any large green areas such as parks and woodland and colour these green. Finally, see whether they can find the areas of waste land which might prove to be a good source for redevelopment. These they can colour red. A general discussion following this exercise should help to confirm a number of key sites.

If possible take groups of children out so that they can

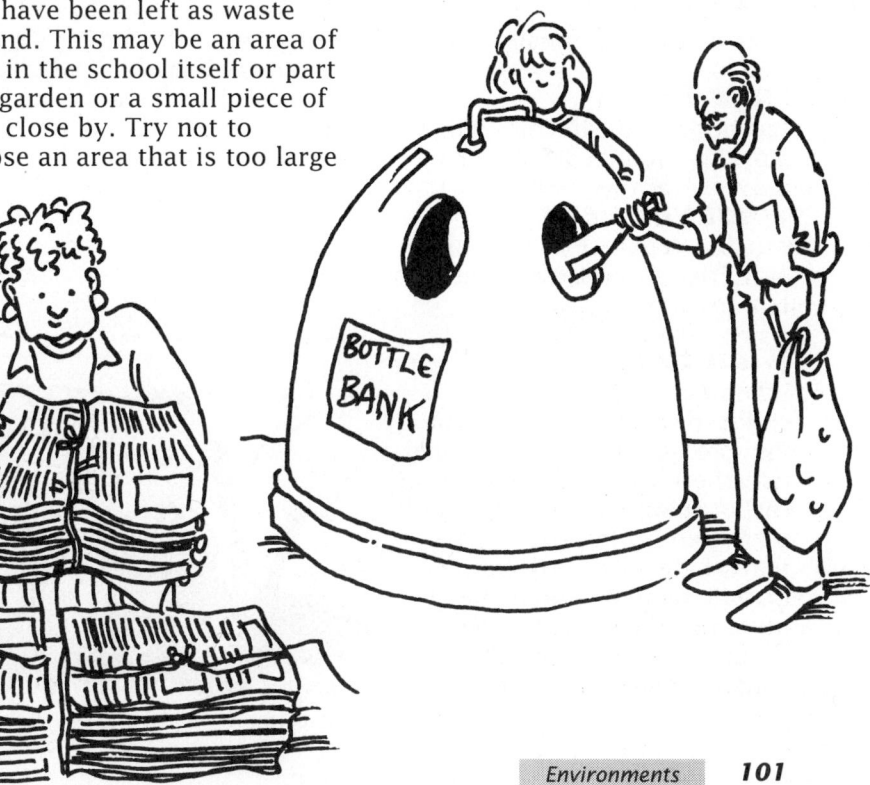

Environments 101

draw and perhaps photograph various sites. Having done this preliminary work, they will need to narrow down their choices. Invite the local planning officer into the classroom or contact her by telephone and let the children find out from her whether anything has been decided at council level about how the land is to be used. (It is pointless clearing land only for it to be taken over for building on.) They must also obtain permission to redevelop the land or part of the land. The children can also survey the local residents to find out whether they support the idea of clearing and improving the waste ground.

From all this information the children will be able to select a site.

## 4. Looking in detail

### Group size
Pairs or small groups.

### Objective
To choose one site and look in more detail at redevelopment.

### What you need
Pencils, paper, results from Activities 1 and 2 (see pages 100 to 101).

### What to do
Having chosen a site, the children will have to examine it in more detail. Explain to them that there will be little or no cash available to help them with their redevelopment so that whatever they decide to do will have to be done by utilising existing resources found on the site. Ask them to consider the size of the site.

Point out to the children, if necessary, that a large area may be difficult to complete and ask them why they think this may be.

Having isolated a single site (chosen from the areas you know to be 'safe' for development), the children should visit the site and look in detail at what is present. The children only need look – there is no need for them to pick up objects or even to touch them. They can observe waste materials which are lying on the ground or poke out objects from free soil using sticks. There is no need for them to dig around in the earth at this stage, but even so it is advisable for them to wear gloves. They should classify the materials they find there as biodegradable, non-biodegradable, recyclable and non-recyclable. Ask them to think about *how* they can reuse the materials they find on the site. This may help them to generate further ideas about how the area might be redeveloped, including their thoughts about what will have to be done to the area, such as tidying up the stream or removing all the rubbish.

## 5. Generating ideas

### Group size
Individuals.

### Objective
To generate ideas about redesigning the chosen area.

### What you need
Pencils, paper, a computer with a graphics facility.

### What to do
You may need to supply the children with a template of the approximate dimensions of the area from which to work. If the waste area is symmetrical or a regular shape this will be less of a problem than if the area is angular or asymmetrical.

Ask the children to list the initial jobs that need to be done to clear the site, but they should keep this list fairly short. Next they can focus on the materials that are available such as old bricks, pieces of wood and stones and let them think of different ways that these materials might be reused, for example, building a rock garden or stone wall with the stones or making a border for a sandpit with the bricks. You will probably be surprised at the innovation shown by the children!

Having looked at these finer details, the children can make one or two drawings of what they think the land will look like when it has been redeveloped. Encourage them to think about what people might like. Would they want a garden area? What about an activity corner for young children? Does the land need to be flat for playing ball games or will it undulate so that it is more interesting? They should also start to think about what exactly will go where.

Once they have drawn a couple of ideas the children can discuss their ideas with other children and local residents. Encourage them to *annotate* their pictures so that they are easier to follow and show reasoning behind their ideas.

## 6. Modelling

### Group size
Individuals or small groups.

### Objective
To generate a design proposal.

### What you need
Paper, pencils or collage material.

### What to do
The children can now start working on their final design proposals. They should draw these, as far as possible, to scale or in proportion. They can then either work as individuals or in small groups to work up *one* design into a model, using collage techniques. The children should label their models so that they show what materials they will use and what the finished work will look like. The advantage of modelling is that it provides a more realistic three-dimensional appearance to the finished model.

Explain to the class that only one design is going to be carried forward to completion so they will have to work hard at making sure their own ideas are realistic and practical. Tell them to write about the different features of their designs and how feasible they think each one is, taking into account available materials, cost and time.

Finally, the children can present their models to the rest of the class as a short talk. On the basis of each presentation a decision will have to be taken on which design will be chosen. This may be done by consensus or you may want to make that choice or let one of the local residents decide.

## 7. Listing the tasks

### Group size
Small groups and the whole class.

### Objective
To plan and organise aspects of the redevelopment design.

### What you need
Pencils, paper.

### What to do
Once one of the design proposals has been chosen, the class will need to look at the design in detail. As a class they

should try to indicate *all* the tasks that need doing – for example, digging over the soil, cleaning up the pond, removing all the glass, sorting out the bricks and stones and so on. Encourage the children to make a list which is long enough for small groups to have a task each to do.

Having allocated the tasks, each group will have to plan what they will do, in line with the chosen design proposal. They will need to allocate jobs for each member of the group and also to list any equipment they will need. Encourage them to think about safety, for example, they must *all* wear gloves. What else will they need? Perhaps some children are going to make a small wall using bricks and mortar or some may be trying their hand at dry stone walling? What equipment will they need to tell them whether their wall is level? They should also try and estimate the time each job will take.

Finally, each group should formulate a plan in the form of a storyboard incorporating all this information.

## 8. Carrying out the tasks

### Group size
Small groups.

### Objective
To carry out the redevelopment of the waste ground.

### What you need
Materials and equipment listed in Activity 7.

### What to do
Before the children begin the redevelopment work, make sure that they are all suitably dressed for the job. It is likely that they will need a change of clothes, reliable footwear and *gloves*. Whether working individually or as a team, make sure they are thorough in all aspects of their work. If materials have to be gathered, they must be gathered up with care and stored safely to avoid accidents. They could place items in plastic bags or alternatively, they may put items in piles on the ground for collection later. Any construction work, whether using wood, hammers and nails, or spades and soil, must be done with precision and finished off properly. They should remove any weeds and make sure that any structures they build are stable and will not topple over.

The children might have to modify and rearrange ideas as they work and they should check with others to find out the most aesthetic positions. Try to allow the children to tackle any unforeseen problems themselves, as far as possible, and encourage them to improvise with the materials and equipment they have. However, you must always pay particular attention in such situations to avoid equipment being used dangerously.

Once work has been completed, make sure all equipment is cleaned up properly and stored safely and securely.

## 9. Finishing off

### Group size
Individuals.

### Objective
To evaluate finished redevelopment and the procedures taken.

### What you need
Pencils, paper.

### What to do
Having completed the redevelopment work, the children should be encouraged to evaluate *all* aspects of it. You can list *all* the decisions the children had to take and identify who did what and

when. Using this information, the children can comment on how successful the venture was, what they enjoyed most and what they enjoyed least. Help them with its evaluation by asking them the following sort of questions:
• If they were to do the work again, how might they make it more interesting, cheaper or easier to complete?
• Are there jobs that still need to be done?
• Has the development met the needs of the residents?
• Can people use the paths?
• Do the residents like what the children have done?
• What comments do the residents have?
• Is the waste ground more pleasing to look at?
• Will the residents utilise it?
• Were there any features of the proposal that they couldn't follow through to completion? What were they? Why couldn't these parts be completed?
• Did the materials perform as expected?
• What were the problems with the materials and equipment used?

# Home: building design

## Age range
Eight to ten.

The context for the activities in this section is the home. In this situation the design and technological work will emerge out of the potentially unfamiliar situation of house design and function and the children will have to identify their own needs and/or opportunities for making. Needless to say, the actual manufacture will not be the 'real' thing, but will be in the form of scaled models using materials which replicate 'real' materials as closely as possible. This in itself will involve a fair degree of skilled craft work.

## 1. Looking at houses

### Group size
The whole class, then small groups or individuals.

### Objective
To investigate living environments.

### What you need
Books and encyclopaedias about architecture and building design.

### What to do
As a stimulus to further activity, start by asking the children to describe where they live. If they live in houses or flats, they should say how many rooms there are and what each one is used for. Ask them whether they have their own bedrooms and whether there are any spare rooms. This should lead into a general open-ended discussion about houses and homes andl living conditions. Is there a need for people to be homeless in this day and age? Why do people live and travel in caravans? What are nomads? In which part of the world do they live? Why do they live this way? What are shanty towns and slums? Why do people live in these areas?

If possible organise a number of visits to a variety of types of home in the area. You may also be able to include a visit to a large stately home or an exhibition relating to how people lived in the past.

Encourage the children to begin to think about the different types of *building*

Environments 105

*designs*, the number of rooms, the function of each room, the number of people who live in the building and the reasons they live like they do.

You could finish this work by allowing the children to choose one type of home and research it in more detail, and then present their findings to the rest of the class.

## 2. Analysing house types

### Group size
Individuals.

### Objective
To generate needs and opportunities for designing home environments.

### What you need
Pencils, paper.

### What to do
Using the material they gathered in the previous activity as background information, the children can analyse each type of home and write a sentence or two about why it has been designed in the way that it has, for example:
• High rise flats can house a lot of people in a relatively small land space.
• Tents allow people to move over large distances quickly and easily.
• Shanty towns are caused by poverty.
• Large mansions can accommodate large numbers of guests and visitors.
• The children's own homes provide them with a comfortable environment with all necessary facilities, such as heating, lighting, electricity and clean water.

The children can then come together as a class and list all their ideas on the board. This should give them a broader perspective as to why homes are designed so differently.

The children now need to identify possible needs and/or opportunities for designing and making a home environment based on the data they generated. Ask them to think of five possible ideas. They must not just copy existing designs, unless they intend using an existing design in a new setting, for example, log cabins as houses on a standard western housing estate. Ideas may include:
• organising shanty towns to make them cleaner and more hygienic;
• putting an extension in their own house to improve living conditions;
• designing low level buildings that are safer in areas where earthquakes and other natural disasters persist;
• setting up portable homes to help the homeless in inner city areas.

From these lists they should finally choose one idea for further development.

## 3. Preparing a database

### Group size
Individuals.

### Objective
To research and develop housing needs further.

### What you need
Books on housing, pencils, paper, a computer with word processing and database or spreadsheet facilities.

### What you do
Ask the children to carry out some further research and development work on their identified housing need. This is likely to involve a visit to the library, but you should also encourage the children to obtain data from other sources such as by writing to, telephoning or interviewing experts and practitioners. If they are looking at developing temporary homes, for example, they might wish to visit a caravan park or equivalent. Wherever they visit or whoever they interview, they will need to have prepared in advance

the questions they want to ask. They should try to write down at least five questions up to a maximum of ten. Encourage the children to include at the beginning of their lists some easy questions which require simple yes or no answers. They can then ask one or two more open-ended questions, for example, 'What do you think about...?' or 'Why do you...?' at the end of their lists. You can check these questions so that the interviewees do not have their time wasted by repetitive and irrelevant questions. It is also important that these people are contacted beforehand to make sure they are willing to be interviewed and to arrange a suitable time for the interview.

The children can prepare the questionnaires on a computer so that they can lay them out with spaces for them to write in the various responses. As part of this exercise, ask the children to use a data collection and processing package on a computer, and present their results, for example, in the form of a spreadsheet. They will have to generate their own titles such as number of people living in the home, size, shape, and so on.

## 4. Data analysis

### Group size
Individuals.

### Objective
To analyse data and refine ideas.

### What you need
Information collected and stored on a computer from the previous activity.

### What to do
As a result of their investigations in the field and using secondary sources, the children can now begin to refine and develop their design ideas. They may have found out that every caravan has Calor gas heating or that most houses have box rooms that are too small and lack space to develop a more comfortable environment. They should study all their findings with the following headings in mind:
• relative cost (for example, high, medium, low);
• time needed to construct;
• skills needed to make;
• ergonomics or how efficiently people work in their environment.

Focusing particularly on the last heading, the children should think about how easily people can move around the available space and how they can include all utilities into this space yet still provide comfort. They should then begin to refine their design ideas. Remind them that they are designing to suit the needs of a particular group of people and their designs must therefore reflect these needs.

## 5. Three-dimensional modelling

### Group size
Individuals.

### Objective
To develop a three-dimensional model of design ideas.

### What you need
Construction kits, junk material, pencils, paper.

### What to do
The children will, by this stage, have spent a fair amount of time investigating and exploring ideas and will probably have come up with various designs and modifications. They should therefore now draw and label

the design that they are going to model. Encourage them to explain why they have chosen this particular idea and then let them make their models. It is interesting to note that while many children cannot yet draw in three dimensions at this age, their ideas normally have a three-dimensional image.

Working with construction kits will allow the children to gain a better picture of what they actually want to achieve. They should be allowed to work with a number of different materials, such as construction kits, card, Plasticine and so on. Introduce the concept of scale and proportion. Many construction kits have model people which can often help as a scale guide and encourage the children to think about how big the actual building is going to be! This can be done to an extent by simple scaling such as using 10cm to represent 1m.

Having completed their models the children should be in a better position to refine and edit their ideas. They should then encourage others to comment on the model's design and ergonomic features.

## 6. The final picture

### Group size
Individuals.

### Objective
To generate a design proposal.

### What you need
Pencils, paper.

### What to do
The children can now generate a final design proposal in the form of a scaled diagram together with a model (the one designed in Activity 5 with adjustments will suffice). Each part of the design needs to be labelled with annotations that explain why particular materials or designs are being used. They will also need to write a short explanation on the design proposal explaining what needs the home has been designed to meet. On a separate sheet ask the children to explain why one or two of their original ideas were not used – perhaps items cost too much or they would be in short supply in that area of the world?

Tell them to write down what materials they would actually need to manufacture this building and from where they might obtain these materials. Are there any decisions still yet to be made? Why can they not come to a decision on these aspects just yet?

## 7. Prototypes

### Group size
Individuals.

### Objective
To develop skills in working with materials.

### What you need
Sheet metal, foil, construction kits, acetate sheets, tape, pot riveter, hammer, nails.

### What to do
Tell the children that they are going to make miniatures or prototypes of their designs. Therefore, if they specified on their design proposals that their buildings would be made from wood, glass and metal, then these materials need to be provided for them. The range of skills needed to work with these materials on a miniature level is not too extensive – for example, scrap wood can be sawn into thin strips in advance to help improve its workability and usefulness (use soft wood rather than hard wood), and thin sheets of metal can be bought from a dealer. Alternatively, baking foil can be used if it is reinforced with thin wooden strips or metallic rods. Thicker sheet metal will have to be bent using pliers or a small hammer. (**NB:** The edges of

sheet metal are quite sharp so the children will need to be instructed how to handle this safety hazard.)

It is advisable not to work with glass, but to use a similar alternative such as clear polyethene. This will have to be stretched tightly to give a realistic effect. Accetate sheets may be a better alternative, but are more costly.

The children may want to use bricks or stones and while stone presents less of a problem it may be better to use bricks from a construction kit.

The children will also need to develop their skills in joining the different materials together – Plasticine can be used instead of putty and if the wood is thin use adhesive instead of nails. Metal foil can be attached with tape or, if the school has one available, a pot-riveter.

# 8. Listing resources

## Group size
Individuals.

## Objective
To plan and make their designs.

## What you need
Pencils, paper.

## What to do
Ask the children to list the resources they require to make their prototypes including both tools and equipment. If some materials or tools are not available then they will have to review their ideas and perhaps think of alternatives.

Tell them to plan and organise their work, making a sequential list of the tasks they will have to do. Although they will be working individually, it may well be that the children will be able to share certain tasks such as cutting. They should always be aware of waste as they work and try to think of ways to minimise it. Also, as with all manufacturing, they should aim at a good quality finish – edges should be level and smooth, and they should be mindful of dangers and safety hazards.

Once they have completed their work they should tidy up properly and with due care and attention.

# 9. How will the prototype function?

## Group size
Individuals.

## Objective
To evaluate products and procedures.

## What you need
Pencils, paper.

## What to do
Once their prototypes have been designed and made, the children must evaluate their products and procedures. How does the building look? Is it finished properly? Do they think it will function as they intended? How easy do they think it would be to build a full sized version? If possible they should ask others to evaluate their prototypes, for example the likely users of the building, or architects.

The children should also assess whether their designs turned out as they intended and if not, how they have changed. How might they be modified or improved in order

**Environments** 109

to satisfy these original intentions?

Ask the children to study the processes and procedures they went through to achieve their prototypes and ask them to think whether they carried out sufficient research. Did they have enough skills to carry out what they wanted to do? Did they make the right decisions? What decisions went wrong? Is their design as ergonomically viable as they had first thought?

# School: ecological garden design

### Age range
Nine to twelve.

The activities in this final section focus around the growing need for us to take on the role of guardians of our environment. The context for these activities is the school and the children will design and create an ecological niche somewhere in or around the school grounds.

The principal focus of these activities is related to the development of a pond habitat, but the same principles could apply to the development of a wooded, shrubbed or heathland habitat. The children will work with their own individual ideas initially, but it should be explained to them that at some point only *one* idea will be carried forward to completion.

## 1. Pond studies

### Group size
Individuals.

### Objective
To study different types of habitats.

### What you need
Secondary resources such as books and encyclopaedias relating to pond habitats, photocopiable page 179.

### What to do
Tell the children that they are going to design and make a pond somewhere in the school grounds. Introduce the activity by getting them to write down a few questions concerning what they will have to research and find out about such a habitat. These initial questions are likely to include:
• What items of flora and fauna will go into the pond?
• Where is the pond going to be sited?
• What will the pond habitat and surrounding environment look like?

To make these decisions the children will need to find out about the ecosystem of ponds. This is best done by making a detailed study of a local pond.

Introduce the children to concepts such as food chains, habitats, groups of similar species and so on. You can use the worksheet on photocopiable page 179 as an introduction to these concepts.

The children really need to grasp the concept that within an environment all the animals and plants need each other to survive. The plants are the producers providing oxygen and food which is consumed by the herbivores who are in turn consumed by the carnivores. The words predator and prey also can be introduced.

A pond study, particularly in the spring and summer months, would help the children to identify all these different species that inhabit a pond and their relative numbers, for example lots of plants, fewer herbivores, less carnivores and very few surface carnivores.

Having completed this initial study, the children can summarise their work by suggesting how what their discoveries might influence their pond. If time allows and local facilities are conducive then perhaps more than one pond can be studied, and the details from each collated.

## 2. Searching for sites

### Group size
Small groups.

### Objective
To look for possible sites for the pond.

### What you need
Pencils, paper.

### What to do
Ask the children to work in groups to make an initial survey of the school grounds with a view to finding possible sites for a pond. Before they go out and look, they will need to discuss the factors that make good and bad sites, for example:
• How safe is it from being vandalised?
• How easily can people visit the site?
• Is it easily accessible yet safe?
• Is there too much or too little light?
• What is the surrounding environment like?
• Are there trees and shrubs there already?
• Is the area grassed or flagged?
• Is it near or far away from buildings?
• How will it be used?
• Will it be used by other pupils?

Armed with a range of such criteria the children will be able to survey a number of likely sites. This information can then be collated on a computer and analysed. This will involve the children in accessing a database of their own or of your creation. Alternatively, such data can be collated on a master sheet on the wall in the classroom. The important factor is that each child should be able to have access to *all* the data once it has been gathered as each child will have to record which site they think has the most viable environment for a pond.

## 3. Landscapes of the past

### Group size
Individuals.

### Objective
To find out how landscaping has been used in the past.

### What you need
Books on different landscapes.

### What to do
Change the children's attention from pond habitats to focus on how people have developed ponds and similar features in the past and in different cultures. From a historical perspective you may want to organise a visit to a stately home, botanical gardens and so on. When on such trips encourage the children to look at the flora and fauna as well as specific design features such as water pumps and waterfalls, the shape and size of ponds and lakes and so on.

If possible, try to organise an interview 'on site' with a gardener or horticulturist. This way they may be able to discover why stones are used (for decoration or to support wildlife) and the purpose of having waterfalls (decoration or oxygenation of the water). They could also ask what they should look out for when designing their ponds and whether these experts can give them any tips.

The two key features to come from such research should be *design* (what items are present and their layout in relation to other items) and *function* (what each item is used for) and back in the classroom the children can make annotated drawings of ponds to show details and functions and write about their trip emphasising the *ideas* they obtained which could be used when designing their own ponds.

Environments 111

## 4. Concept sketches

### Group size
Individuals.

### Objective
To generate a few design ideas based on information collected.

### What you need
Pencils, paper and/or a computer with a graphics facility, photocopiable page 180.

### What to do
Despite having carried out research into ponds there will still be many gaps to fill and problems to be resolved. Ask the children to draw a few sketches of how they see their pond developing. These will be in the form of *concept* sketches showing parts of their initial annotated diagrams and how they may be changed or altered. Try to encourage them to draw three-dimensional pictures alongside two-dimensional plans.

From these ideas the children should identify any problems with their designs such as how to build the pond, what its function is to be and where it is to be sited, and generate a design brief. This initial brief need only be in the form of a short paragraph and having written it, the children can try writing a more comprehensive design brief under the title: 'Design and make a school pond which can be used for studying pond-life'. On the basis of this focus the children can identify and list all the items they need to research in more detail before they can set about making.

Brainstorming is perhaps the easiest way to go about this task. Use photocopiable page 180 to help you. For each item in the bubbles the children will have to think of aspects they will need to research and find answers for. Having listed their ideas they can then systematically look at each item in turn and tick or cross whether they need to know more about it.

## 5. Scrutinising details

### Group size
Individuals.

### Objective
To research in more detail certain aspects of their ideas.

### What you need
Various catalogues and sources of information regarding costs of ponds.

### What to do
Tell the children that they can now work on aspects of their design ideas that need closer scrutiny. They will need to measure the area they have chosen or that is available to them. Will they want a large pond to fill the bulk of the space or will they want a smaller pond so that people can walk around it easily?

Connected with this problem is the cost factor and a catalogue from a garden or DIY centre or a telephone call will give the children information about how much moulded ponds cost. They might also like to find out whether it would be possible to make a pond that costs hardly anything by using scrap materials. (This is feasible but involves much more preparation!) At this juncture you should add a financial constraint and this will limit the size of the pond unless they have decided to make one themselves.

The children will also need to think about where they are going to get materials from. Are these going to be bought or donated? What materials are readily available? What materials will they need? Do the two lists match up? If not, decisions will have to be made. They should record all this research together with the decisions they make and their reasons for making them.

**NB:** it may be worth contacting your Local Groundwork Trust for advice.

## 6. Drawing up plans

### Group size
Individuals.

### Objective
To generate a design proposal using modelling techniques.

### What you need
A variety of modelling materials, adhesive, card, paper, scissors, straws, coloured paper and so on.

### What to do
Tell the children that although they have all worked hard drawing up designs for a pond only *one* proposal can actually be used. Therefore, they must each draw up a plan of their proposal which they will eventually present to the rest of the class. These plans should indicate what they want to do in terms of relative costs, the materials needed and those readily available, size, dimensions and an indication of time and manpower. They can be done as architectural plans or as a series of drawings/pictures that show what the children intend to do.

Following on from this, ask the children to spend time on making a mock-up model of their planned pond and its environment. Try to encourage them to make the model and the drawings to scale. The models can be created using a collage effect, for example, they might use blue cellophane for the pond or shredded green paper for the grass. The collage effect of the model will be a design in itself.

Finally, the children should be encouraged to 'sell' their products to an invited audience. This means that they must emphasise the positive features of their designs and also submit all their research and development work in the form of a portfolio to show how well they have recorded the project.

## 7. Production plans

### Group size
The whole class and individuals.

### Objective
To draw up a production plan prior to the manufacture of the pond.

### What you need
Pencils, paper.

### What to do
Start off by introducing the children to the concept of a production plan whereby they plan and organise how they are going to carry out the work. Ask them to identify what they will need to know, for example:

- the materials they intend to use;
- where they are going to get them from;
- how they are going to get them;
- what equipment will be needed;
- who will get this and distribute it;
- whether there will be enough equipment for one each or whether they will have to share;
- how they will make sure everybody takes part.

All these factors need to be discussed and decisions reached, including when and how long each part will take to complete! It may be worthwhile brainstorming all these as a class and then allowing the children to organise and sequence the details into a logical plan of campaign. This will ensure that you retain control of all the arrangements.

Once the final plans have been reached they can be put up on the class notice board so that they are accessible to everyone. These plans should include who is doing what and when, so that all the class

*Environments*

know their role in the overall construction. They should also include details of any possible safety hazards and these need to be emphasised so that all the children are aware of them. Hazards are likely to include the risk of infection through cuts and therefore all the children must wear gloves. The working area should also be cleared of other children and fenced off in some way. You should also talk through possible risk situations with the children and make sure they all know what to do in case of an accident.

## 8. Making the pond

**Group size**
Various.

**Objective**
To make the pond environment.

**What you need**
Materials and equipment as listed by the children in Activity 7.

**What to do**
With a strong reminder about safety controls and likely hazards, the children will now be able to follow their production schedules. Make sure only a few children work on the project at any one time and that they are properly supervised when at work. This will probably mean that you will have to enlist the help of other teachers and parents. Make sure that the area selected is cordoned off and this will no doubt add to the air of excitement.

You will probably have to instruct the children how to use certain materials and equipment properly, for example, how to dig properly using a spade, how to plant flowers, and possibly how to make a small wall using bricks and mortar (such an exercise as this may involve skill development of a more thorough nature).

It is also likely that they will meet with problems during their construction, for example, they may run out of materials or perhaps the moulded pond won't fit properly at first. Rather than spoon feed the children, consult with them to find out how they think these problems can be solved. Often with a little more thought they will deal with the problem without much help. If the problem proves to be insurmountable such as pipes running underground that they were not aware of, then you may have to act and give directives.

## 9. Evaluating the job

**Group size**
Individuals.

**Objective**
To evaluate the work done.

**What you need**
Pencils, paper.

**What to do**
Once the pond is completed, ask the children to evaluate all aspects of the exercise, from their initial research to the manufacture. To do this they should list all the features of the work they undertook, including their initial research, making their models, drawing up plans, making the pond and so on. Ask them to comment on each item in the list under the headings:
• Did it work?
• How well did it work?
• What problems were there?
• If the work was carried out again, how might it be made to work better?

This last question implies a need for criteria, for example, how might it be made more cheaply, quickly, to function better, smaller, larger and so on. Also as a part of this overall evaluation the children will need to justify decisions that have been made by them and others. This may be included as part of the criteria outlined earlier, for example, what was the reason for having a smaller pond? Why was only *one* pond chosen?

# CHAPTER 5

# Systems

Traditionally, technologists associate systems with computers, electronics, mechanisms and control. However, systems also occur in many other situations such as business, living organisms and living processes. The concept has fundamental principles that are common to all contexts and therefore can be taught in a variety of ways.

The basic principle of a system is that it involves a set of interdependent tasks that together perform an overall job. For example, management systems involve people taking on different roles in order that a product sells or that work operates efficiently, while a gambling system involves a series of moves and decisions based on sequential events in order to maximise the chances of winning as an end result. At its simplest, a system will have an **input** (what goes into a system such as energy and artefacts), a **process** (a job or task that converts the input into an output) and an **output** (what you get from the system such as different forms of energy or a parcelled artefact). This simplistic approach to systems will be a more than adequate introduction for young children. Later on details such as feedback and control can be introduced to complicate the picture.

The themes in this chapter include a range of different systems, hence a range of different materials to work with and develop skills in.

Systems  115

# ACTIVITIES

## School: production systems

### Age range
Five to seven.

Young children tend to be egocentric, working and carrying out tasks alone. However, technology often demands that children work together as a team, conversing and interacting as they carry out their 'roles'. This process of working out who does what is a simple form of system.

The activities in this section are intended as a means of introducing the concept of systems and the terms *input*, *process* and *output* using the production of a greetings card as the product to be manufactured. A process can satisfy a need just as the manufacture of an artefact can. Here, craft skills are still used and developed, but the focus is not so much on the product as on how the procedures are organised.

## 1. Printing

### Group size
Individuals.

### Objective
To develop basic printing skills.

### What you need
Printing blocks such as potatoes, paints, inks, Plasticine, sponge and leaves; paper.

### What to do
Show the children how to use printing to produce different effects. The children can explore a variety of methods, but it may be a good idea to start off by making hand prints. They can explore printing with flat hands, fingers, the side of their hands and so on. Encourage them to talk about what the shapes resemble.

Having explored printing with their hands the children can use potatoes and other media to create a design. They should specify their design before they work on it. Even if the end result turns out differently they will have at least thought about a design and tried to reproduce it. This internal conceptualisation or 'imaging' is of great importance and significance to the young 'technologist' as it is a direct link between creative thought and creative activity.

Finally, the children may like to add other features to their prints, turning them from collages to pictures with identifiable features.

## 2. Thinking about greetings cards

### Group size
The whole class, then teams of three or four.

### Objective
To brainstorm ideas about greetings cards.

### What you need
Pencils, paper.

### What to do
Tell the children that they are going to make greetings cards – depending on the time of year the need for such cards may be more obvious than at others. If a particular event or festival is forthcoming then it is likely that the children will have lots of ideas about the type of card to make. If not, then a visit to a local shop to look at the range of cards that are available might be useful.

Help the children to brainstorm different types of card such as 'good luck', 'birthday', 'get well soon' and so on. The children must then decide as a group what they want to make cards for. Encourage them to come to a collective decision, trying to avoid one person dictating to the others. Having decided on the type of card the children can each write a sentence about it, for example, 'We are going to make greetings cards for *Ramadan*'.

## 3. Studying greetings cards

### Group size
Pairs or small groups.

### Objective
To find out about and examine a variety of greetings cards.

### What you need
Various examples of different greetings cards, pencils, paper, photocopiable page 181.

### What to do
This activity is principally a lesson in observation. The children should work together in their groups, looking at the different cards and writing down at least ten observations concerning them. Guide the children towards what they might look for or alternatively use this guidance as a backup tactic if the children get stuck, perhaps starting by providing no help at all. Observations should include:
• a description of what is on the front, for example, a picture, picture and writing or just writing;
• the type of picture, for example, cartoons, collages, photographs and so on;
• key essentials such as 'most Christmas cards have a fir tree, holly, robin and/or religious images on them';
• how the card is made, for example, from thin card folded in four to provide support so that the card stands up.

Ideas concerning such things as cost or ease of manufacture need not be considered unless they are mentioned by the children themselves.

To conclude this work ask the children to complete an annotated sketch of a typical card using photocopiable page 181.

Systems 117

## 4. Front cover

### Group size
Small groups.

### Objective
To begin developing ideas for card designs.

### What you need
A computer with a graphics program.

### What to do
The children can now begin to think about the picture that will go on the front of their cards. They must discuss the details of their pictures in their groups before they start to do any other design work. Encourage them to think simply. Children often tend to include too many objects and images in design, making them look cluttered. This can be avoided if you restrict the number of images the children are allowed to use in the picture. However, it is important to allow *some* choice even though a broad constraint has been imposed and there is certainly no need to stipulate exactly what must be in the picture!

The children can sketch their initial ideas in colour on paper. Encourage them to come up with a few different possibilities, maybe one card each and then decide on the *best* design. This can also be done using computer graphics. The computer can be set up for each group to experiment with. They will need to practise using a mouse, but given time they should be able to produce a reasonable picture. If their pictures are successful the children can print them out and colour them in.

## 5. What is a system?

### Group size
The whole class.

### Objective
To introduce the concept of systems.

### What you need
Paper, pencils, photocopiable page 182.

### What to do
Tell the children that they are going to work in their groups to make greetings cards and they must decide who in the group will do what. To do this they will have to operate and organise a 'system' for working. Tell them that what goes into a system, for example, energy or a letter, is called an *input*. This is then altered or moved along a route until it emerges from the system as an *output*. Within a system certain jobs take place and these are called *processes*.

Once you have explained the basic principles to the children let them work through photocopiable page 182. They should talk about what each system does and then work backwards to discover the input.

After developing the children's awareness of these fundamental concepts, ask them to focus on how they will make their greetings cards. Tell them that they will use their printing skills to make the pictures, while the title and/or the message inside can be handwritten or stencilled so that it is neat and well presented. Finally, they will need to fold the card and place it in an envelope ready for sending.

## 6. Organising the work

### Group size
Small groups.

### Objective
To organise work by producing a plan.

### What you need
Pencils, paper.

### What to do
Ask the groups of children to make a few, say about ten, copies of their greetings card designs. Each group will have their own design and should plan how to make their cards so that they are all made in the same way. Their ideas for each stage of the process can be placed on the board so that the children can write them out in sequence. The list should include for example:
- Print __ on the front in ___ (colour).
- Print __ on the front in ___ (colour).
- Print __ on the front in ___ (colour).
- Write/stencil the message on the front.
- Fold the card.
- Write/stencil the message inside.
- Place in an envelope.

Obviously, the number of times the children print will vary according to how many are in the group and how complicated the picture is.

Ask the children to write and draw their lists in the form of a series of instructions and once they have done this they can begin to think in terms of *input* (printing, writing and folding) and *output* (the finished card). This can be recorded on their instructions.

## 7. Gathering materials

### Group size
Small groups.

### Objective
To gather equipment, prior to manufacture.

### What you need
Pencils, paper.

### What to do
Ask the children to talk about the materials and equipment they, as a group, will need to make their card. At this stage they do not need to provide a list, but they need to begin to think about the resources they will need.

With teacher input they should organise themselves so that they make sure all the equipment is ready. This will involve somebody making the printing blocks and cutting the card so that when folded it will fit into the envelopes provided. This is yet another exercise that can be negotiated with the children or at the very least, discussed with them to raise their awareness of planning.

## 8. Following a storyboard

### Group size
Small groups.

### Objective
To make cards using a production system.

Systems 119

### What you need
Printing blocks, stencils, paint, inks, card, envelopes.

### What to do
Ask the children to arrange their materials along a table in the order they will use them. Encourage them to follow their design 'storyboards', as they set out the equipment and you can help them by offering advice if particular items are missing.

Having set out their equipment the children will have to decide who will do what job. Encourage them to discuss this between themselves and come to a conclusion. If they cannot agree then you can suggest that they each take a turn at each stage. They may also find that there are too many stages for the number of children in the group. If this is the case they can double up on some stages or leave certain jobs until the end – for example, everyone can help to put the cards in envelopes themselves.

To see how well their system works, ask the groups to carry out an initial trial run, making one card only. Once they've completed this run ask them to stop and evaluate their systems. They may find that the paint is too runny or that one job is holding up the next (stencilling is likely to be quite slow). Try to encourage the children to think of ways around their problems as far as possible. Once they are satisfied that all is in order, they can set to and put the system into full operation.

## 9. Evaluating inputs and outputs

### Group size
Individuals and small groups.

### Objective
To evaluate finished products and systems.

### What you need
Pencils, paper.

### What to do
Once each group has made their ten cards, ask them to talk about what they did. Who did what in each group? What were the inputs? What was the output? What processes took place?

Ask them to study all the cards their group made. Are they all the same? Are they slightly different? Which is best? Which is not so good? Why is this one the best or worst? Did their system work well? Did everybody have a job to do? Did anybody have more than one job? Were there any hold ups? Did any job take longer than another? If so, then why?

Encourage the children to talk about the production lines that are used in industry. Explain to them how lots of products are made using systems very similar to the ones they worked out. Have they ever seen real production systems in operation?

Finally, ask the children to record what they did and what they made, using a combination of writing and drawing.

## Recreation: mechanical systems

### Age range
Six to eight.

The activities in this section revolve around the use of pulleys. The children will be asked to design and make a working *model* of a fairground ride. The only criterion required is that the ride should involve the use of a pulley system or a pulley as part of a system. At this level the pulley system will be straightforward and relatively easy to construct. There is no need to complicate issues by looking at ratios and such like. The children should also be able to use a combination of various modelling mediums to produce an effective finished product.

# 1. Pulley systems

## Group size
Pairs or small groups.

## Objective
To explore pulley systems.

## What you need
Construction kits with pulleys such as LEGO and Meccano, thin string, photocopiable page 183.

## What to do
It is important that the children are introduced to pulleys before they have to use them in their work. Show them how pulleys evolved from the wheel and how they make lifting or moving objects smooth and easy. The string, rope or belt used with a pulley is not pulled over any edges or corners and so there is less friction, which in turn means that the rope does not fray very quickly.

Once you have explained to the children how a pulley system works it is important that the children are able to set one for themselves. Using photocopiable page 183 ask them to set up, investigate, explore and play with one of the pulley systems shown on it. They might also like to try building cranes, chair lifts or other equivalent pulley systems.

This work could be organised as a round robin exercise, with each group in the class spending a fixed amount of time on every task. Leave each group with all the necessary parts and see whether they can construct their models by following the pictures on photocopiable page 183.

# 2. Evaluating pulley systems

## Group size
Individuals.

## Objective
To write about and evaluate pulley systems.

## What you need
Pulley systems (as made in Activity 1), pencils, paper.

## What to do
On the basis of their practical exploration in Activity 1, the children can write about and/or draw each of the pulley systems they have made. Ask them to identify each part of each system, for example, the belt, the pulley, the axle, the housing and so on. Then ask them to explain what each part does; for example, the belt moves around the pulley, the pulley makes the belt move more easily and so on. Can they also identify the input(s) and the output(s) of each system?

Tell the children to list each system as a flow chart. You will probably have to help them do this. A good way to do this is to discuss and identify the *processes* involved in each system and then to list these on the board for the children to sequence and order for themselves. Ask them to suggest how each pulley system might be used and/or how it might be used differently. (Don't mention fairground rides yet!)

Finally, the children can write a sentence about each system underneath their flow chart(s).

## 3. How can pulleys be used?

### Group size
The whole class, then individuals or small groups.

### Objective
To brainstorm ideas for using pulleys in context.

### What you need
Pencils, paper.

### What to do
Tell the class that they are going to design and make a fairground or fun ride using pulleys for part of the ride. Talk with the children about the various types of rides they have seen or have been on at theme parks and ask them to say whether they think these rides used pulleys or not. If pulleys were used, how were they used? If they were not used, how might the ride be changed to incorporate a pulley.

After this initial class discussion let them talk within their groups about how pulley systems might be used for rides. If the children are unsure about how to start, focus their attention on one type of pulley system, for example, a lift or counterweight idea. Also many theme parks have chair rides that travel around the park, how might the children develop this idea further?

As a conclusion to this work, the groups of children must try to come up with one idea that they feel is worth investigating further and draw a rough sketch and write a little about it.

## 4. Courting opinions

### Group size
Pairs or small groups.

### Objective
To research other people's ideas and opinions concerning fairground rides.

### What you need
A computer with a word-processing facility, pencils, paper.

### What to do
Emphasise to the children that it may be possible to find some good ideas for their designs from other people. However, to do this they must think up the right questions to ask them about fun rides. These may be as basic as, 'What is your favourite ride?' or more abstractly, 'Which rides have you found boring and why?' Encourage them to think of new places where such rides could be put, for example, in the local park or in their backgardens. They should try to think of at least five questions which may help them to come up with an idea for a ride.

The children should type their questions into a computer and work on the layout, leaving spaces for people's answers. Once these have been printed out they should use them to survey as many people as they can.

Having collected their data the groups can analyse them and write a short piece about their results.

## 5. Visiting a park

### Group size
The whole class.

### Objective
To visit a local park and/or theme park.

### What you need
Pencils, paper, clip-boards.

### What to do
It would be useful for the

children to visit a theme park at this point. They can then experience the rides for themselves and actually see which rides use pulleys. Ask them to sketch and write about some of the rides too.

If supervised, they may also be able to use the questionnaire from Activity 4. If you contact the park beforehand they may be able to provide guest speakers and experts to describe how the rides are designed and maintained.

## 6. Modelling pulley systems

### Group size
Individuals, pairs or small groups.

### Objective
To explore ideas using modelling kits.

### What you need
Construction kits such as LEGO, Meccano or Fischer Technic.

### What to do
Having experienced pulley systems, and developed ideas about how such systems might be used as a part of fun rides in a fairground or theme park, the children will be ready to explore the mechanisms of their ideas. To do this most effectively they ought to work in groups, particularly if construction kits are scarce. If, however, there are enough pulley wheels and a variety of sizes available, then the children will be able to work individually on their own projects.

To help them focus their ideas, ask them to build a moving system using pulleys and describe how it works. They need not provide any other details to their models such as chairs and so on. These extras can be represented by pieces of card, paper or clips fixed to the pulley system to mark where they will go.

At the end of this exercise the children should have gained a better idea of how their fun ride will operate. Finally, they should make a sketch of their idea so that they do not forget it.

## 7. Designing surroundings

### Group size
Individuals, pairs or small groups.

### Objective
To design the surroundings to go with the ride.

### What you need
Pencils, paper, crayons or felt-tipped pens.

### What to do
Focus the children's attention on the housing for their rides. Theme park rides usually have names such as 'The Beach' or the 'Tower of Terror' and so the children's rides will also need names. The names will need to be shown prominently somewhere on the facia and so the children will have to decide what colours they will use, what sort of graphics they will use and so on.

They will also need to think about extras such as chairs. How will these be joined to the model? They may need to investigate this in detail and on the basis of their findings draw or paint their final designs. Encourage them to sketch a number of ideas before deciding on their final one.

Your role in this process will depend on the creative instinct of the children themselves and you should also encourage them to seek the opinions of other children in the class concerning their sketches.

## 8. Making pulley rides

### Group size
Individuals, pairs or small groups.

### Objective
To make their pulley rides.

### What you need
Construction kits, card, paper, pencils, coloured crayons, sticky tape, scissors.

### What to do

Having produced a final sketch the children can set about making their models. They should make the mechanism first and make sure that it is working properly. The main problem they are likely to encounter as they fix their fittings to the belt is sagging. Therefore, they must make sure that the pulley is tight enough to support suspended weights, yet loose enough so that it does not jam and/or pull the ends that the pulleys are fixed to, towards each other. This may take time to resolve!

However, once the pulley system is working properly, the children can turn their attention to the rest of the model. They can fit additions and extra features to the pulley using Blu-Tack, sticky tape or metal fasteners and clips. Encourage them to measure accurately, use rulers to draw lines and cut along lines carefully. They should continue to check their work as they build and make sure that they work to scale.

Once everything has been completed, the children must try out their systems to check that they work as they expected.

## 9. How does the ride look?

### Group size
Individuals.

### Objective
To evaluate work completed and tasks undertaken.

### What you need
Pencils, paper.

### What to do

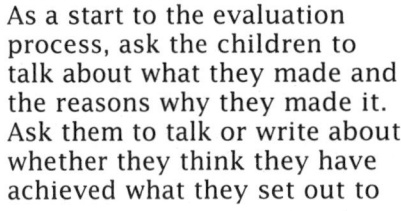

As a start to the evaluation process, ask the children to talk about what they made and the reasons why they made it. Ask them to talk or write about whether they think they have achieved what they set out to make. Does it work as they expected? What problems did they meet? Did they solve the problems? If so, how? Does the ride look good? What do other people think?

The children should also consider how the pulley system might be made automatic. How might it be speeded up or slowed down? What would happen if it were speeded up or slowed down? What would be the safety hazards? Point out to the children that all fairground rides are extensively tested before they are used and are checked frequently to ensure high safety standards.

Finally, ask the children to point out the inputs, the processes (jobs done in the system) and the output parts of the system. This can be done as a written piece or by discussion. Ask them to say how they might make the system work.

# Business: office filing systems

### Age range
Seven to nine.

The activities in this section focus on the filing system. The context is business and therefore the children's work should reflect this influence. Office filing systems are very varied, from computerised data storage through to more traditional filing cabinets and bound manuscripts. Although the children taking part in these activities will be of a fairly young age, there is no reason why they shouldn't have their awareness revised with respect to the possibilities for designing and making in this area of work.

# 1. Introducing filing systems

### Group size
The whole class and individuals.

### Objective
To introduce the idea of filing systems.

### What you need
A telephone directory, class register.

### What to do
When children visit the doctor or dentist, the receptionist usually asks for their names and addresses. This information is then used by the receptionist to locate the children's files within a filing cabinet. This or an equivalent example can be used to introduce the idea of filing systems to the class. Explain to them that such cabinets may be labelled A – L and M – Z. Why is this? Why put the details in such an alphabetical order? Why order them at all?

This opening discussion should help the children to realise that files are arranged so that they can be found (retrieved) easily. Ask the children to think of other items that are arranged in such a way, for example, the class register or the telephone directory. What happens if two or more people have the same surname? Use extracts from the telephone directory to show them what really does happen. The children should scan a page and find names, addresses and telephone numbers.

This can easily be turned into a game if you like. One child should look for a name while the others have to find the person's telephone number and address without being told their name!

# 2. Generating data

### Group size
Pairs or small groups.

### Objective
To generate data that can be stored or filed.

### What you need
Pencils, paper, rulers, tape measure.

### What to do
Start by telling the children that they are going to create a filing system for use in the classroom or possibly in an office. The information that is to be filed will be about the children in the class. What sort of information do they think they will need? What other information might be useful? They will need everyone's full names, addresses and telephone numbers and they might also want to include their sex, height, hair colour, shoe size, eye colour, hobbies, interests and so on. Make sure that the information required will not be embarrassing. You can let the children decide on the headings but make sure that you retain the power of veto! The files that the children compile will not be 'confidential' but introduce this term to the children anyway.

Once the children have decided on the information they need to obtain they can set about gathering their data. They can work in groups or with partners and they should record their findings on paper.

Systems

## 3. School survey

### Group size
Pairs or small groups.

### Objective
To research the design of filing systems.

### What you need
A computer with word-processing or desk top publishing facility, pencils, paper.

### What to do
Having gathered some data about themselves, it might be useful for the children to explore other details that they may put on their files. They might ask the headteacher, the school secretary, the kitchen assistants and so on about what other information about the class might be usefully kept in a filing system. They should think of five or six questions that will help them carry out their research, for example:
• What information about our class would be useful for you in your work?
• Would you want, or could you use data about children's height, eye colour, or hair type in your files?

At least *one* of their questions should be about the type of filing system they might use. Would they want a box file of a card index, or would they want the data stored on a computer file? The children can collate and analyse the data they collect and on the basis of this research, they should gain a good idea of *who* they would be designing the filing system for. By doing this they will have identified a specific need or opportunity.

## 4. Types of filing systems

### Group size
The whole class and small groups.

### Objective
To observe office filing systems.

### What you need
No special requirements.

### What to do
The objective of this activity is to extend the children's knowledge of the range of filing systems available. Show them that diaries and Filofaxes are also forms of filing systems.

Try to organise a visit to a local office so that they can be shown other types of systems such as card indexes on desks, computer storage and retrieval database facilities, cabinet files, lateral filing and so on. However, before the children visit the office ask them to make a numerical list against which they can record and describe as many different systems as possible. They should be able to list at least five and possibly more. The children may also want to sketch and draw each system as a reminder when they return to the classroom.

On returning to the classroom the children can talk about and describe each of the systems. What was good about it? What would be its drawbacks for what they wanted to do? They can then draw any conclusions about which type of system will be most appropriate for them.

## 5. Layouts

### Group size
Individuals.

### Objective
To establish a layout for individual records.

### What you need
A computer with desk top publishing or word-processing facilities, pencils, paper.

### What to do
Up to this point the children have worked in groups, but now they should use their

collective information to establish their own designs. Ask the children to work individually on the likely layout of the information that will be stored in their systems. They will probably have already decided roughly what details they want to appear on the sheet, for example name, address, telephone number and so on. Their research will also have given them some new and different angles on their designs. At this stage ask them to state for whom the filing system will be, for example the classroom, the school office or the canteen. Different groups may decide to focus on different areas, if this is the case then there is likely to be some variation of file design depending on individual needs.

Encourage the children to think about what information will go where. They may decide to put the data which will dictate the filing system, such as last names at the top of the card, or it may be that, for example, dietary needs are the priority. The children need to be aware of these priorities as they work on their layouts and they may have to consult with the people for whom they are designing the system before any idea is fixed.

The children will then need to play with their ideas, perhaps using a computer. Remind them that they are designing a system and so they will need to consider inputs, processes and outputs.

## 6. Which system shall I choose?

### Group size
Individuals.

### Objective
To develop ideas about their storage systems.

### What you need
Construction kits such as Stickle Bricks, LEGO and so on, card, sticky tape, scissors.

### What to do
Tell the children to look at and think about whether they will keep their system in a filing cabinet, drawer, index, book or possibly on a computer. To an extent their survey of needs and opportunities (see Activity 3) will influence their choices. You may want to decide what sort of system the class will use or you may allow the class to discuss the matter and reach a consensus of opinion. Perhaps if they are given the constraint of it having to be a box of some sort they can then explore variations on this.

The children should make models of such cabinets and drawers using matchboxes. They can then consult the people for whom they are designing the system and find out their opinions and ideas. This will help them to reach a firm decision about what to choose and what not to choose. Encourage them to talk with each other as well and to seek advice from you if problems arise.

## 7. Designing

### Group size
Individuals.

### Objective
To generate a design proposal.

### What you need
Pencils, paper, ruler.

### What to do
Ask the children to generate a design proposal. This proposal will consist of a labelled diagram showing how the individual records will be laid out and a diagram showing what the storage cabinet/box will look like. They will need to label items such as moving drawers, but the diagram need not be too complicated, although it does need to be informative. Explain to the children that people need to be able to understand from the diagram what they will be making.

Tell the children what materials will be available to them. Card is probably the easiest material to work with and the children may suggest utilising a cardboard box or other available boxes. This is acceptable so long as the box is the correct size for the files. Point out to the children that the 'cabinet' has to be the correct size for the files so that they can be stored and accessed easily. Ask the children to write a few sentences about each aspect of their design – why they have made the choices they have and why they have decided not to use other ideas. Remind them that their design is a *system* and so they must identify the *input(s)*, *processes* and *outputs* of the system they have planned. How will it work? How do the parts function together?

## 8. Planning

### Group size
Individuals or groups.

### Objective
To plan how they will make their system.

### What you need
Pencils, paper.

### What to do
Tell the children to formulate a 'plan of attack' before they set about making their filing systems. First they will have to list everything they need. This can be done in the form of a check-list and they can study their design proposals to help them make this list. Encourage the children to think where they will get the materials from, for example, scissors in the class and a box from home. This will ensure that they start to plan in detail.

Next ask the children to produce a plan showing how the work will be done. They can do this individually or collectively and perhaps brainstorm a list of stages which they can formulate into some sort of sequential order. This may be produced as a flow chart or as a storyboard, depending on how much time is available. The children will need to know what time is available for them to complete the work in and they can then work out what they will do and when. The children will also need to be aware that the targets they are setting will have to be adhered to – although in reality some flexibility has got to be allowed to ensure a quality finish and to avoid unnecessary pressure and frustration!

When the children have finished their plans you should check them and advise the children so that nothing has been overlooked!

## 9. Making the system

### Group size
Individuals.

### Objective
To make the filing systems.

### What you need
Materials as specified in Activity 8.

### What to do
By this stage the children should have gathered together all the materials, tools and equipment that they require. Remind them that they may need to organise themselves so that they can share tools and

materials. If they will be sharing equipment remind them that they must try to be diplomatic and thoughtful as they work. Point out that if everyone has to waste time searching for equipment then they may not complete the work in the time available. Therefore all tools and equipment should be returned to their proper places after use.

Encourage the children to measure and mark out their work before they start to cut. When they are cutting they should observe the appropriate safety procedures, for example, using tools correctly, not leaving rough edges, not leaving tools lying around and so on.

Once the children have completed their filing systems they should finish off the work neatly, snipping loose ends, pencilling, colouring, removing smudges and so on. Finally, they should clear up properly making sure that any parts that can be reused are kept safely and not thrown away.

## 10. What do others think?

### Group size
Individuals.

### Objective
To evaluate completed work.

### What you need
Pencils, paper.

### What to do
Having completed their filing systems, the children should try to evaluate their finished products. The best way for this to happen is for the people for whom the system has been designed to assess it. What do they think? Is it as good as they expected? Can they find any problems with the design? Will it require any modifications? Can these modifications be made without damaging or ruining the whole product?

Let the system be tried out and then it can be assessed to see if it works properly or as well as was expected. Can data be accessed easily? Ask the children to examine the technical details such as the moving parts. Do they stick or open smoothly? They should also look at their systems from an aesthetic view point. Does the artefact look good or can its appearance be improved?

Ask the children to write about how they reached their final design. They could include any visits they made and whether these helped them when planning their designs. Can the children think of other data which might have been useful to them?

# Community: electronic systems

### Age range
Eight to ten.

The type of system highlighted in this section is associated with electrical circuits. The activities will focus on fairly large and bulky electrical circuits, but would equate just as easily to electronic circuit design. The principal feature of the system is the use of an electrical membrane panel or pressure pad, although the work could equally focus on other types of sensory devices.

To succeed in this work the children will need to have a certain amount of knowledge of electrical circuits already. As

Systems 129

the context for the activity is the community, the work will revolve around situations which will be unfamiliar to most children.

## 1. Introducing circuits

### Group size
Pairs or small groups.

### Objective
To build up awareness and knowledge of electrical circuits.

### What you need
Circuit boards, insulated wire, tape, HP10 battery, lamp switch, 2.5V torch bulb, bulb holder, adhesive, copper sheeting, aluminium, plastic, wood, paper.

### What to do
Ask the children what they think the word 'circuit' means – for example, motor racing tracks, horse racing courses, athletics tracks and so on. Point out to them that these are all types of route from one point to another. In view of this what do they think an electrical circuit is? Explain to them that it is the path that electricity takes as it moves from one point to another, just like any other circuit.

Having discussed what an electrical circuit is, the children should be given the opportunity to discover for themselves what one is. Therefore, set them the task of making a bulb light up by making a circuit using a battery, two wires and a switch. Some children will discover the answer by chance, others by previous experience. How the children arrive at the answer is not so important, it is establishing the principle that electricity travels around a circuit that is of greater importance.

Discuss with the children from where the electricity starts (the battery (–)) and where it returns (+). Why does the electricity not work if the switch is off? Explain that if the circuit is broken the electricity cannot pass through.

Ask the children to record all the data they have discovered in this activity. They should use the correct symbols to describe the circuit – battery ⊣⊢ , bulb ⊗ , and switch ⌐⌐ . They may need help initially to draw the circuit.

Once this has been completed finish off by talking briefly about what their circuit might be used for.

## 2. Conductors and insulators

### Group size
Pairs or small groups.

### Objective
To explore conductors and insulators.

### What you need
Circuit board equipment, plus a variety of conductors and insulators.

### What to do
Ask the children to set up and test an electrical circuit. Once it is working they can place various materials in turn into the circuit. If the wires have crocodile clips this is easy to do but if not, then each material can be placed between the wire and the battery using tape to hold it in place. Ask the children to record which materials stop the circuit working and which don't – perhaps using the headings 'works' and 'doesn't work'.

The concept of electrical conductors and insulators can now be introduced to the children. Make sure that they identify the link between metals as conductors and non-metals as insulators. How do they think that this information might be used? They might suggest designing an electrical 'tester' which can be used to establish whether a material is metal or not, or perhaps a game where correct answers complete a circuit and incorrect ones do not. The intention is that the children apply their newly acquired knowledge. There is no need to go into design details, but rather to explore possibilities. At the end of the session the children can present their ideas to the rest of the class as part of a broader discussion about conductors and insulators.

## 3. Making a pressure pad

### Group size
Pairs or small groups.

### Objective
To construct an electrical pressure pad and place it in a circuit.

### What you need
Three 10 × 10cm pieces of thin card, two 10 × 10cm pieces of foil, circuit board equipment, photocopiable page 184.

### What to do
Ask the children whether they think card and foil will be conductors or insulators. Tell the children that they will use these two materials to make the pressure pad shown on photocopiable page 184. Give them the pieces of card and tell them to cut three or four holes in *one* of the pieces of card. Then they must sandwich the three cards together using pieces of foil to separate them, placing the card with the holes in the middle of the sandwich.

The sandwich can be fixed together using sticky tape. Tell the children to remove a small square from the corner of the top and bottom pieces of card, so that the foil is exposed.

Once the pad has been completed it can be fitted into an electrical circuit by attaching the wires to the exposed areas of foil. To make the circuit work the children should press down on to the pad. However, unless they press over a hole, joining the two pieces of foil, the circuit will still not work. There are likely to be a few teething problems with the equipment and the children should talk through each problem and try to solve it.

Finally, discuss how such pads are used in real life, for example, on calculators, copiers, cash tills and so on. Can they think of some other uses for such devices? A burglar alarm system or other warning device for instance, may use pressure pads to trigger off particular responses. Tell the children to record all their ideas using pictures, writing and the correct symbols.

## 4. Creating a database

### Group size
Pairs or small groups.

### Objective
To research electronic systems in the community.

### What you need
A computer with word-processing and database facilities.

### What to do
Introduce or revise information regarding systems (see page 118). What are the input(s), the processes and the output of their electrical circuits? Introduce the terms 'sensor' and 'control'. A sensor could be a pressure pad used to detect pressure and control will control the flow of electricity through a circuit. The input(s) are the electrical power of the battery and the pressure placed on the pad,

Systems

the processes are the electrical current, switch, connections made and the output is the lit or unlit bulb. Ask the children to show this system information as a flow chart and discuss different sensing devices and different output devices that could be used or achieved instead. For example, they might use temperature sensors and bells.

Give the children the task of looking for needs and opportunities for using a pressure-pad circuit. They can do this by exploring how sensor-effective systems are used in real life and perhaps, more significantly, people's feelings about such systems. Are they too loud? Do they go on for too long? Do they satisfy the needs required? For example, visual output is no use for somebody who is sight impaired!

Let the children start to discuss ideas for a questionnaire or survey which will help them to discover the views of people in the community. The questions should be mainly closed, in other words, requiring yes or no responses, with one or two more open questions. The children can produce question sheets on the word processor and carry out a supervised survey in a local shopping centre questioning about 20 to 30 people. The responses the children obtain should be analysed, sorted and amended as they accumulate and compiled into a database.

## 5. Looking for opportunities

### Group size
Individuals.

### Objective
To identify needs and/or opportunities for using pressure pads and other sensory devices.

### What you need
Pencils, paper.

### What to do
Encourage the children to compare pressure pads with other types of sensory device for example, infra-red beams, push button switches and so on. Which type operates best where? Where are different types unlikely to be of much use? Could one type of sensor replace another in a system? If so, what new opportunities for the system does this option give? The children may have found out from their research that people do not like noisy alarms or alarms which ring for a long time. How might a pressure pad be used to alleviate those problems? What other outputs might be used instead of a bell?

Ask the children to think about incorporating a time delay or some sort of timed system which switches off after a certain time. Would the children be able to devise such a device using a pressure-pad system or is such a development beyond their skills and knowledge?

Encourage the children to identify such a need or opportunity within the context of the community for which they can devise a system. The only constraint that they must consider is that it must have a pressure-pad control and be electrically worked. Once the children have decided on the system, they should write a design brief, for example, 'I will make an electrical pressure-pad system to help deaf people cross the road' or 'I will make a pressure-pad system to teach blind children how to get about in a room'.

## 6. Analysing parts

### Group size
Individuals.

## Objective
To identify and research parts of a design.

## What you need
Materials specified by the children.

## What to do
Having drawn up a design for a pressure-pad system, the children should research each section of their design – input(s), processes and output. To help them accomplish this, ask them to list the component parts of their systems. They can then complete a web diagram for each part. This is a quick and easy way of brainstorming ideas and identifying possible angles for further research. For example, children may identify a variety of possible insulators which can be used in the pressure pad or they might want to research different types of foil and if possible different thicknesses.

All this research will need to be carried out, recorded, tabulated and amended as the work progresses. Encourage the children to use this research to decide what is needed and what materials best meet their needs within the system they are designing.

# 7. Final plan

## Group size
Individuals.

## Objective
To generate a final design proposal.

## What you need
Pencils, paper.

## What to do
By this stage the children will have researched most if not all of the parts of their design and will be in the position of being able to draw a final annotated diagram showing the finished system. It might be useful to display these plans so that they can be seen by the rest of the class or other interested parties, particularly if the system is being designed for a particular group of people. The children might like to present their plans, explaining each part and why they have made certain choices in preference to others. Encourage them to talk about any difficulties which they may have yet to resolve and invite ideas or comments from the audience. These comments may involve the children in having to edit their proposals, but will result in a more balanced and successful design.

The children should also draw a flow diagram that shows the sequence of events as they occur in the system. Finally, they will need to check that all the materials they need to make their system are readily available.

# 8. Making the electronic system

## Group size
Individuals.

## Objective
To plan and make their designs.

## What you need
Materials as listed by the children (see Activity 7).

## What to do
The children can now set about making their electronic pressure-pad systems. Before they begin however, impress on them the need to use materials accurately and safely, paying particular attention to the avoidance of waste. Where possible they should work together, perhaps tidying up or setting out equipment.

Systems 133

*Are you pleased with your design? Does it work?*

It might be a useful aside to allocate a specific resource to a certain group of children and let them work out a plan for the management of this resource. For example, the children may have to share a large sheet of paper and so one person might be allocated to cut out the pieces to suit the needs of everyone else in the group – they may have to work out a routine so that everyone in the group has access to a soldering iron or scissors or wire strippers.

The children must use tools that are appropriate to the tasks being undertaken. When faced with problems they should try to resolve them logically and seek help to make sure that what they intend to do is safe. Tell them that marks will be given for quality of finish, appearance, how well the system functions and efficient use of the resources available. Encourage them to *use* their design proposals during manufacturing as a reference and a plan for proceeding. They may also make further sketches or models to help them resolve problems during making.

## 9. How well does the system operate?

**Group size**
Individuals or the whole class.

**Objective**
To evaluate their finished systems.

**What you need**
Pencils, paper.

**What to do**
Once the children have completed their systems they can evaluate their designs.
• How does it look?
• Does it work?
• Does it satisfy the needs/opportunities identified?
• What do others think about the design?

This review can take the form of a written appraisal, but also encourage the children to include the procedures that they undertook before they made their models. Did everything go according to plan? What were the problems they encountered? How were they solved? If they were going to make another one of these, how would the design have to be altered? Why would each alteration have to be made?

It is also useful to carry out such an evaluation as part of a general class discussion before the children write their reviews in order to provide them with a stimulus.

# Home: electronic feedback systems

**Age range**
Nine to twelve.

The activities in this section again focus on electronics, but this time they incorporate more complex electrical circuits and the use of gates, sensors and feedback (and hence control) in the work. The equipment that is required for these activities has been kept quite basic, but if the school is well resourced then there are many possible adaptations which can be incorporated.

## 1. Making different electrical circuits

**Group size**
Pairs and small groups.

**Objective**
To introduce the concept of electrical circuits and variety of components.

### What you need
Insulated wire, paper-clips, torch bulb and holder, AA 1.5 volt battery, thick cardboard, paper fasteners, photocopiable page 185.

### What to do
Ask the children to follow the instructions on photocopiable page 185 to make a complete circuit and light the bulb. If the lamp flickers then there is a faulty connection and if it does not light, the bulb or the battery may not be working or one of the connections may be faulty. Remind the children that for the electricity to flow there must be no breaks in the circuit and metal must always be touching metal.

Ask the children to talk about conductors and insulators, system inputs (the electricity) and outputs (the bulb lighting up). Talk about how the switch controls the circuit and let them draw the circuit using the correct symbols. Underneath the diagram they can draw a simple flow chart to show how the system operates.

Finally, tell the children to speculate on how this circuit may be used in the home.

## 2. Challenging circuits

### Group size
Pairs or small groups.

### Objective
To look at AND, NOT, and OR, circuits.

### What you need
Insulated wire, paper-clips, torch bulb and holder, AA 1.5 volt battery, thick cardboard, paper fasteners.

### What to do
This activity can be tackled in two ways. Either it can be presented as an open-ended challenge to the children, or if time is at a premium, it can be given to them in the form of instructions. If presented as a challenge ask the children to set up a circuit like the one in Activity 1, but this time using two switches which both need to be *on* for the bulb to light. What should evolve is a *series* circuit with two switches and bulb in series with each other.

The next challenge will be to set the children the task of setting up a circuit using two switches, either of which can be on for the bulb to light. This will present greater problems for them as principally they will need to make a parallel circuit.

Finally, ask the children to set up a circuit where the bulb is *on* all the time but when the switch is switched on the bulb goes off. This final one is likely to be the most difficult as it uses only *one* switch which is in parallel with the lamp.

After the children complete each circuit they should draw them and write brief comments about how each operates. Try to make sure that they include the word 'control' in their description.

If the activity is presented as a series of instructions, then ask the children to explain why each system works as it does. Tell them that the three gates are called AND, OR and NOT – the first, needing both switches, is AND, the second, needing either, is OR and the third, with the switch working opposite to expectations, is NOT.

## 3. Switches and sensors

### Group size
Pairs and small groups.

### Objective
To study switches and sensors.

### What you need
Bimetallic strip, pressure pad, relay (electromagnet), light sensor, push button, toggle switch or equipment catalogues and books.

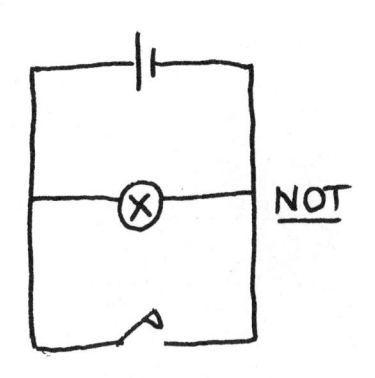

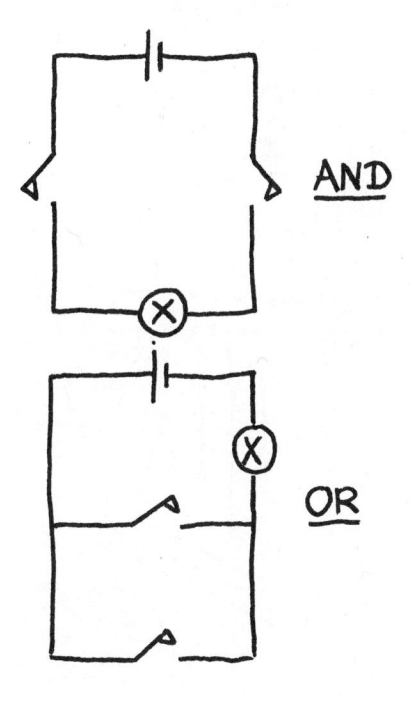

### What to do

Let the children research through books and catalogues or experiment with actual equipment to find out about different types of switches. Someone in the class may have *sensory* switches at home, such as ones where the lights come on when you walk into the room. If the children have tried out the pressure-pad activity on page 131 they may want to look at this again.

The objective here is for the children to gather information about a wide variety of switches. This data can be recorded on paper or stored as a database on a computer. The data will help them to become more aware that switches or indeed the part of a system that controls the energy flow, need not be operated manually. The implication of this is that sensors can act as switches. The children should be able to use this information to think about what sensors might be used in place of the paper-clips in their circuits from the previous activities.

## 4. Feedback

### Group size
Pairs and small groups.

### Objective
To study a sensory device and introduce 'feedback' as a concept.

### What you need
Simple circuit equipment plus a compatible sensing device such as a pressure pad or push switch.

### What to do
Introduce the children to the concept of 'feedback' in a system. Feedback is a method of control where the data that comes through the output is fed back to the input in order to control the system. This can be achieved by adding a simple sensing device to their circuit. (It is important that the device is compatible with the current and voltage in the circuit.) The pressure pad that was made on page 131 would suffice for the circuit boards used so far or they could use a bimetallic strip. If the circuits being used are microelectronic then light sensors, thermistors and relays will be good choices to make. If none of these are available then the children will have to imagine that one of their original switches is a sensor.

As the sensor detects pressure, heat or whatever, it acts as a switch to make a circuit so that the bulb lights. Once the children have been able to achieve this effect they can draw a flow diagram to show how the sensor operates the system. The loop that appears in the flow diagram is called a feedback loop because the incoming information is fed back through the system to make it work. Can the children think of any such systems that are used in the home (heating thermostats, warning lights and so on)?

## 5. AND, OR and NOT gates

### Group size
Individuals and small groups.

### Objective
To research ideas for needs and opportunities for AND, OR and NOT gates in the home.

### What you need
Paper, pencils.

### What to do
Tell the children that they are going to design and make an electronic system that uses feedback (this implies the use of a sensor). Let them talk through what they might design in small groups. They should provide reasons as to why they might design it and how it might operate. These will only be initial ideas. Once the children have finished discussing in small groups

they can bring their ideas back to the whole class. Try to discourage copy-cat ideas, but encourage innovation and creativity. They will find that they have a lot of information from previous studies to draw upon.

The children need to research out how some of these principles of AND, OR and NOT circuits might be used in the home. For example, they may come up with a device to tell them when a little brother or sister is in their room, or a basic smoke alarm to discourage people smoking in the house. Ask them to include in their research why they prefer some ideas to others – for example, because it will be cheap to make; it will help the environment; it will reduce running costs, and so on. All these ideas should be recorded together with their reasoning and which idea they think is the most realistic.

# 6. Research ideas

## Group size
Individuals.

## Objective
To research and develop ideas for using a feedback circuit further.

## What you need
Circuit apparatus, pencils, paper.

## What to do
Tell the children to focus their ideas. You can help them to do this by asking them to work through a sequence of instructions, for example:
• Write a short sentence about what they are going to make and their reasons for making it. (This in technological terms is called a design brief.)
• Ask them to list all the parts of the brief (specification) and come up with various possibilities for each part (an analysis). It would be useful to carry this out on computer and process the data.
• Tell them to research each part of the analysis in as much detail as is necessary in order to find the optimum solution for each part. If equipment is not available this should be recorded, together with anything that can be used as a replacement.

This research can be concluded by drawing a circuit diagram of the final system, together with appropriate annotations and a flow chart explaining how it will operate; the sensor that will be used; whether the gate is AND, OR or NOT; how the feedback will operate and so on. A list of likely equipment can also be added.

# 7. Setting targets

## Group size
Individuals.

## Objective
To plan the procedures prior to making the system.

## What you need
Pencils, paper.

## What to do
Before the children start to manufacture their systems they must work out a schedule for making. To help them, tell them how long they will be given to complete the work, for example, they might be given every Friday afternoon until half term or, more precisely, one hour per week for five weeks. On the basis of this constraint, the children will be able to formulate a plan of work. They can set targets for each lesson which should help them monitor the progress they are making. They may choose for the first lesson to just gather material together and for the next lesson they might set up a rough circuit and evaluate it. The next lesson they might try out other ideas and/or retry ideas.

Finally, tell the children that one part of their schedule should include a trial out for their system at home to gauge opinion and feasibility of how well their idea actually works.

## 8. Making with care

### Group size
Individuals.

### Objective
To make their designs.

### What you need
Materials and equipment listed in the previous activity.

### What to do
Having completed their work plans the children can set about making their designs. Encourage them to avoid wastage while making, and to think about any safety problems that may occur. There are likely to be problems that hinder their progress and encourage them to fault-find as they work. Faulty connections are the most common fault that will occur and the children will need, therefore, to be skilled in systematically looking for such faults. It may be that a circuit has a number of faulty connections and one way to help sort out these problems is to set up a reliable 'tester circuit' where they can check bulbs and batteries. This will save a lot of time. Where sensing devices are not available, allow the children to use an ordinary switch instead.

Finally, the children can try out their circuits at home (under supervision if necessary) to see how well they work. Emphasise that *no* circuits should ever be attached to the *mains* supply at home (or in school).

## 9. Which parts need evaluating?

### Group size
Individuals.

### Objective
To evaluate work carried out.

### What you need
Pencils, paper.

### What to do
Before the children evaluate their systems, ask them to think about what they should pay particular attention to. How well did the circuit work? How did they plan what they wanted to do? Did they work efficiently?

Encourage the children to consider some hitherto unmentioned criteria such as cost and design. As a class they can then establish a range of criteria which they feel is relevant in order to evaluate their own product and procedure. These can be listed on the board and then copied down and used as a basis for evaluation. Ask them to read out the results of their evaluations. What were the problems? How were they solved? If there was an opportunity to do the work again, how might they alter, adapt or modify the work and procedures to be more efficient? What lessons did they learn?

The children can read out their evaluations and these can form the basis of a general summing up. Finally, all the work can be displayed for the whole class to see.

# CHAPTER 6

# Energy and control

The concept of energy is very difficult to explain to young children. Rather than try to define it, it is perhaps easier to help children to recognise energy in its various forms such as heat, light, electricity, sound and so on. Even very young children will be able to recognise that energy is needed in order for things to move and that when that energy 'runs out' the object no longer moves. The conceptual progression is therefore about recognising and understanding the wide variety of energy types and how they interrelate through the use of artefacts, systems and our environment.

Control, on the other hand, is a much easier concept for children to deal with. It has few abstract interpretations and at its simplest, it is a matter of using an on/off switch. Such things as switches, gates, dials and meters are all features which are used to control the artefacts, systems and environments we find around us. Therefore, the ability to control the environment is bound up with technological advances. We can control our environment within our houses to a large extent – we have thermostatic heating systems, comfortable furniture, well organised and equipped kitchens and our societies are controlled through rules, laws, good practice and so on. However, we still cannot control such things as the weather and earth movements.

Energy and control are natural partners. By controlling energy flow, we can control how it is used, how it is changed and how much of it is used, for example, using a gas cooker means that we can control the strength of the flame and insulating a building limits how much heat is wasted.

Energy and control

# ACTIVITIES

## Home: making balloon rocket vehicles

### Age range
Five to seven.

The activities in this section are concerned with introducing the two major concepts of energy and control. The children may already have had some association with either or both concepts and this can be focused on during the work. Many toys are motorised in one form or another, for example, they may be clockwork, use springs, magnets or electric motors. These are all potential energy sources and can be used as examples of such for the children. Once they have learned these basic principles they can use them in the manufacture of balloon rocket vehicles.

## 1. Moving toys

### Group size
The whole class or individuals.

### Objective
To introduce the idea of 'energy' and movement.

### What you need
Various toys that move.

### What to do
Ask the children to bring from home, any toys they have that move by themselves such as clockwork models, toys that are spring-loaded, battery driven or motorised – some of the toys may just have moving limbs. Let each child, in turn, describe to the class how her toy moves, what makes it move and how she can control its movement. This control may be in the form of a switch, a key and so on.

Ask the children to group the toys, placing them in sets according to what makes each toy move, for example, one group may consist of battery driven toys, while another clockwork and so on. Once all the toys have been placed in a set explain to the children that all moving toys need some sort of energy to move.

Demonstrate this by using one of the toys and ask them where they think the energy comes from for each group of toys. For example, the motorised toys get their energy from batteries while the clockwork and elasticated toys get their energy by being wound up. What happens if the energy is not there? Take out the batteries, let the clockwork wind down.

To finish, ask the children to draw a picture of one of the moving toys and label from where it is controlled. They can also write a few sentences about how it works.

## 2. Controlling energy

### Group size
Individuals.

### Objective
To reinforce ideas of energy and control.

### What you need
Coloured pencils, photocopiable page 186.

### What to do
Using photocopiable page 186, ask the children to identify what energy is being used in each picture and how it is being controlled. The emphasis of this activity is on movement relating to energy, but some of the pictures are intended to promote discussion and thereby broaden the children's experiences of energy types.

The children may need help initially, to identify the energy types, although the control types are more obvious. Ask them to describe the controls, in terms of switches, knobs, dials, push-buttons, handles and so on.

Having talked through the worksheet with the children, they can colour from where the energy is manifested in red and the control in blue. They could also cut out the pictures and group them according to the type of control they use. Ask them to talk about how the controls work, for example, a switch that turns on and off, a knob or dial which makes finer adjustments, a push-button and so on. The children can then go back and consider the toys they looked at in the previous activity. What types of controls did they have?

## 3. Balloon rockets

### Group size
Pairs and small groups.

### Objective
To make a balloon rocket vehicle.

### What you need
Balloons, a balloon pump, LEGO, string, photocopiable page 187.

### What to do
Ask the children to build the balloon rocket shown on photocopiable page 187. Any basic LEGO vehicle can be constructed, and the children can be allowed to investigate and explore various chassis types to see which will move and which will not. (It is important to get the correct size ratio between the size of the balloon and the vehicle if the vehicle is to move at all.)

Very young children may have difficulty in blowing up balloons so you may have to do this for them or provide them with a balloon pump. There is also likely to be a problem fixing the balloon to the chassis. This can be done with string, Blu-Tack, or incorporated into the vehicle design. If you like you can set this as a challenge for the children. This will provide lots of fun and excitement as they tackle each problem.

Once all the vehicles are finished you can hold a vehicle race. Which rocket goes fastest and the farthest? Which is the biggest, smallest, widest? Encourage the children to talk about what they have made and how they solved the different problems that occurred.

Finally, ask the children to draw a picture of their rocket, labelling the different parts and writing what each one does.

## 4. Controlling the rocket

### Group size
Pairs or small groups.

### Objective
To investigate how air release might be controlled.

### What you need
Balloon rockets (see previous activity), bulldog clips, string.

### What to do
This activity can be presented to the children in two ways, either as an open-ended discovery lesson where the children are challenged to try and control the release of the air from the balloon, or it can be treated as a structured lesson where the children are shown each possible way to control it. Whichever form of lesson is chosen, the children must try each possibility and record through notes and sketches their opinions about how the 'control' works. Does it release enough power to move the chassis? How easily does it control the release of the air? Does it work on an 'on/off' principle or is there more control? An example here might be given by demonstrating the slow release of the air by using your fingers to produce a rather 'rude' or a more high-pitched squeaking noise. The bulldog clip can also be used to facilitate such a release and the gentle release caused by tying a piece of string loosely will have much the same effect.

The children should finish up with at least one method of controlling the air release from the balloon, even if it is just an 'on/off' bulldog clip release.

## 5. Rockets at home

### Group size
Individuals.

### Objective
To look for opportunities to use a balloon rocket.

### What you need
Paper, pencils.

### What to do
Having made the balloon rockets 'move' and 'controllable' (to an extent), the children can be asked to think of ways that such a vehicle can be used at home. Start off with a brainstorming session to generate and discuss ideas. Examples might include taking notes from room to room, delivering drinks and food from the kitchen or perhaps they will look for a model that travels across the room to switch on the television, a lamp or a light switch. They should be discouraged from discussing any scenarios which are potentially dangerous. Are there likely to be spillages? Will it knock anything over? Ask the children to go home and find out about any other possibilities.

Finally, from all this research the children should decide on one idea for their balloon rocket.

# 6. Adding a chassis

## Group size
Individuals.

## Objective
To design the balloon rocket vehicles.

## What you need
Pencils, paper, coloured crayons or felt-tipped pens.

## What to do
Ask the children to draw their design for their balloon rockets.
• What will they look like?
• How will they be different to the models they made before?
• Will they have to have extra parts? If so, where will they go?
• Will they have to hold something? If so, how will it be held?
• Will the designs be safe? Will they tip over?

Tell the children to label their drawings and you can put appropriate words on the board to help them. Those who can write and read to a greater extent can be encouraged to annotate their pictures, showing what each piece will do. Let them colour their drawings to make them look more realistic and when they have finished, ask them to describe how their design will work. Sensitive questioning will provoke positive criticism and will likely lead to a better thought out design.

# 7. Making the rocket

## Group size
Individuals.

## Objective
To make from designs.

## What you need
Balloons, construction kits, other materials listed in the previous activity.

## What to do
Let the children set about making their designs. If construction kits are at a premium they might be able to substitute them with 'junk' materials or by combining the two. If they use a chassis and wheels from construction kits this will solve the technological problems involved in making moving axles. However, if these are not available, then they can fit dowelling through cotton bobbins and use Plasticine plugs to stop the bobbins from falling off!

Lightweight packaging on top of a kit chassis will reduce weight and increase the chances of the vehicle moving. If the children have designed vehicles to carry drinks then make sure that plastic cups are available. Will they work with a drink inside? Make sure that this is tested in a safe space as spillages are likely!

Once built and tested, the children can take their vehicles home to see how well they work there.

# 8. Do rockets work on all surfaces?

## Group size
Individuals.

## Objective
To evaluate work carried out.

## What you need
Pencils, paper.

## What to do
Having had the opportunity to test their designs at home, the

children should be given the opportunity to assess how well they worked there. The vehicles may have worked at school on low-friction surfaces, but how did they fare on carpet?
• Did they move at all?
• Did they move as they were intended to?
• Did they move smoothly?
• Did they travel in the direction they were intended to?

For each of these questions ask the children to talk about how their models could be changed in order to make them work as intended. Tell the children to draw and/or write a little about how they worked and/or how they might have to be modified. If time is available let them carry out and trial the modifications to see if the model works any better.

Finally, ask the children to comment on how well they think the whole task went, from their initial ideas right through to trying out their model at home. Do they think that they worked well? Did they put in enough hard work, thought and effort into the project?

# School: levers and linkages

### Age range
Six to eight.

The activities in this section deal with the principles of levers and linkages. At this age there is no need to get into the details of first, second and third class levers or the hard physics of 'moments'. The aim is for the children to become more aware of levers and related linkages, through exploration and investigation. Some technical language is introduced in the first couple of activities (with future development in mind). The activities use construction kits almost exclusively, but other media, such as card and paper fasteners are appropriate, if perhaps a more fiddly, option.

## 1. See-saws

### Group size
Pairs and small groups.

### Objective
To explore and make lever systems.

### What you need
Pivots, rulers, slotted masses, photocopiable page 188.

### What to do
Introduce the children to levers by using the concept of a see-saw. This system will have a *pivot fulcrum*, a *load* (that which is to be moved), and an *effort* (the force needed to move the load). Ask them to set up a lever/see-saw system using a ruler and pivot from a construction kit as shown on photocopiable page 188. The children can then carry out the experiments on the sheet.

Ask them to place a 1kg mass at one end and then force down the other end. Is this easy or hard to do? Tell them to move the pivot closer to the weight. Is it easier or harder to push the weight down now? What happens if they move it closer still? Ask the children to predict what will happen when the pivot is moved away from the weight. Will it be easier or harder to push?

The children can then start to explore the two lever systems shown on the bottom of the sheet (second and third class) and compare these with the previous ones (first class). There is no need to talk about first, second and third class levers, but it would be useful to get them to draw pictures of what they have set up and label the load, effort, fulcrum and so on. An extension might be to get them to add arrows that show the direction of the load and effort.

As a final exercise, ask the children to set up all these different types of levers using construction kits. They should draw pictures of their constructions, label them and write a sentence about how each might be useful.

## 2. Linkages

### Group size
Small groups.

### Objective
To investigate linkage systems.

### What you need
Card, paper fasteners, construction kits, photocopiable page 189.

### What to do
Depending on the manipulative ability of the children, they can carry out this exercise using either thin card and paper fasteners or construction kits. Ask them to make each of the linkage systems shown on photocopiable page 189. Where fulcrums are used attach these to a backboard.

When they have made each linkage the children should cover the mechanism apart from the *input* and *output* parts. By doing this they will be able to see what job the linkage does and thereby speculate about what job the linkage might do! They should jot any ideas down together with diagrams and sketches. Some children might also like to try to identify where the load, effort and fulcrum for each linkage are, and draw force direction arrows.

## 3. Looking at levers and linkages

### Group size
Individuals and the whole class.

### Objective
To look at existing lever and linkage systems.

### What you need
Card, paper fasteners, construction kits, pencils, paper, photocopiable page 190.

### What to do
As an introduction to the generation of ideas about how levers and linkages might be used, the children should be given an opportunity to look at how some existing designs utilise levers and linkages. Ask the children to examine the systems shown on photocopiable page 190 and if it is possible, bring some examples of these objects in for the children to examine more closely. Ask them to consider the following questions about each object:
• Is it a lever?
• If so, where is the fulcrum? Where is the effort? Where is the load?
• Does the lever system make the job easier or harder?
• Is it a linkage system?
• If so, what is the input? What is the output?
• Can they follow the linkage system to see how each part interacts?
• Can they describe through verbal, written and/or

diagrams how one or more of the systems work?
• Do they have a control mechanism? If so, how does it control the linkage system? Why does it control the linkage system?

Finally, the children can be given the opportunity to make one of the lever and/or linkage devices using card and fasteners or construction kits.

## 4. Sketching and making

### Group size
Pairs or small groups.

### Objective
To make their own lever/linkage system.

### What you need
Construction kits, paper fasteners, card.

### What to do
Ask the children to work in groups and design and make their own lever or linkage system. Insist that they sketch their ideas on paper first and describe on their drawings how their systems will work before they make them. It might be that they explore aspects of the mechanism first to see how it will function and this should be encouraged. Point out to them that they may mix and combine media for manufacture. For example, they may use a construction kit to make the linkage mechanism, but then attach card or paper to it in order to get it to look more like the 'real thing'. Encourage innovation, but do not prevent copying at this stage. Although the children may have copied ideas from elsewhere these can be used later on to seek out new opportunities for use.

Encourage the children to solve their own problems related to getting the mechanisms to function as they want them to. It might be that they have set out to produce something that is too complex. In this exercise let them realise the error of their ways, then stress simplicity!

## 5. Evaluating

### Group size
Individuals.

### Objective
To evaluate their design and identify new opportunities for use.

### What you need
Pencils, paper.

### What to do
Having designed and made their mechanism ask the children to describe how they work.
• Are there inputs and outputs?
• Do they work properly?
• Have they turned out the same as expected or differently?
• If they are different, how are they different?
• Why did they have to make changes?
• Could they be made better? If so, how would they improve upon their existing designs?

All these questions are fundamental to any technological evaluation process. It is likely, because the previous exercise was set as a design and make task, that the children will not have had specific uses in mind as they designed and made. However, as they worked their ideas may have changed – 'Perhaps we might use it for...', or 'What about...?'. Now is the time to focus their attention on to this aspect of the process. It can be put as simply as 'What might your design be used for in school?' They should list at least five possible uses and then choose one of their ideas and give reasons for their choices; for example, 'It looks easiest to make!' or 'It's the most useful one'.

## 6. Word processing

### Group size
Individuals.

### Objective
To research and develop ideas further.

### What you need
A computer with word-processing facilities, pencils, paper.

### What to do
Ask the children to conduct a survey concerning their choice of system. This may involve questioning people like other teachers, the caretaker, the headteacher and so on, or it might simply be a matter of asking themselves questions. The children may require guidance when deciding on their questions to ensure that they obtain a breadth to their research. Add the constraint that they must think up a minimum of five questions.

Once the children have written their questions out in pencil, they can use a word processor and print them out ready to be used. Encourage the children to leave big enough spaces after the questions to write in the answers. They may also want to add line guides for people to write on.

Let the children conduct their surveys themselves although you should remind them that they must not barge into rooms uninvited and that they should ask their questions politely or if it is not convenient, to negotiate a convenient time and return later. The results of their surveys can then be analysed and the resultant information used in developing their ideas.

## 7. Modifying/ justifying

### Group size
Individuals.

### Objective
To modify design to suit new needs/opportunities, and to add a control unit to ideas.

### What you need
Construction kits, pencils, paper.

### What to do
The children should, by this stage, have a good idea of how their original designs will need to be changed to suit the need, or new opportunities their research has identified. Changes may be as simple as changing the colour to suit the decor of the room, or more complicated like making a part of the design differently. Whatever the reason(s), ask the children to justify their proposed changes to you.

Introduce a constraint on their designs. Stipulate that their designs must control something such as controlling how far a door opens, or have a control mechanism built into it, for example, a ratchet to alter height or extension, or perhaps just a peg to act as a locking device. The emphasis should be placed on the concept of control and how their lever/linkage systems function as a consequence of that control.

## 8. Final drawings

### Group size
Individuals.

### Objective
To generate a design proposal.

### What you need
Pencils, paper.

### What to do
Tell the children to generate a final design proposal. Ask them to produce a large drawing, labelling the key features such as fulcrum, load, effort, input, output and control. They can also add colour, either for effect or to represent the actual colour(s) of what they are going to make. Having labelled their drawings they should then annotate them, or at least some of the parts of the drawings, explaining how they will work. If colour is a key essential this should also be explained in the drawing. The annotations need only consist of a short phrase or sentence. Encourage the children to pay attention to details, using a ruler where necessary and giving their drawings titles. If they are colouring they should do this carefully, trying to keep within lines and so on.

Having finished their drawings the children can explain their designs to the rest of the class. This process should help them to identify labels and annotations that they have missed and perhaps need to add.

## 9. Making and evaluating

### Group size
Individuals.

### Objective
To make and then evaluate designs.

### What you need
Card, paper fasteners, construction kits.

### What to do
The children have already explored the process of making part of their designs, albeit as a group, and therefore it might be that all they have to do this time is to add on to or take away from what they have already made. On the other hand, it might be that everybody has to start again from scratch. Whatever the situation, encourage safe and accurate work and an attention to detail. Encourage the children to respect other people's work and working space. If equipment is shared then the children must be reminded of this fact.

Ask them to describe how they propose to go about their work and perhaps invite the headteacher or other interested parties to come and see the children working so that they can describe what they are doing as they work. Question them about why they are working as they are. Why does this go here? What does that do? What needs to be done to make it do this?

Once they have finished, ask the children to evaluate their work by saying how satisfied they are with their efforts. How have their designs been modified? Do these modifications work? Do they work as well as expected? What problems were there? How were they solved? This can be done as a verbal exercise or as a series of short written questions and answers.

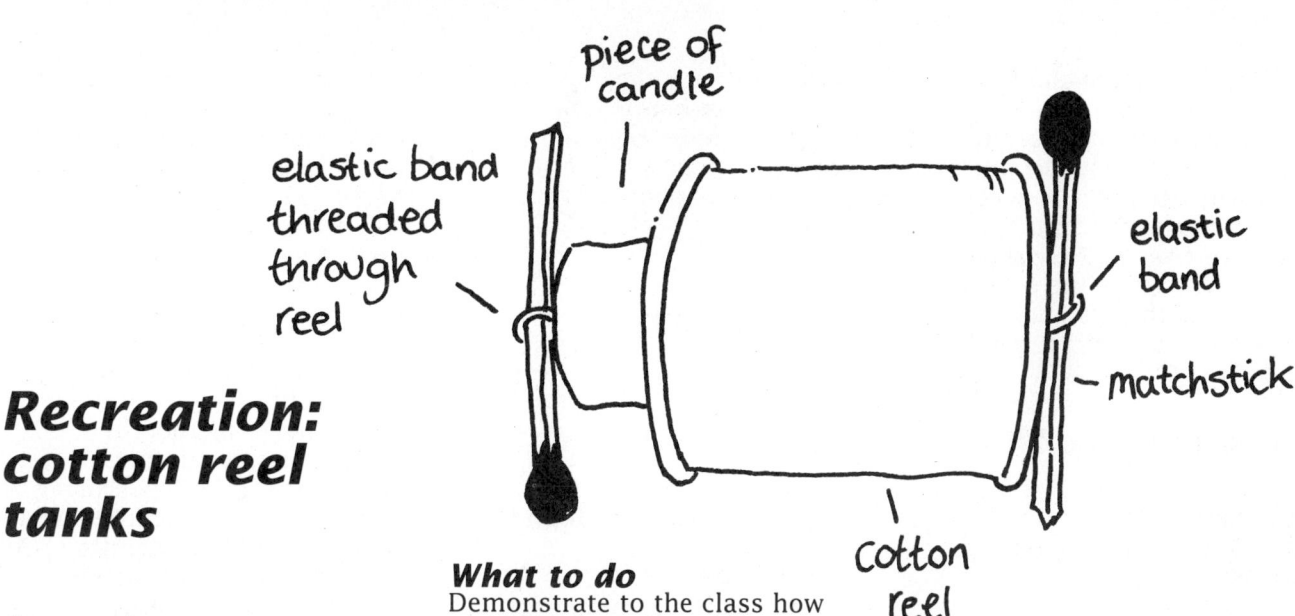

*Diagram labels: piece of candle; elastic band threaded through reel; elastic band; matchstick; cotton reel*

# Recreation: cotton reel tanks

### Age range
Seven to nine.

The cotton reel tank is a classic example of a well-used and documented piece of mechanical technology. The traditional model uses a cotton reel, a matchstick, and a piece of candle and is powered by an elastic band fixed at one end through the hole in the cotton reel. A modern equivalent uses a tin can to replace the cotton reel, a plastic bead instead of the candle, and a paper-clip as the winder. Despite such technological advances this series of activities will emphasise tradition in order to develop technological activity.

## 1. Making cotton reel tanks

### Group size
Pairs and small groups.

### Objective
To build up construction skills.

### What you need
Cotton reels, elastic bands, pieces of candle, matchsticks.

### What to do
Demonstrate to the class how to make the cotton reel tank and then let them make their own. Once made, they can try them out. Do they work? How well do they work? How can they get their tanks to go faster and further?

Ask the children to record their conclusions. They might like to hold tank races, recording and charting how each tank performs. Encourage them also to try and get their tanks to move up increasingly steep slopes, recording their successes and failures. Finally, ask them to draw and label a sketch of their final construction.

## 2. Improving designs

### Group size
Pairs and small groups.

### Objective
To explore and modify designs.

### What you need
Cotton reel tanks, different sizes of elastic bands, sharp knife.

### What to do
Having made and tried out their tanks, the children can now be asked to think how they might get their tanks to go faster, further, or up and down slopes.

Tell them to explore the design itself. Why is the candle there? Does the tank work without the candle? How does using a thicker elastic band affect performance? Ask the children to explore what happens when they use different lengths of matchstick or cut serrations around the edges of the cotton reels. How does this affect performance? Do the tanks go uphill any better? Do they travel downhill any better?

For each adjustment the children should sketch the change and write a little about how it worked. They can also test their changes by holding different competitions. For example, they could design a tank to travel a certain distance in a certain time, or one to travel up the steepest possible incline.

Finally, ask the children to talk about their tanks as systems. They will need to look at what each part does and why each part is needed. Which parts control the system? How do they control it? Which part is the energy source? Is the system controlled and, if so, how?

## 3. Using tanks

### Group size
Individuals, small groups or the whole class.

### Objective
To look for opportunities to use cotton reel tanks.

### What to do
Help the children to brainstorm ideas for how their tanks can be used. This can be done as a whole class discussion or in groups with the children discussing their ideas as a class afterwards. Point out to them that they should look for opportunities in a leisure or recreational context, for example, games, toys or other playthings. They might even want to turn their tanks into kits so that they can be used like other construction kits.

Introduce the idea that a frame or housing might be attached to a tank so that its workings are hidden and it looks more like, for example, a car or truck. Encourage the children to think about making it into something other than a vehicle such as a wind-up mechanism where the turning matchstick could be used as a dial or a clockface.

Having explored lots of possibilities each child should choose a favourite idea, or better still, one that is worthy of further research, being based on sound reasoning. Their decisions can then be expressed as pictures and short written explanations.

## 4. Research

### Group size
Individuals.

### Objective
To research and develop ideas.

### What you need
Pencils, paper, a computer with word-processing facilities.

### What to do
Having isolated one idea, or at least, having narrowed down the field, the children can begin to research their ideas in more detail. The first area for research will be to find out the feasibility of their choices. If they decided to make a game, who will it be for? How will they find out if people will like it or not? If the children cannot come up with an answer to either of these questions themselves, you should direct them towards devising a questionnaire and carrying out a survey to find out opinion. As well as or alternatively, they may look to see what similar toys or games are available in the shops. This may involve a visit to a local toyshop to question the proprietor or writing a letter to a major toy manufacturer.

Whichever method of research is chosen, the questions can be typed using word-processing facilities on a computer, and the children will have to think about the layout of the questionnaire.

## 5. Concept drawings

### Group size
Individuals.

### Objective
To research the housing for 'tank' designs.

150 Chapter 6

### What you need
Pencils, paper, coloured crayons or felt-tipped pens.

### What to do
Introduce the children to the idea of concept drawings. This phrase need not be used directly, but might be described as ideas or pictures. The essential objective is to sketch a few ideas for the housing (outside) of their tanks. What colours will each part be? What other design variations can be included? If you have been directing much of the work the children have done so far, now is a prime opportunity for them to express their own creativity.

Limit the number of pictures each child draws to five or ten and once they have completed the required number, they can carry out a survey to see which drawing is the most popular. They must direct this survey at their target market and thus this may involve the children having to go out on supervised visits. Once they have collected their data the children can construct a database which can be used to help them analyse the information.

## 6. Proposals

### Group size
Individuals.

### Objective
To generate a design proposal.

### What you need
Paper, pencils, coloured crayons or felt-tipped pens.

### What to do
The children should, by this stage, by ready to start working out how they will make their designs. Paper or thin card will be useful here, as they explore how the housing is going to fit on and not impede the tank mechanism. They should also consider the materials that they will eventually use to construct the housing. If the material is too heavy the tank will not move and if it is too flimsy it might be easily damaged. Can it be painted and if not, how can it be coloured? You can introduce these aspects of the developmental work to the children as their work begins to take shape.

The children's final choices can be represented as an annotated diagram, showing parts, materials and so on and their reasons for each choice.

## 7. Storyboard plans

### Group size
Individuals.

### Objective
To plan out a schedule of work.

### What you need
Pencils, paper, a computer with word-processing facilities.

### What to do
Tell the children how long they will be given to make their designs. This can be presented as a *fait accompli* or it can be negotiated. Whatever method you take, the children will have to plan their work schedule to fit into the allotted time. Their ideas may be presented as a flow chart or if time allows, as a storyboard. Their plans should show what will be done, in what order and approximately how long each activity will take. They will also need to write a list of materials and equipment they will need. Their choice of materials and equipment should reflect their knowledge and understanding of materials and processes involved and they will need to check what is available to them.

The children can draw up their plans on a word processor.

*Did I plan accurately?*

*What problems occurred?*

*Did I keep on target?*

## 8. Making

**Group size**
Individuals.

**Objective**
To make from designs.

**What you need**
Materials and equipment listed in the previous activity.

**What to do**
Let the children begin to make their designs. They must use their design proposals as a guide and follow their planning schedules. It is likely that the classroom will have most of the equipment they have asked for (this will have been taken into account in the previous activity), but if you feel that other items can be added then make sure the children are aware of what is available. They should already have developed in the first two activities in this section the necessary manufacturing skills, but they will need to take care when they come to making the housing and attaching it to the tank.

Let the children improvise when they come up against problems and try to encourage and advise them, using direction only as a last resort. Encourage them to be aware of safety hazards and to look for quality in all aspects of their work, from efficiency in the use of materials to looking for a good finish.

## 9. Does the design work?

**Group size**
Individuals.

**Objective**
To evaluate work and working procedures.

**What you need**
Pencils, paper.

**What to do**
Once the children have finished making their designs, the first evaluatory step will be to see if their designs actually work.
• Do they move?
• How well do they move?
• How does the housing alter their movement?
• Could they be improved and if so, how?
• Can any minor adjustments be made so that they function better or more efficiently?
• Does the market they were intended for like them?
• Are they user-friendly?
• Are they sturdy?

The children can evaluate all these questions without having to write down their answers. Instead they can write a general piece about the work they did and include in it how well their designs worked and how they could be improved.

Finally, the children can comment on how well the schedules they wrote functioned. Did they keep to their target times? Did they plan accurately? Did they need more equipment and materials? How did they avoid wastage? What did they do to avoid problems occurring? What problems still occurred?

# Business: mechanisms and control

**Age range**
Eight to ten.

The activities in this section will involve the children in carrying out a design and technology package involving an introduction to gears and mechanisms. The early part of the work will focus on skill development and research, through investigation and evaluation. From the assimilated data the children can then identify their own opportunities for using mechanical systems within a business setting.

# 1. Introducing gears

## Group size
Pairs and small groups.

## Objective
To introduce gears and types of gears.

## What you need
Modelling kits which have gear systems, photocopiable page 191.

## What to do
Most retail construction kits will include in them a variety of gears and these kits can be used to show the children what a gear looks like. Point out that the protrusions on the wheel are called 'teeth' and the children can count the number of teeth on each gear wheel. They can then draw a picture of a gear and label the teeth, wheel and so on.

Next, using photocopiable page 191, introduce the children to a range of gear systems including bevel gears and rack and pinion. Let them find the components for each type of gear system and construct each type so that they function properly. They can then describe, in their own words, how each works.

It is important that the children learn that the gears need to 'mesh' properly in order to function efficiently. Some will turn, but the gears may slip because they are too far apart. Other attempts may result in the gears locking because they are too close or out of synchronisation. With advice the children should be able to surmount these problems. Encourage them to attach other pieces on to each gearing system, so that it starts to resemble a 'real' item such as a windmill or a moving toy.

Let the children use their imagination. You might want to use this as an opportunity to visit a local factory or museum to see how gears are used or were used in the past.

# 2. Gearing principles

## Group size
Pairs and small groups.

## Objective
To study gears in more detail.

## What you need
Large and small gears.

## What to do
Having gained an insight into the range and types of gears, the children can begin to look at some of the principles behind gear systems. Ask them to set up a large gear wheel (40 teeth) and a small gear wheel (10 teeth). They may need to introduce a handle into the system so that both turn smoothly together. They should then mark one tooth on each gear wheel and this will enable them to study gear ratios. Which wheel turns the quickest? If the children turn the large gear wheel, how many times does the small gear wheel turn for one complete rotation?

They should find that the small wheel moves round four times to each full rotation of the large wheel. How far do they think the big wheel will move during one rotation of the small gear wheel? Ask the children to see if they can recognise any link.

The children can move on to explore another two gear mechanisms, for example, a 30 tooth wheel and a 10 tooth one and a 40 and a 20 tooth one. Ask them to record their results and draw any conclusions. There is no real need to talk about 'gear ratios'

as a concept so long as the children have an idea about which gears to use together to make a system, for example, 'double its speed' or 'half its speed' and so on.

## 3. Changing direction

### Group size
Pairs or small groups.

### Objective
To explore directional changes in gearing systems.

### What you need
A variety of gear systems, including bevel and rack and pinion.

### What to do
Ask the children to set up a two-gear system (as in Activity 2). As they turn one gear wheel one way what can they see happening to the other gear wheel? They will notice that it turns in the opposite direction. They should record their findings as a drawing. Now ask the children to explore a mechanism using three gear wheels set so that they are parallel to each other. Ask them to draw what happens using arrows to show the direction each wheel turns. Encourage them to make suggestions for how this sort of gear system could be used – a list of two or three will suffice.

Tell the children to set up a bevel gear system. Point out that the movement is at 90° to the force being applied. How might such a system be used? Ask them to draw and write a little about such movement.

Tell the children to set up a rack and pinion gear system and record how this system moves. This time it is from a rotary to a linear movement and such a mechanism is used to steer vehicles. Can the children turn the rack and pinion system into a rough, but functioning steering system? Encourage them to explore and record how else this system might be used.

## 4. Turntables

### Group size
Pairs and small groups.

### Objective
To make a mechanical turntable.

### What you need
Construction kits with gear wheels, photocopiable page 192.

### What to do
As a focal point for design and manufacture ask the children to make a turntable mechanism. This will mean constructing a gear system that works at 90° to the force applied. They will also need to attach a large plate to the horizontal gear and this will turn with the horizontal gear. The children should use photocopiable page 192 to help them make this turntable and once they have made it they can begin to think how this can be used in a business setting – for example, a crane or a display unit in a shop.

Ask the children to think about how else the turntable might be allowed to move. It could be turned on its side to become a clockface, and possibly a rack and pinion would make it move in a linear rather than a rotary fashion – the variations are endless. The children should be encouraged to come up with several different ideas and write about why a business might want a turntable display or why a company might require a turntable crane.

## 5. Using turntables

### Group size
Individuals.

### Objective
To generate ideas for using turntables.

### What you need
Pencils, paper.

### What to do
Having built a turntable as part of a group the children can now be encouraged to work individually, focusing on one of their ideas. It might be appropriate to take this opportunity to review the children's choices and help them to select achievable targets. Encourage them to think 'simple' even if this means going back to the drawing board and starting again. Most likely though, it will mean refining ideas so that the children will be able to make them work. Ask them how they see their turntables functioning. Will the gearwheels be showing or will they be hidden? This early child/teacher interaction will help to narrow down the focus considerably for each child. The children should record and explain all their ideas.

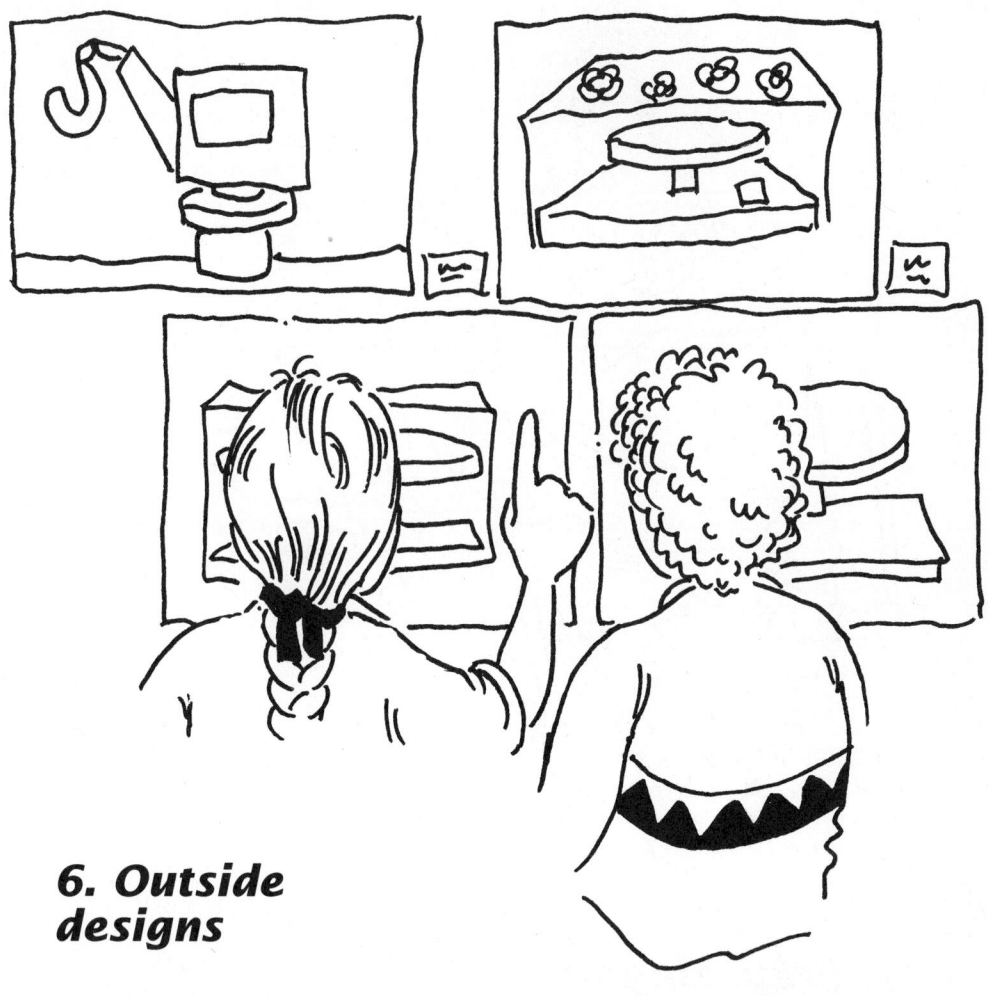

## 6. Outside designs

### Group size
Individuals.

### Objective
To design the outside housing for a turntable.

### What you need
Pencils, paper, coloured crayons, paints or felt-tipped pens.

### What to do
To change the children's direction of thought from mechanisms, ask them to think about what the rest of their design is going to look like. If it is to be a display what colours will they use? Is the mechanism going to be hidden? If so, then the cover will have to be built to achieve this purpose. What materials might be used to achieve this?

Let them draw their ideas on paper. Encourage them to draw more than one and then consult with you or their classmates to help them decide which is the best. These drawings can be thought of as concept drawings and they will not only have to show shape, but colour, pattern and so on. They might also want to construct their ideas using paper, in order to gain a better perspective of their overall design. All their ideas, opinions and conclusions should be recorded with explanations and reasons for their choices.

Energy and control

## 7. Preparing to make

### Group size
Individuals.

### Objective
To plan the manufacture from designs.

### What you need
Pencils, paper.

### What to do
The children will now be in a position to draw a final design proposal. This may be a single picture or a combination of diagrams, but whichever form is chosen, the children will have to show the mechanism, how it will work and how the housing will fit around the mechanism. Their diagram(s) need to be labelled and the children should use this as a basis for drawing up a list of requirements. Also tell them to plan what they will do and in what order they will work. Will they make the mechanism first and then place the housing around it or will they construct the housing first?

Finally, each child should produce a schedule, however rough, of how they will carry out the work and how long each activity is likely to take.

## 8. Making

### Group size
Individuals.

### Objective
To make the turntable designs.

### What you need
Construction kits, card, scissors, sticky tape, rulers, pencils, paint or coloured pencils.

### What to do
The children will now be ready to start making their designs. Encourage them to work to their schedules. Insist that they use their design proposals, studying them and following them as closely as possible. Although they are working individually, they might have to share tools and equipment, particularly consumables such as paper, card and paints. The greatest demand is likely to be for the construction kit pieces. There is no easy way around this problem except by buying in or making gearwheels. Pre-cut gears can be bought and fixed on to dowelling or alternatively, notches can be cut or dowelling glued on to cotton reels to make gearwheels. However, such work will take time and a reasonable degree of skill will be needed to produce quality gears that will function properly.

Encourage the children to finish their work carefully, removing all rough edges, applying colour evenly and smoothly.

## 9. Demonstrating the product

### Group size
Individuals and the whole class.

### Objective
To evaluate products and procedures.

### What you need
Pencils, paper.

### What to do
Once all the work has been completed, the children can

demonstrate to the rest of the class how their products work. Do they meet the needs or opportunities the children identified? This demonstration can be done in the form of a role-play exercise, under the guise of a sales pitch, for example, 'Buy my product because...'. The children can then comment on the pros and cons of each product. Their comments can then be written up in the form of an evaluation.

Following on from this each child must then review the processes and procedures they undertook to make their products. Where did they have most problems? Where did they need most help? How might they have worked more quickly or more efficiently? What decisions did they make? Why did they choose this material instead of that one? How might their product be made more successfully next time?

# Community: robots

### Age range
Nine to twelve.

There are so many different types of computer and related software packages on the market that this series of activities will not attempt to go into details of computer programming. However, there is much preparatory work involved with planning and investigation that runs alongside specific programming skills, and this will form the emphasis of these activities. The context is 'the community' and so the children will be guided towards seeking opportunities for 'using robots' within their local community.

## 1. Following instructions

### Group size
Pairs or small groups.

### Objective
To introduce the concept of 'programming'.

### What you need
Pencils, paper, ruler.

### What to do
Tell the children that computers do not actually 'think' for themselves, but only follow instructions, and the way computers are 'told' what to do is through programming. Programs are sets of instructions which the computer can understand and different makes of computer understand different computer languages such as BASIC and PASCAL. Therefore, it is important to get the language appropriate for the particular computer being used.

Ask the children to role-play writing a computer program. Begin by asking each group to decide on a task that a robot might do. Emphasise to them the need to keep the task simple, for example, boiling a kettle of water, lifting up a cup and moving across the room. Having decided on a task they should list, sequentially, all the moves the robot will have to make – lift arm... bend arm... move arm forward and so on. To itemise every move will take a lot of work, but once they have been listed, the instructions can be written as a flow chart.

Ask the children to try out their program on a volunteer. What commands are missing? How might they be simplified?

*Energy and control*

## 2. Computer programs

### Group size
Pairs or small groups.

### Objective
To introduce computer language.

### What you need
A computer, interface to control outputs, associated software.

### What to do
The children will need to practise writing 'simple' computer programs. To introduce a computer language ask them to write a simple program using the relevant computer commands. The program may be as simple as drawing a line on screen or printing a sentence or some equivalent task. Following on from this they can then practise this skill by writing their own simple program, perhaps a line in a different place or a different sentence.

Introduce the children to the relevant software that will be used to instruct their robot. They will need to be given time to become acquainted with the language – what the commands are and what they can do. They might also need to practise recognising and searching for faults in a program and it would also be wise to show them how to load the software into the computer. All this will avoid problems later on and by the end of this activity the children should be able to operate a simple program effectively, writing up each command and what it means.

## 3. Writing a computer program

### Group size
Pairs or small groups.

### Objective
To encourage the children to use their programming knowledge.

### What you need
A computer, interface, associated software.

### What to do
Ask the children to try out their programming knowledge by writing a program to switch on (and off) combinations of the light emitting diodes (LEDs) on the interface (most interfaces will have eight LEDs, one for each output to the interface). If the program has an associated timer, the next step will be to write a program that will switch on and off specific combinations of the LEDs at various time intervals. (The relevance of this work will become more apparent in later activities.)

Each program attempt should be preceded by a flowchart showing the sequence of instructions. This will encourage a disciplined approach to computer programming. It will also help each child to fault-find if his program does not function as expected.

## 4. Programming a robot

### Group size
Pairs or small groups.

### Objective
To program a buggy or robot to move.

### What you need
A computer, interface, associated software, buggy or robot, for example, a turtle or LEGO buggy with a motor.

### What to do
Introduce the buggy or robot to the children. Point out that because it is going to be controlled by the computer it is not just a mechanical buggy, but a robot. For movement, the buggy will have two motors. To go forward both motors will have to be switched on. If both motors are switched off the buggy will remain stationary.

To make the robot turn one way or the other, either one of the switches should be on and off. Motors have the capacity to turn clockwise or anticlockwise and reversing the current will cause the buggy to go backwards.

Ask the children to explore how to get the buggy to move forward, to turn right and then left and to reverse. Alternatively, if you have developed your own interface, show the children how to write the appropriate program to command the buggy. This will differ depending on what type of computer is in use. All this work should be recorded and noted for later use.

Following on from this, the children should draw a simple chalk line on the table or the floor – the line need not be straight and can have angles and turns. They must then write a program so that the buggy will follow the line.

## 5. Useful robots

### Group size
Individuals.

### Objective
To identify opportunities for using a robot.

### What you need
Pencils, paper.

### What to do
Ask the children to brainstorm all the possible uses for their robot within the community – for example to help old people, to improve communications in the local health centre, to be used as a delivery service along their street, to help a sight-impaired child move around a building, and so on. It is likely that children will think up many imaginative settings for using their robot.

Running parallel to this or as a consequence of this work, the children might then evaluate a specific area such as a house, a day centre, or the street as part of a feasibility study. Is the intended route too complicated for a robot to follow? Will the service the robot supplies be needed? This initial study will be of great value in their deliberations and they must record all their ideas and conclusions as a sketch, picture, map or route plan.

## 6. Designing the route

### Group size
Individuals.

### Objective
To design and model a proposed route for a robot.

### What you need
Pencils, paper, modelling kit, a computer, interface, buggy.

### What to do
Having sketched a rough route for their buggies (Activity 5) the children can set about modelling the route using a kit or junk material to represent possible obstacles and hazards. They should also write a brief program and test it using the model. It is important that they work to some sort of scale, not necessarily exact, but it does need to reflect angles, corners and so on. All this data can be recorded and the children can base their decision on the emerging evidence. This will encourage each child to refine her ideas accordingly.

Talk to the children about their work. How well do their programs operate? What are the problems they are coming up against?

Energy and control

## 7. Adding details to the design

### Group size
Individuals.

### Objective
To research consumer needs.

### What you need
Pencils, paper.

### What to do
The children's buggies should now be functioning at the model stage, but they must begin to think about the job their buggies will be doing. To do this, the children will need to find out what people want in their chosen section of the community. They will then have to think about how to house their buggies. (They will already have identified a route in Activity 5 but here the intention is that they think about the buggy design (housing) in order to carry out the tasks.) What is the maximum weight they will take? Will they hold liquid without spilling it? How can these likely problems be resolved?

All these ideas will have to be researched and solutions proposed. This can be done by modelling and the children will have to record their results and conclusions.

## 8. Planning to make

### Group size
Individuals.

### Objective
To design a final proposal and plan what resources will be needed.

### What you need
Pencils, paper.

### What to do
The children can now generate final design proposals. These should show the computer program as a schematic flow chart and they will also need to list all the resources they will require. The children will need to know what other tools and equipment are available to them and whether any are likely to be in short supply. Will anybody receive preferential treatment in terms of resources or will they negotiate or search for alternatives? These potential pitfalls should be discussed beforehand in order to avoid any arguments.

Finally, the children will have to identify their own course of action and draw up production schedules. Encourage them to sequence the stages in making and to think about any time constraints.

## 9. Making and evaluating

### Group size
Individuals.

### Objective
To make and evaluate their robots.

### What you need
Equipment listed in the previous activity.

### What to do
The children can now set about writing their computer programs and making the housing for their buggies. They will already have ironed out many problems, but there are likely to be others that will need to be tackled as they realise their designs.

Encourage the children to be sparing in the use of consumable resources and encourage them to keep manufacture as simple as possible. If they have problems let them try and solve them on their own or through discussion with their peers. They must only come to you as a last resort.

Once they have made their robots the children need to try them out. Do they work and look as well as they were planned? If not, how might they be modified? What do the people they were designed for think about them?

# CHAPTER 7

# A framework for assessment

Assessment of children in technology is needed in order to allow teachers to record the skills, tasks and concepts which have been covered and to measure how well each child has achieved in each area. This then allows groups of teachers to map progress and continuity from one year to the next for each child. It will also allow them to map out tasks that are relevent to each child and thus ensure progression of learning.

There are two main aspects that need to be assessed within a technology curriculum. First there are the individual skills and concepts, such as being able to cut accurately with scissors, using a hand saw and understanding such things as structures and forces. The second aspect to be assessed is the children's ability to operate within and use the design and technology process. That is, to be able to identify needs and opportunities (AT1), to generate and develop designs (AT2), to plan and to make (AT3), and finally to evaluate (AT4).

## Assessing skills and concepts

To test the level of children's skills and their understanding of particular concepts short practical and written tests can be compiled. For example, to test a child's ability to cut card using a pair of scissors, the child might be asked to cut out a pre-drawn template from card. You will then be able to assess the child's accuracy, speed and the overall quality of the child's effort. To test concepts, short written tests of multi-choice type questions are quite sufficient.

Practical tests can be grouped together and organised on a carousel basis, where each practical activity is carried out in turn, by each child. The children may be given a fixed time for doing each activity, say two minutes, and then they must move on to the next test. The main problem with this method of organisation however, is that it is difficult to make up different tests which all last for a similar duration. Also time constraints are less important for successful practical work, for example, a child may be a slow and meticulous worker, but producing work of a consistently high quality! Assessing craft skills is about assessing quality and accuracy, not necessarily speed.

Alternatively you may decide to assess in situ, thus providing a more realistic assessment of children's capabilities without imposing unnecessary time constraints. If the children are working individually on a similar piece of practical craft work, their efforts can be compared against the criteria that they were set.
• Can they accurately measure a shape which is to be cut out?
• Can they cut along a line accurately?
• Can they colour in without going outside the lines?

These and many other criteria can be ticked off simply by watching the children at work.

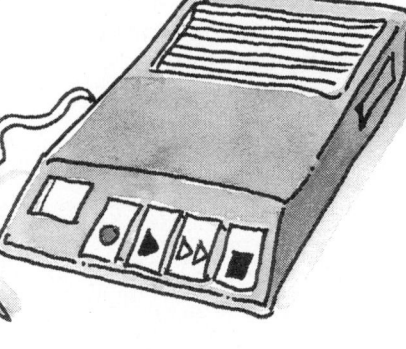

A framework for assessment

# BACKGROUND

Another option might be to ask the children to work on specific short craft tasks, but without a time limit. The children then simply work through each activity as set out by the leader. The advantage of carrying out practical assessment like this, is that there is likely to be little opportunity for the children to copy each other or cheat even though they will not be working under strict examination conditions. This is not the case with written tests that are intended to examine concepts and non-practical skills. These do need to be examined in silence.

## Assessing the process

To assess the design and technology process as a whole, the teacher needs to build up a picture of how each child's ideas have developed. All the activities in this book have been written with this in mind. Most brainstorming activities and the process of generating ideas include writing and drawing elements and this work can be collated and assessed as can any evaluation work the children do. With the final design proposals and the finished object the child's progress can be seen easily and assessed at leisure, either on your own or with a colleague to help moderate the work.

Group work, in the main, should be restricted to the skill development work which is needed in order for the children to progress and succeed in particular design and technological activities. The children will usually work as individuals when actually generating a design and making a final product. For example, they may be asked to brainstorm ideas on their own, but then work together as a class to compare ideas. This will allow them to refine their own ideas accordingly and might lead them towards writing a sentence or two to justify their own reasons for the refinements they have made.

This constant dipping in and out of designing and making activities is crucial to design and technology work, but it does present problems when you come to assess. It is often impossible to isolate one child's ideas from another since they will have borrowed, copied and improved upon their efforts as they have worked through a project. However, if the children can be encouraged to sketch, draw or write a little each time they come up with something new or change an aspect of their work and justify changes, then this evidence can be assessed easily once the project has been completed.

## Assessing the final product

If the final product is not a consumable such as a sandwich, then the children's work can be put on display together with an 'ideas file' showing the work they carried out during the project. A display of this kind can then be assessed using the statements of attainment. To enhance this assessment further, you could include any relevant short tests, observations or notes you made during the work. Together this will provide a fairly comprehensive picture of each child's performed.

If the product is a consumable then assessment of the product may have to be immediate. Alternatively you could take photographs of each finished piece and place these in a portfolio with the rest of the children's work. Creating such a file, will in itself be interesting to the children. It will encourage and develop their own organisational skills.

By using this portfolio you and the children will be able to maintain continuity in terms of areas to be improved and so on. It will also allow you much more flexibility in being able to complete, and reinforce what has gone before. If you feel that certain children are not capable of being so responsible, then you can collect each piece of work from them and file it accordingly. Little touches such as dating pieces of work and/or numbering pages will help in the final analysis and it goes without saying that such work should be stored in a safe place!

# AT CHART

## England and Wales

The chart on this page refers to the National Curriculum for England and Wales. Use this chart to identify the attainment targets covered by the themes in this book. The chapters in this book have been divided into various sections entitled Home, School, Recreation, Business and Community. Therefore the numbers in bold refer to the relevant chapter while the letter refers to one of the above themes; for example, **3**/H refers to the theme Homes in Chapter 3.

| AT / Level | 1 Identifying needs and opportunities | 2 Generating a design | 3 Planning and making | 4 Evaluating | 5 Information technology capability |
|---|---|---|---|---|---|
| **1** | **1**/H, **3**/H, **4**/R, **5**/S, **6**/H | **1**/H, **3**/H, **4**/R, **5**/S, **6**/H | **1**/H, **3**/H, **4**/R, **5**/S, **6**/H | **1**/H, **3**/H, **4**/R, **5**/S, **6**/H | **2**/H, **3**/R, **4**/B, **6**/H |
| **2** | **1**/S, **2**/H, **3**/R, **4**/B, **5**/R, **6**/S | **1**/S, **2**/B, **3**/R, **4**/B, **6**/S | **1**/S, **2**/H, **3**/R, **4**/B, **5**/R, **6**/S | **1**/S, **2**/H, **3**/R, **4**/B, **5**/R, **6**/S | **1**/S, **2**/H, **3**/R, **4**/B, **5**/R, **6**/S |
| **3** | **1**/B, **2**/S, **3**/S, **4**/C, **5**/B, **6**/H,R | **1**/B, **2**/S, **3**/S, **4**/C, **5**/B, **6**/R | **1**/B, **2**/S, **3**/S, **4**/C, **5**/B, **6**/R | **1**/B, **2**/S, **3**/S, **4**/C, **5**/B, **6**/R | **1**/B, **2**/H,S, **3**/S, **5**/B, **6**/R,C |
| **4** | **1**/R, **2**/R, **3**/C, **4**/H, **5**/C, **6**/B | **1**/R, **2**/R, **3**/C, **4**/H, **5**/C, **6**/B | **1**/R, **2**/R, **3**/C, **4**/H, **5**/C, **6**/B | **1**/R, **2**/R, **3**/C, **4**/H, **5**/C, **6**/B | **1**/R, **2**/R, **3**/C, **4**/H, **5**/C, **6**/C |
| **5** | **1**/C, **2**/B,C, **3**/B, **4**/S, **5**/H, **6**/C | **2**/B,C, **3**/B, **4**/S, **5**/H, **6**/C | **1**/C, **2**/B,C, **3**/B, **4**/S, **5**/C, **6**/C | **1**/C, **2**/B,C, **3**/B, **4**/S, **5**/H, **6**/C | **1**/C, **2**/R,B, **3**/B, **4**/S, **5**/H, **6**/C, |

# PHOTOCOPIABLES

The pages in this section can be photocopied and adapted to suit your own needs and those of your class; they do not need to be declared in respect of any photocopying licence. Each photocopiable page relates to a specific activity in the main body of the book and the appropriate activity and page references are given above each photocopiable sheet.

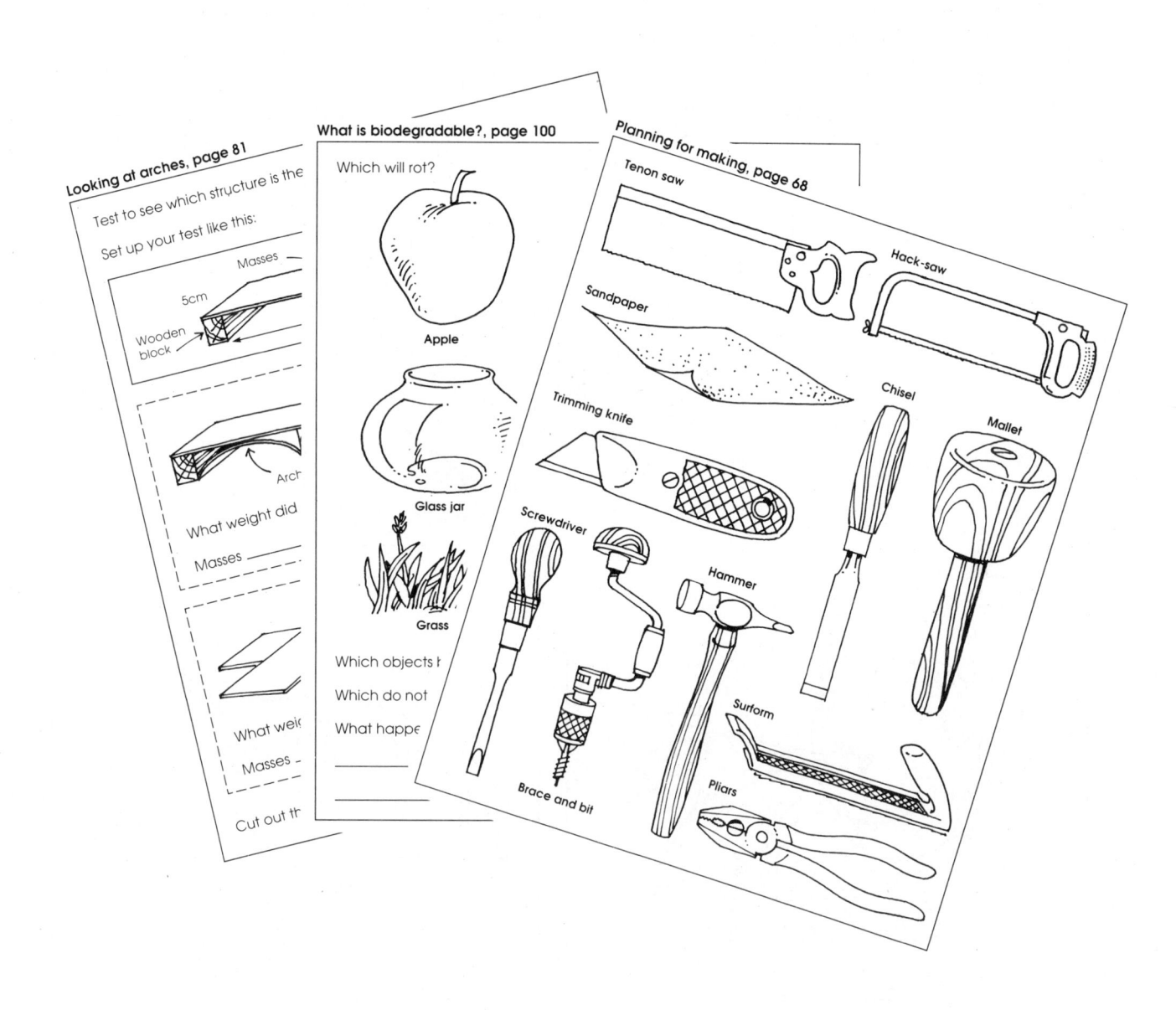

Photocopiable pages

## Detailed planning, page 19

Cut out these pictures and stick them in the order you will do them.

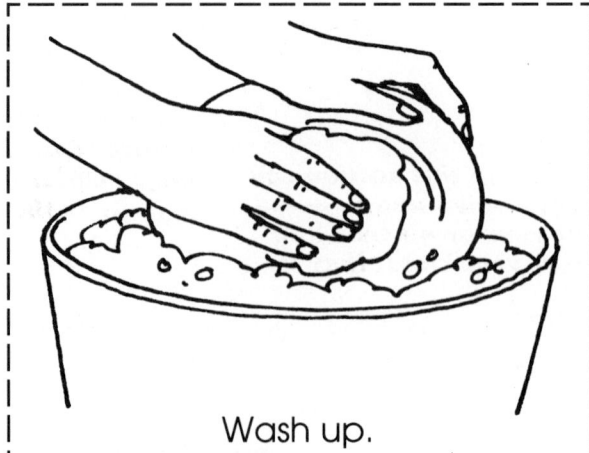

Cut the vegetables.

Wash up.

Mix the vegetables and sauces.

Taste my side salad.

Measure sauces.

# Components, page 33

**Mains** – colour this red.
**Filler** – colour this yellow.
**Fruit and vegetable** – colour this green.
**Drink** – colour this blue.

Water

Beef

Peas

Potatoes

Chicken pieces

Vegetables

Bread

Vegetable soup

Apple

Cheese sandwich

Orange juice

Bangers and mash

Orange

Carrots

Meat

Beans

Rice

Wine

# Shoe design, page 41

Colour the sole black.
Colour the heel red.
Colour the upper green.

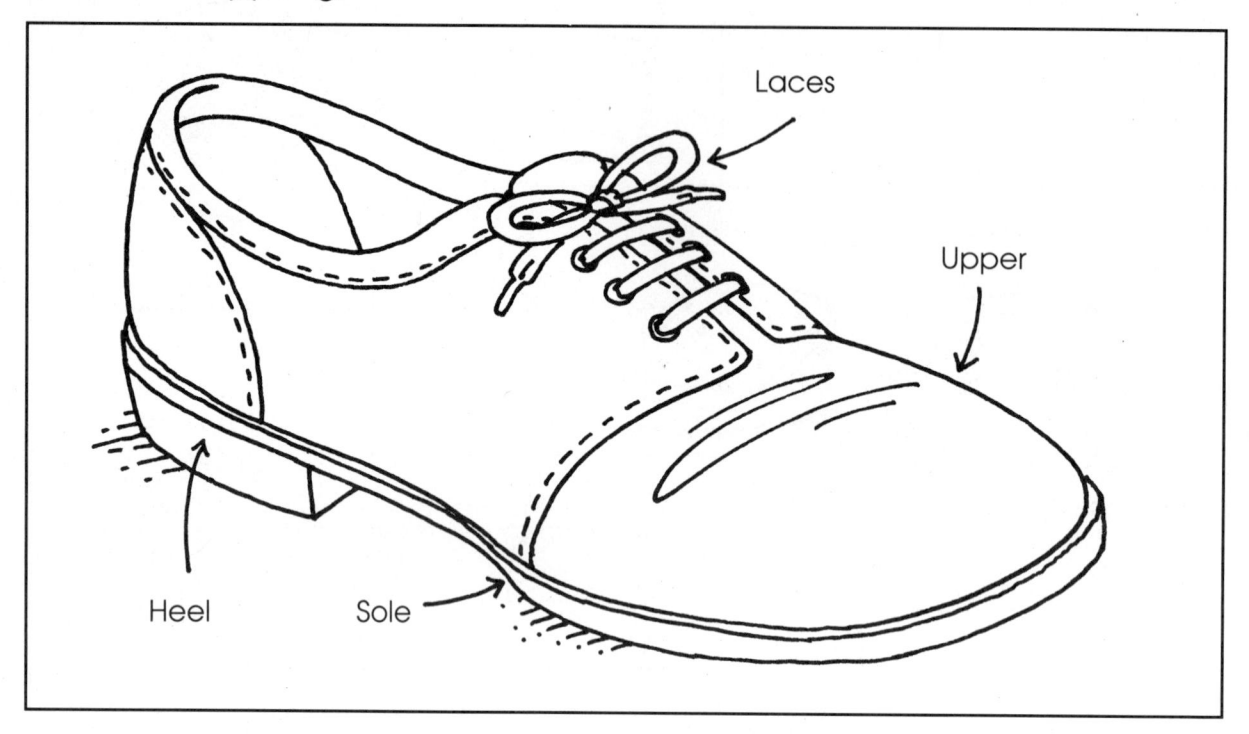

Laces

Upper

Heel    Sole

Now colour this shoe in the same way.

Draw your favourite shoe and colour it.

# Joining materials, page 43

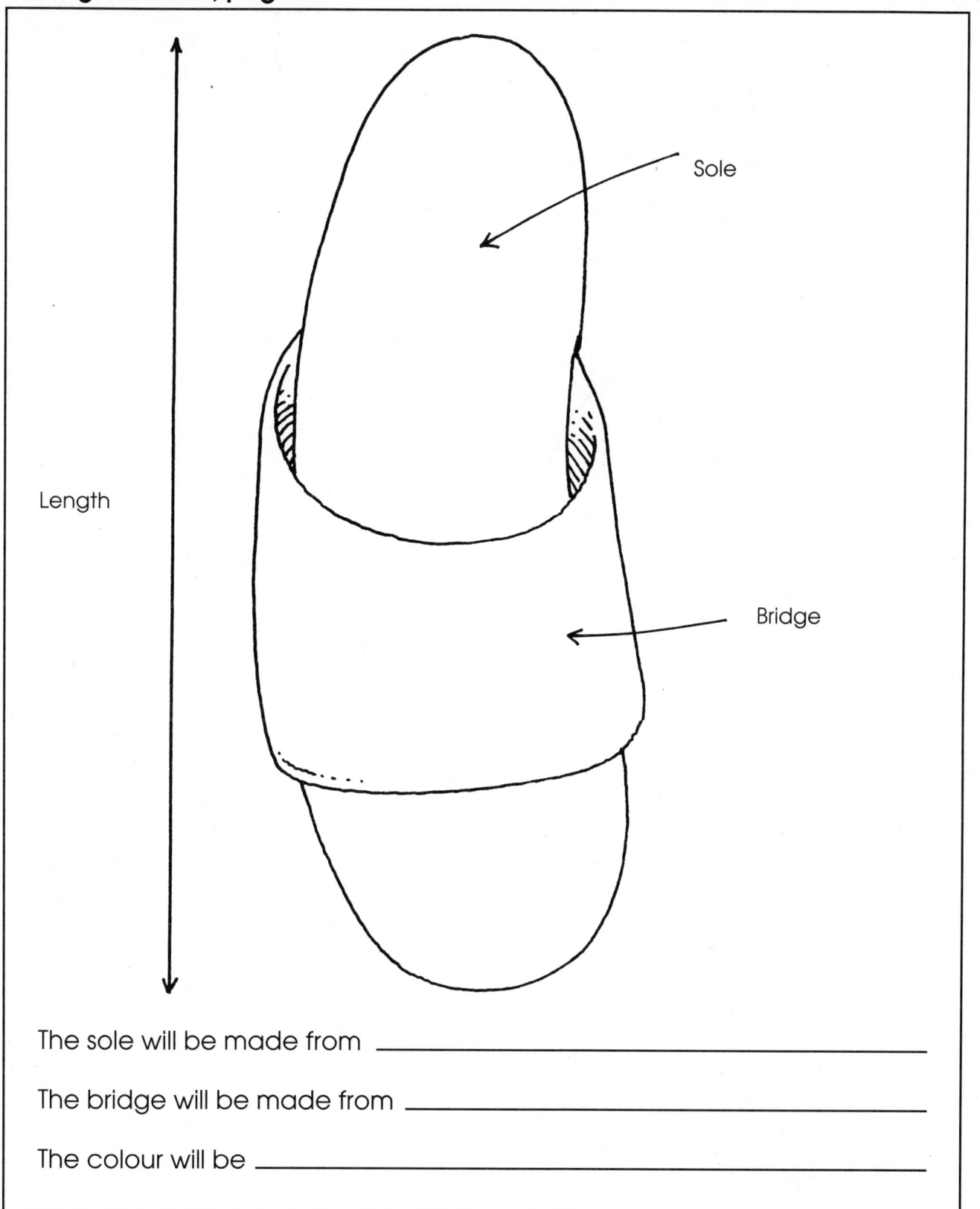

Length

Sole

Bridge

The sole will be made from _____

The bridge will be made from _____

The colour will be _____

# Templates, page 47

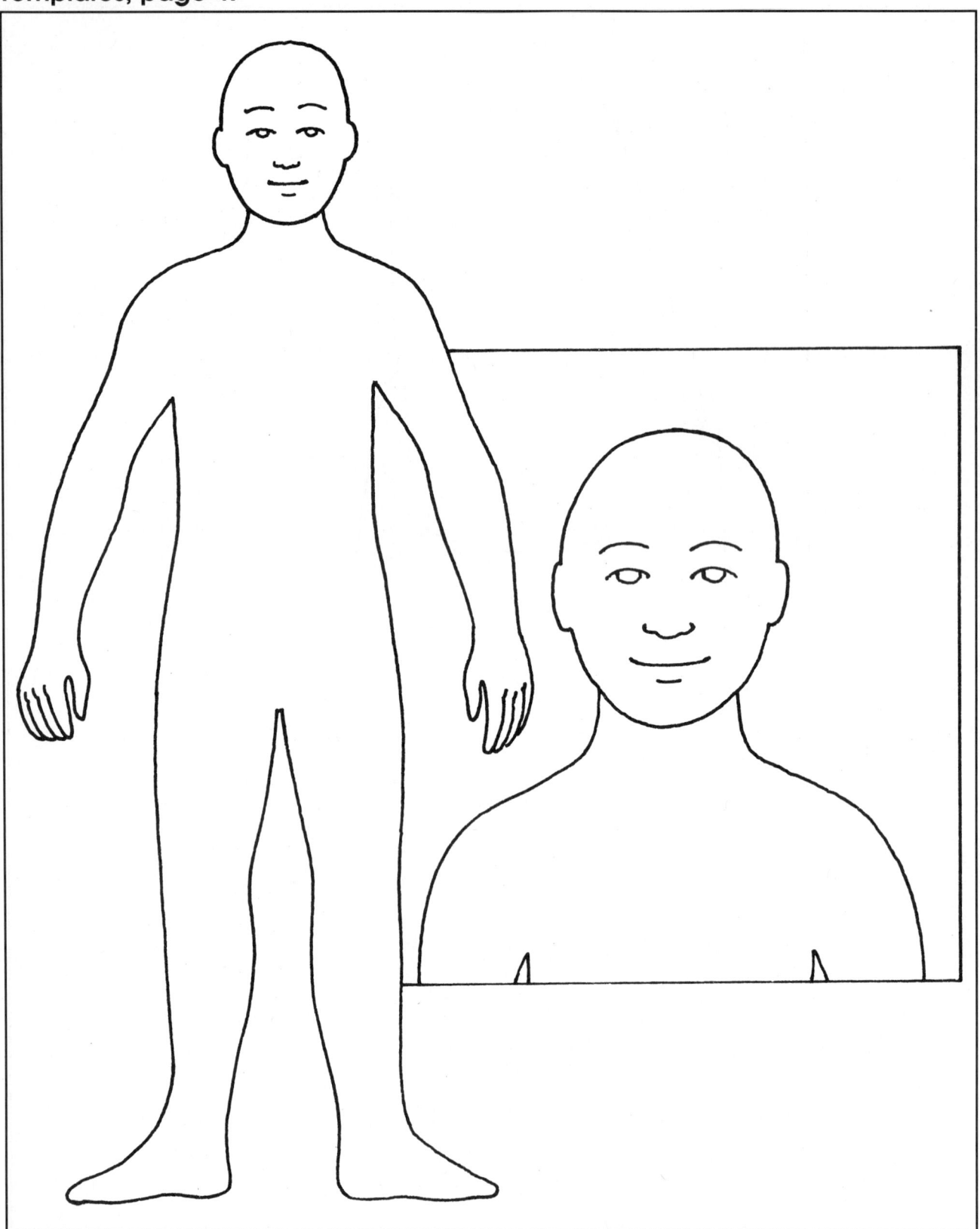

**Testing materials, page 55**

Use this grid to record your test results.
Space has been left for you to add tests and materials of your own.

| Test / Materials | Soaked in water | Stained | Washed and dried | | |
|---|---|---|---|---|---|
| Wool | | | | | |
| Cotton | | | | | |
| Nylon | | | | | |
| | | | | | |
| | | | | | |

Use your results to answer these questions.

1. Which material absorbs water: • quickest? _____
   • slowest? _____

2. Which materials: • stain easily? _____
   • stain a little? _____
   • do not stain at all? _____

3. Which materials: • lose their shape when washed and dried?
   _____
   • do not lose their shape when washed and dried? _____
   _____

Photocopiable pages

# Planning for making, page 68

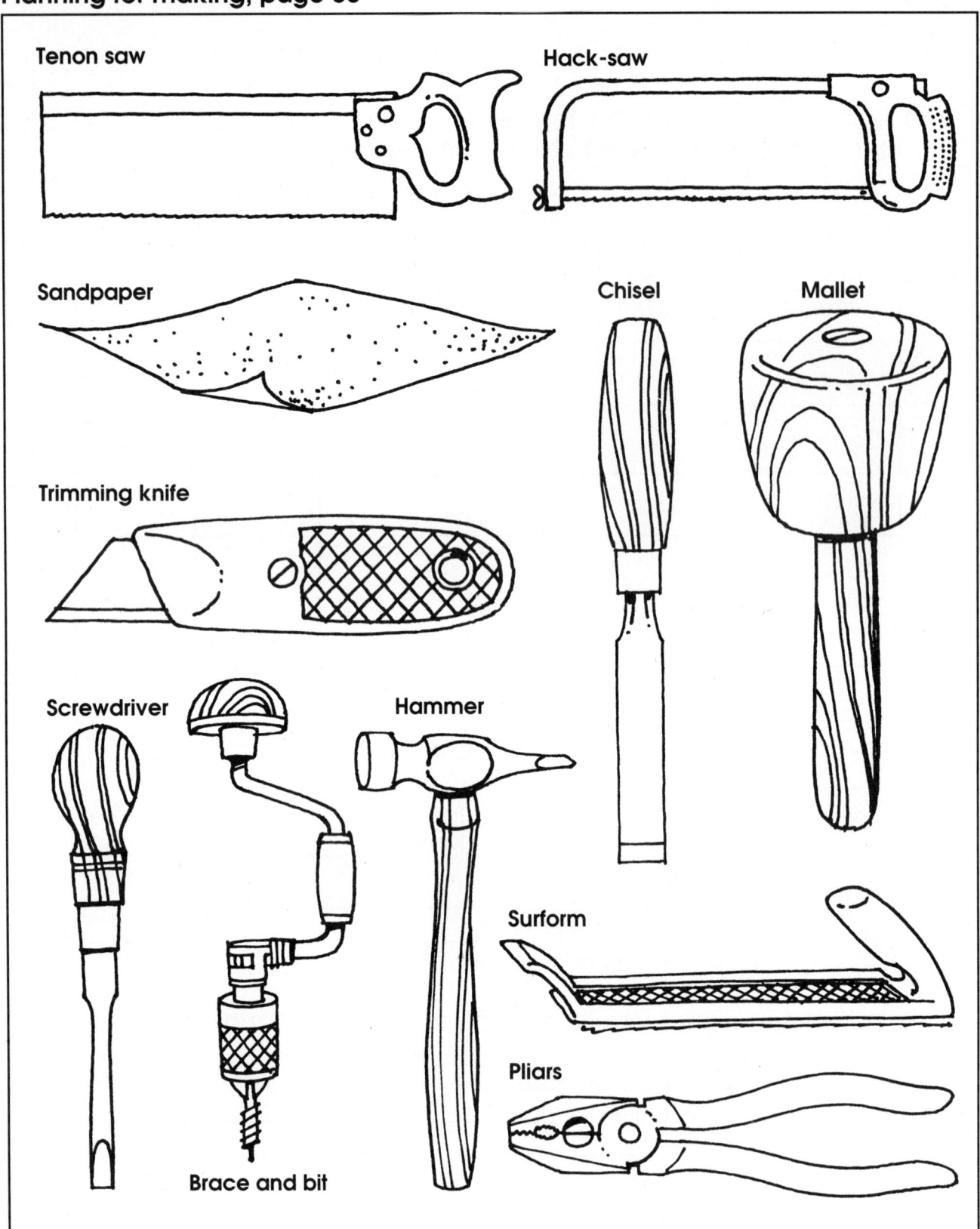

Tenon saw

Hack-saw

Sandpaper

Chisel

Mallet

Trimming knife

Screwdriver

Hammer

Surform

Pliers

Brace and bit

# Investigating structures, page 70

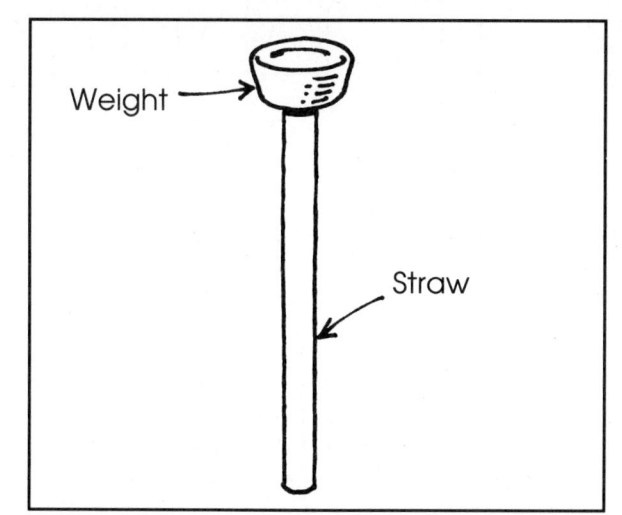

**Weight** → *(bowl on top of straw)*
**Straw**

Does it stand up? _____

Is it knocked over easily? _____

Is it strong? _____

**Weight** → *(bowl on top of tripod of straws)*
**Sticky tape here**

Does it stand up? _____

Is it knocked over easily? _____

Is it strong? _____

**Sticky tape here** *(pyramid structure)*
**Sticky tape here**

Does it stand up? _____

Is it knocked over easily? _____

Is it strong? _____

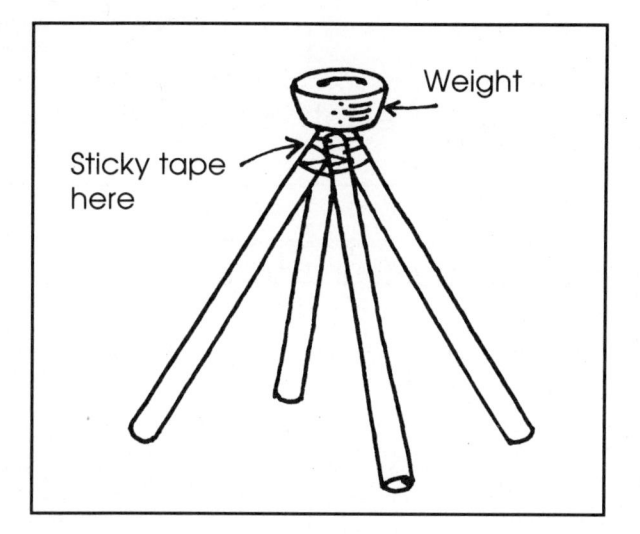

Does it stand up? _____

Is it knocked over easily? _____

Is it strong? _____

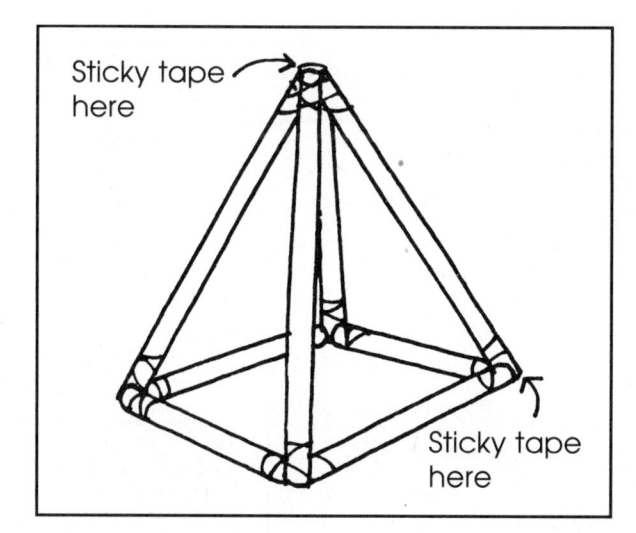

*Photocopiable pages* **173**

# Cutting and sticking, page 71

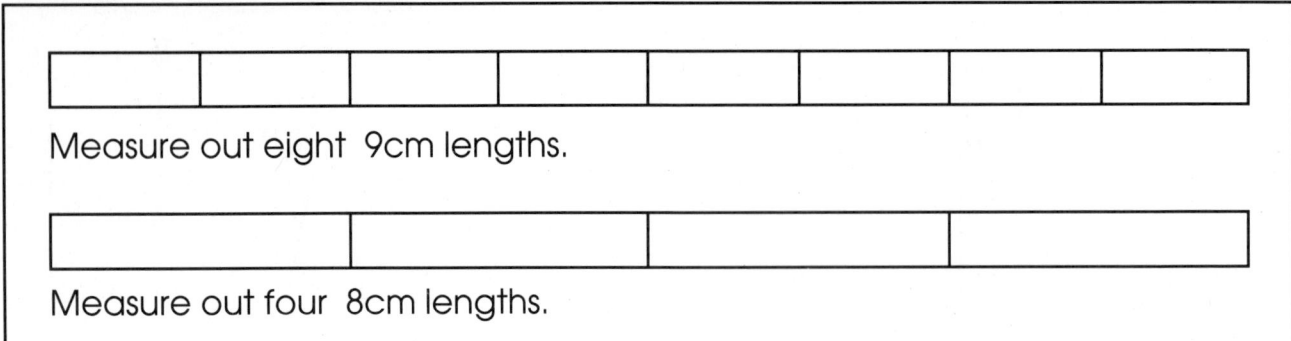

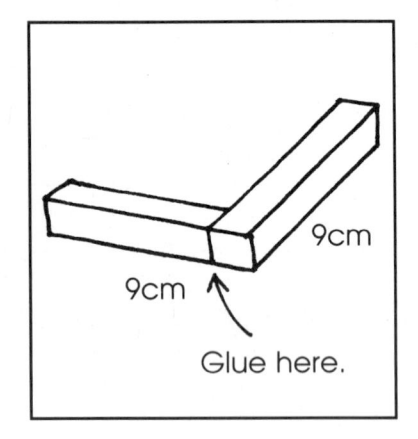

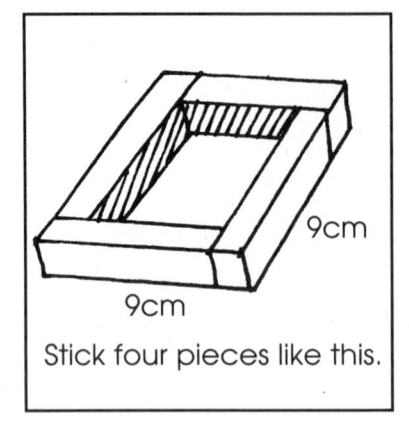

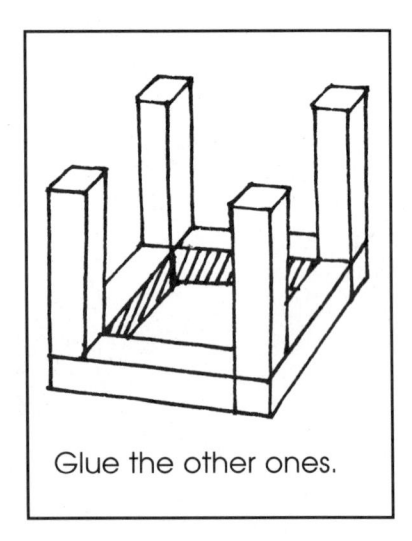

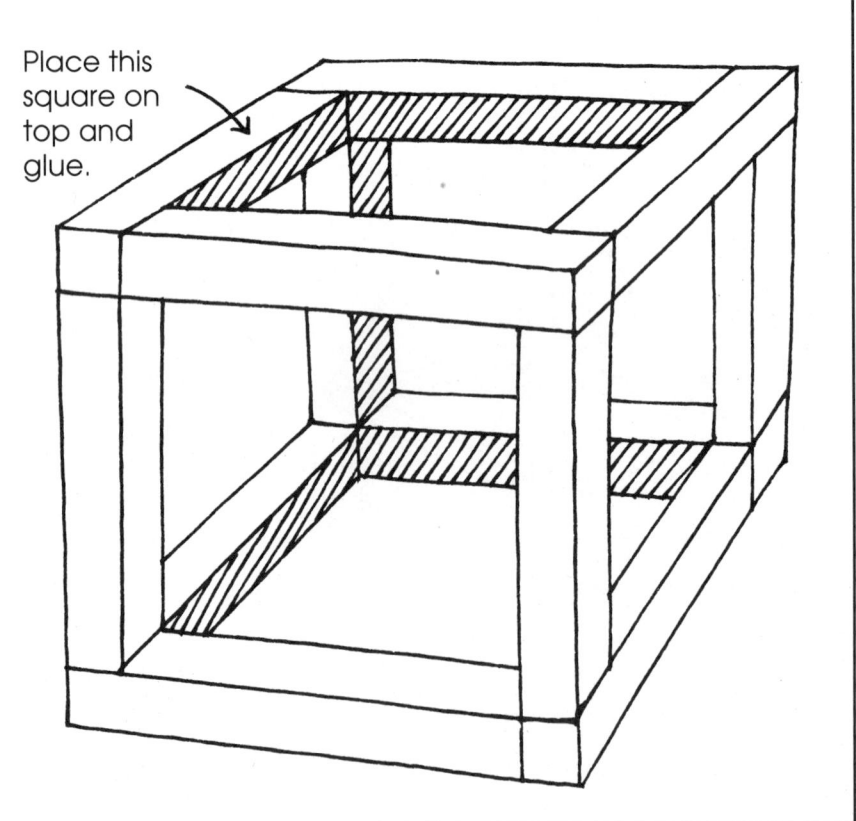

Measure out eight 9cm lengths.

Measure out four 8cm lengths.

9cm
9cm
Glue here.

9cm
9cm
Stick four pieces like this.

Glue on an 8cm piece.

Glue the other ones.

Place this square on top and glue.

*Photocopiable pages*

# How do others design for 'quakes'?, page 80

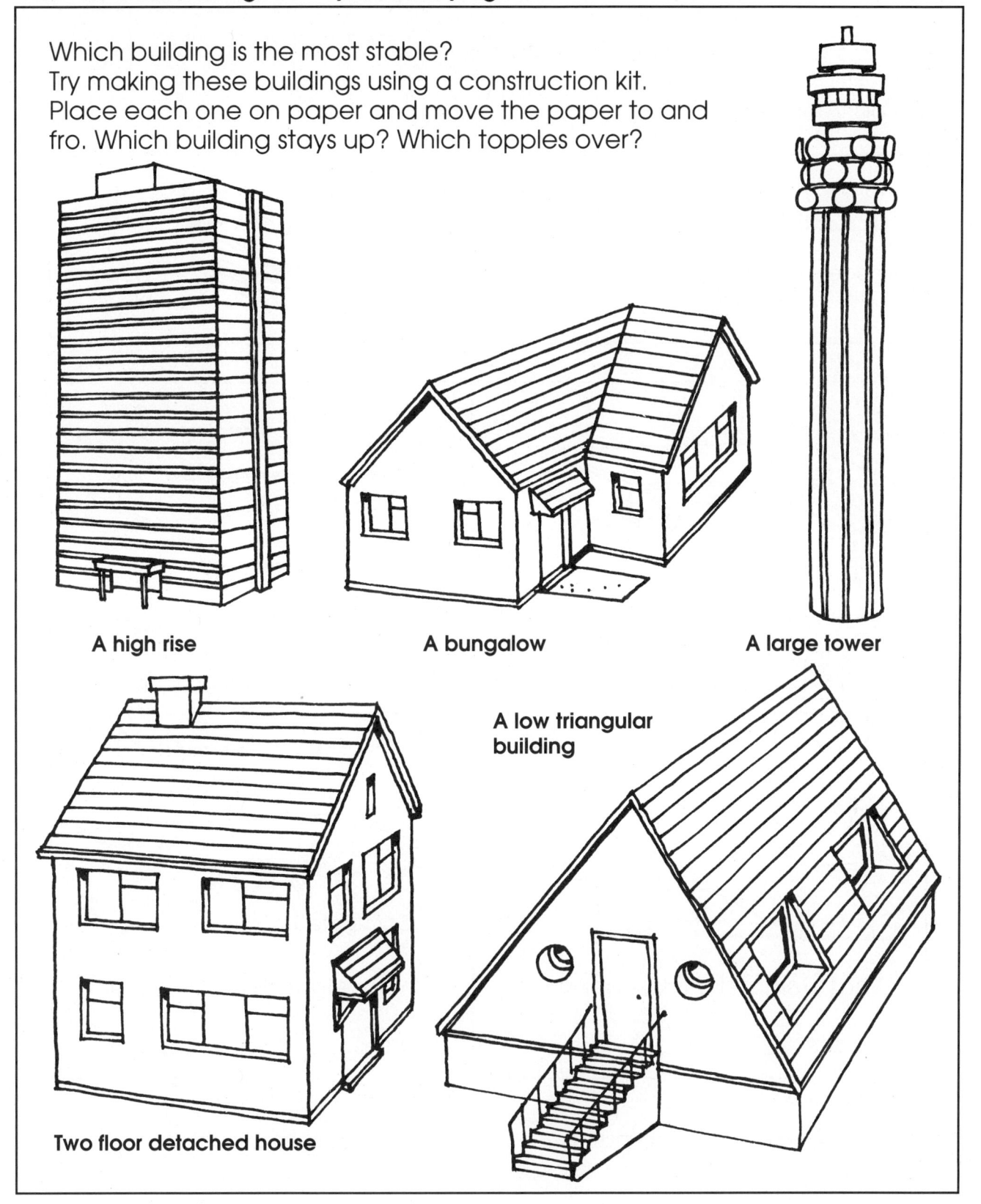

Which building is the most stable?
Try making these buildings using a construction kit. Place each one on paper and move the paper to and fro. Which building stays up? Which topples over?

**A high rise**

**A bungalow**

**A large tower**

**Two floor detached house**

**A low triangular building**

Photocopiable pages   175

# Looking at arches, page 81

Test to see which structure is the strongest.

Set up your test like this:

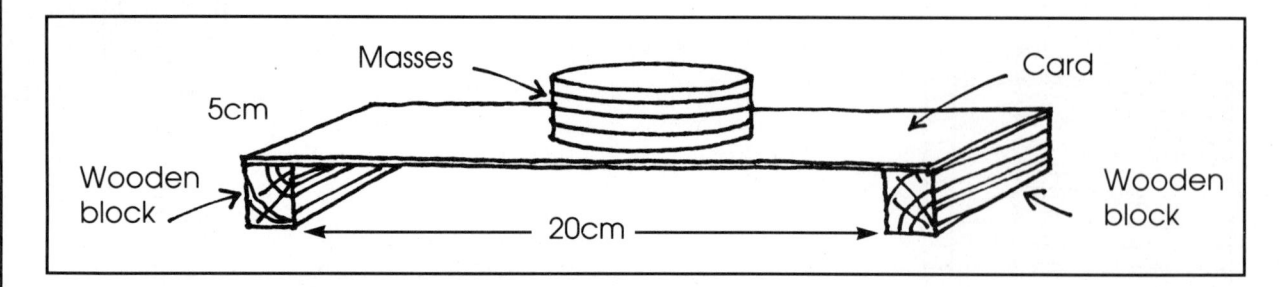

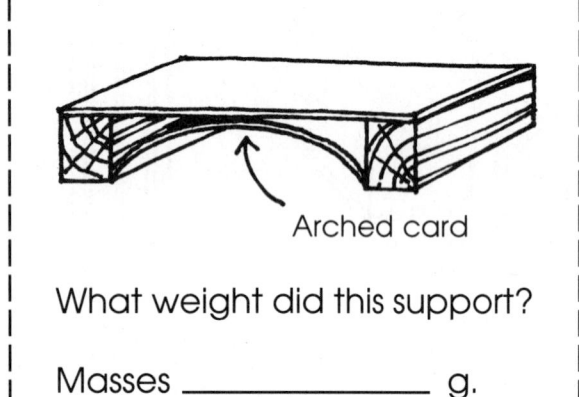

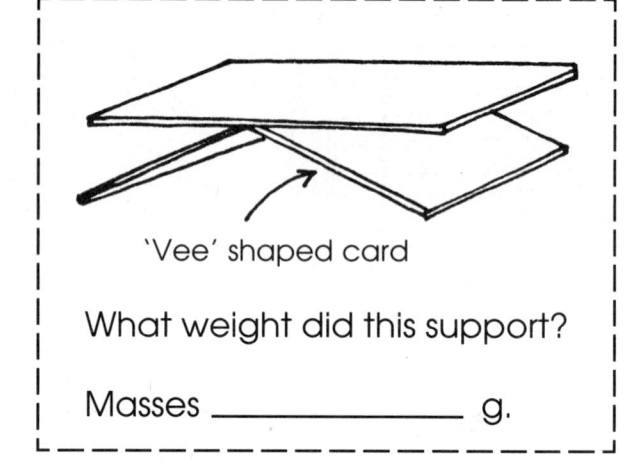

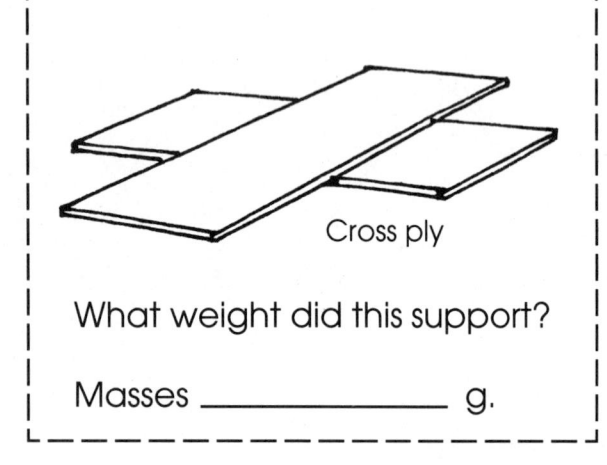

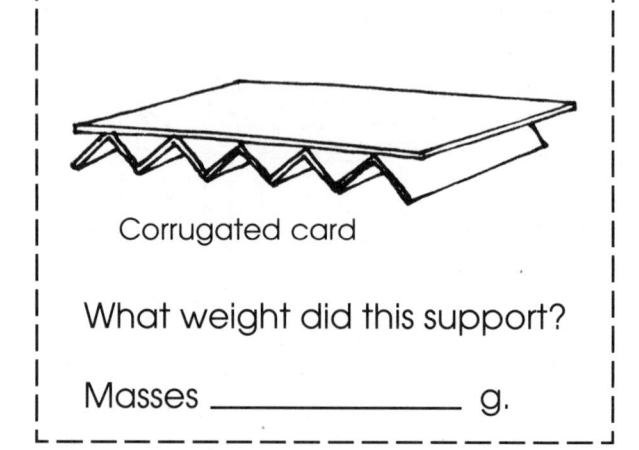

*Masses, Card, 5cm, Wooden block, 20cm, Wooden block*

**Arched card**

What weight did this support?

Masses _____ g.

**'Vee' shaped card**

What weight did this support?

Masses _____ g.

**Cross ply**

What weight did this support?

Masses _____ g.

**Corrugated card**

What weight did this support?

Masses _____ g.

Cut out the pictures and put them in order, strongest to weakest.

# What is biodegradable?, page 100

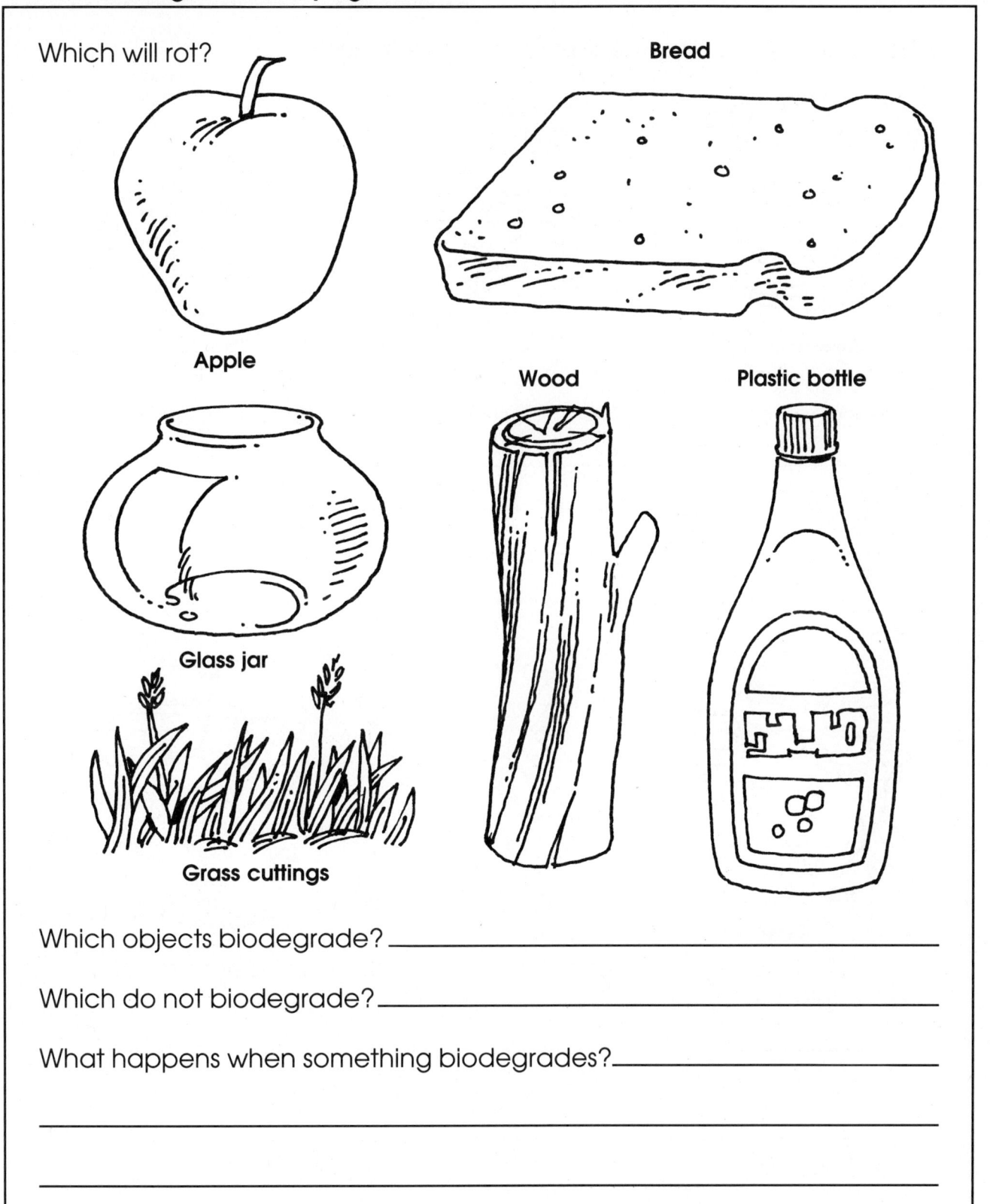

## Which will rot?

**Apple**

**Bread**

**Glass jar**

**Wood**

**Plastic bottle**

**Grass cuttings**

Which objects biodegrade? _____

Which do not biodegrade? _____

What happens when something biodegrades? _____

_____

_____

*Photocopiable pages*

# What can be recycled?, page 101

What new uses can you think of for all these things?

Used yoghurt pot.

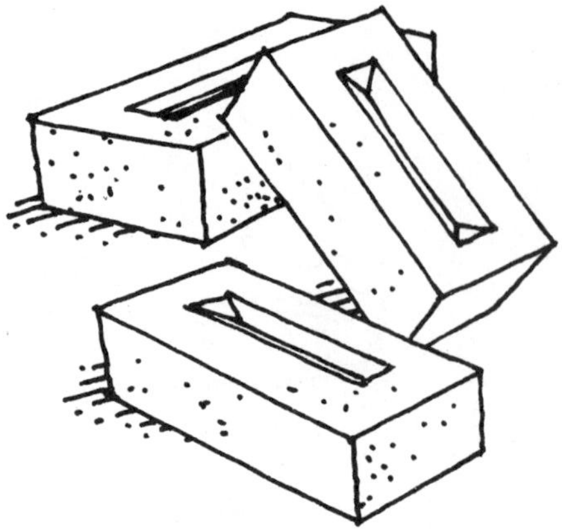

_____
_____
_____
_____

A few loose bricks.

_____
_____
_____
_____

Supermarket trolley.

_____
_____
_____
_____

Old plastic bags with holes in them.

_____
_____
_____
_____

Long planks of wood.

_____
_____
_____
_____

Different sizes of stones.

_____
_____
_____
_____

# Pond studies, page 110

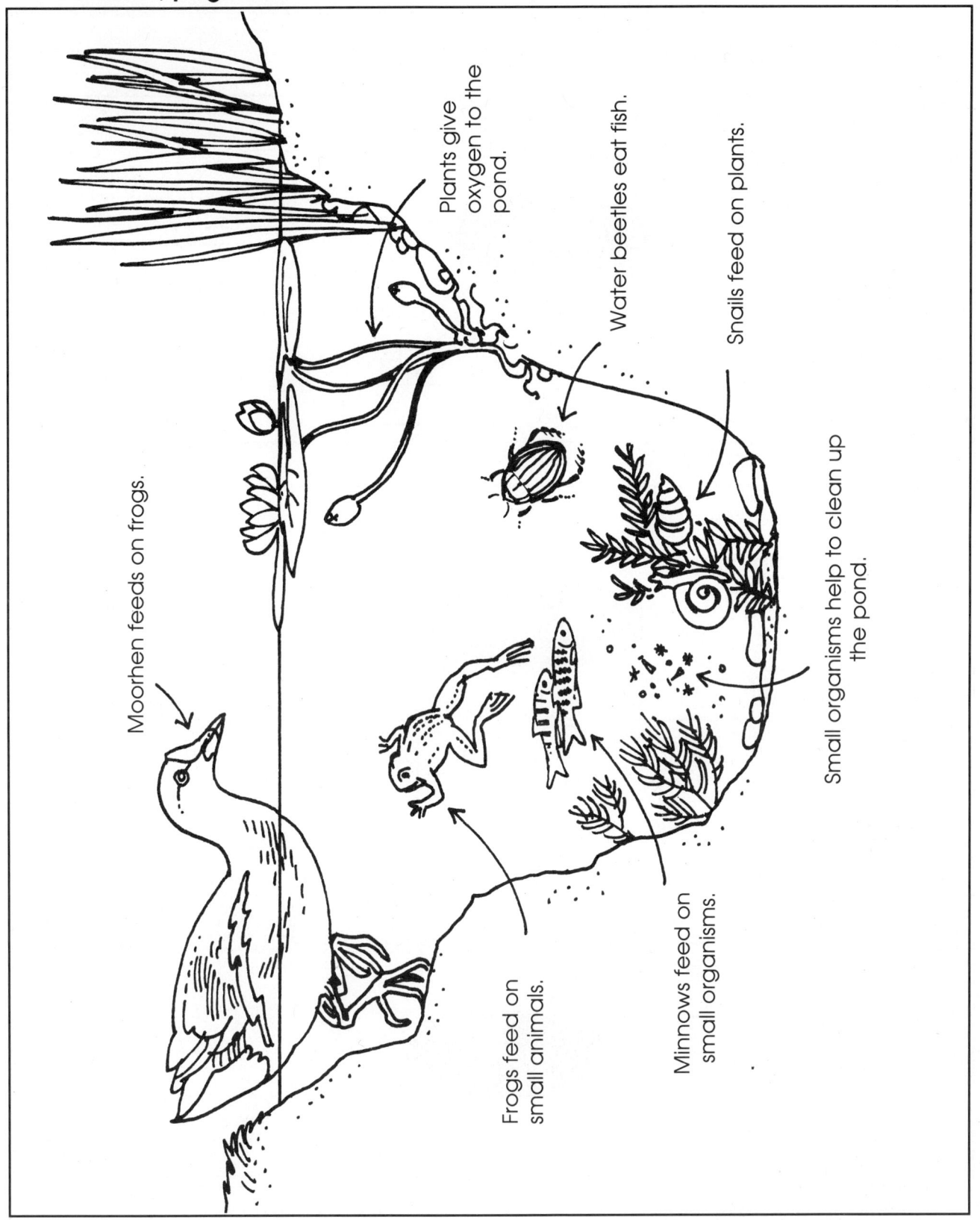

- Plants give oxygen to the pond.
- Water beetles eat fish.
- Snails feed on plants.
- Small organisms help to clean up the pond.
- Minnows feed on small organisms.
- Frogs feed on small animals.
- Moorhen feeds on frogs.

# Concept sketches, page 112

Fill in the missing spaces.

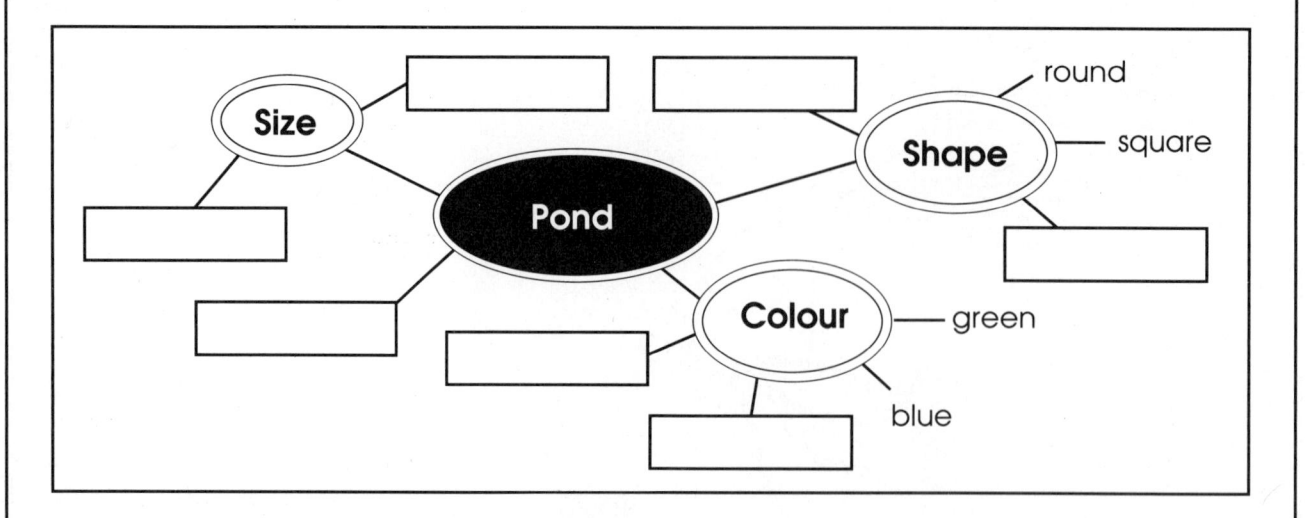

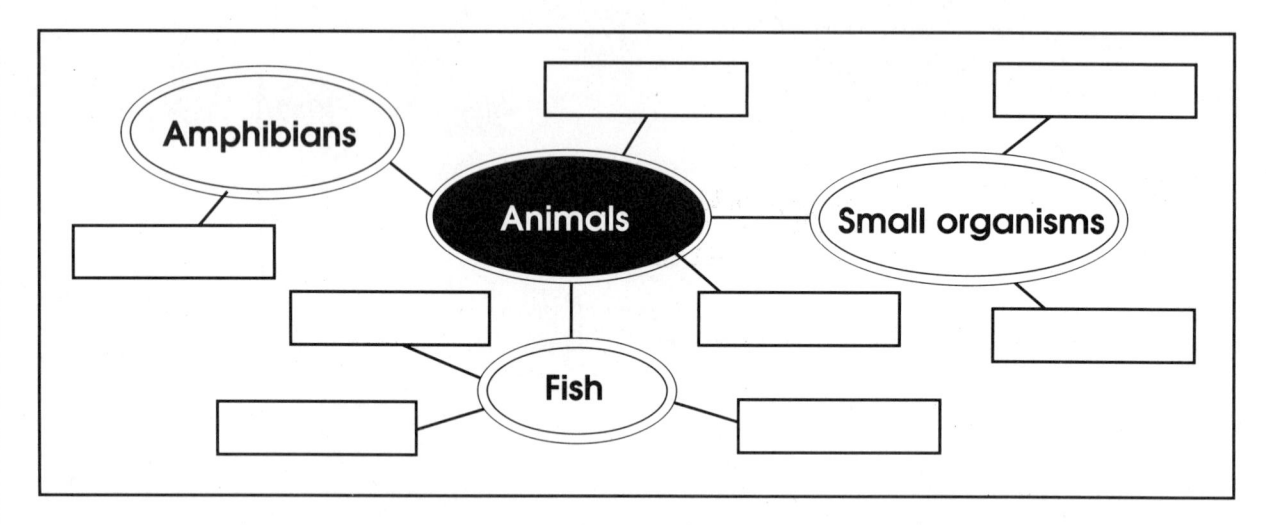

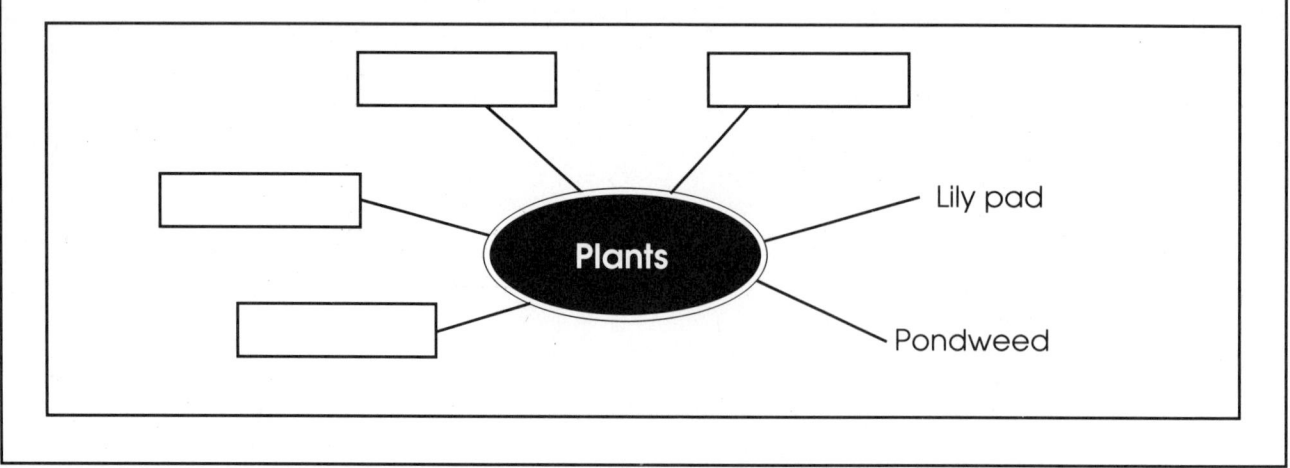

**Pond** — Size, Shape (round, square), Colour (green, blue)

**Animals** — Amphibians, Small organisms, Fish

**Plants** — Lily pad, Pondweed

# Studying greetings cards, page 117

The card has been _____

This is the_____ inside.

This is the
_____

To a Special Person...

Happy Birthday

Most cards have a _____

Choose from these words:

folded    title    picture    message

# What is a system?, page 118

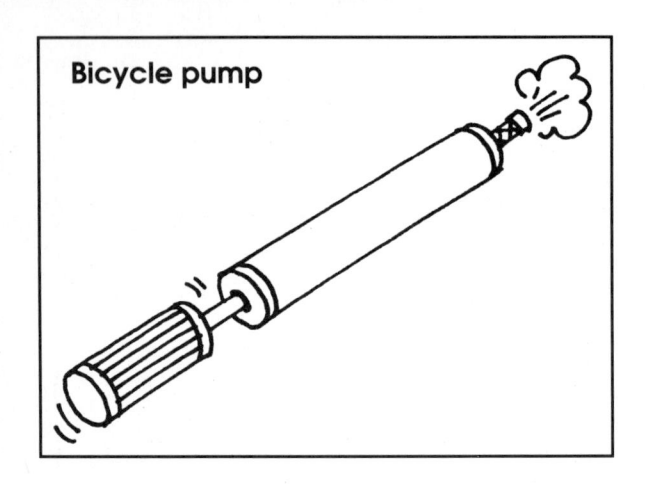

**Bicycle pump**

**Riding a bike**

The input is _____

The input is _____

The output is _____

The output is _____

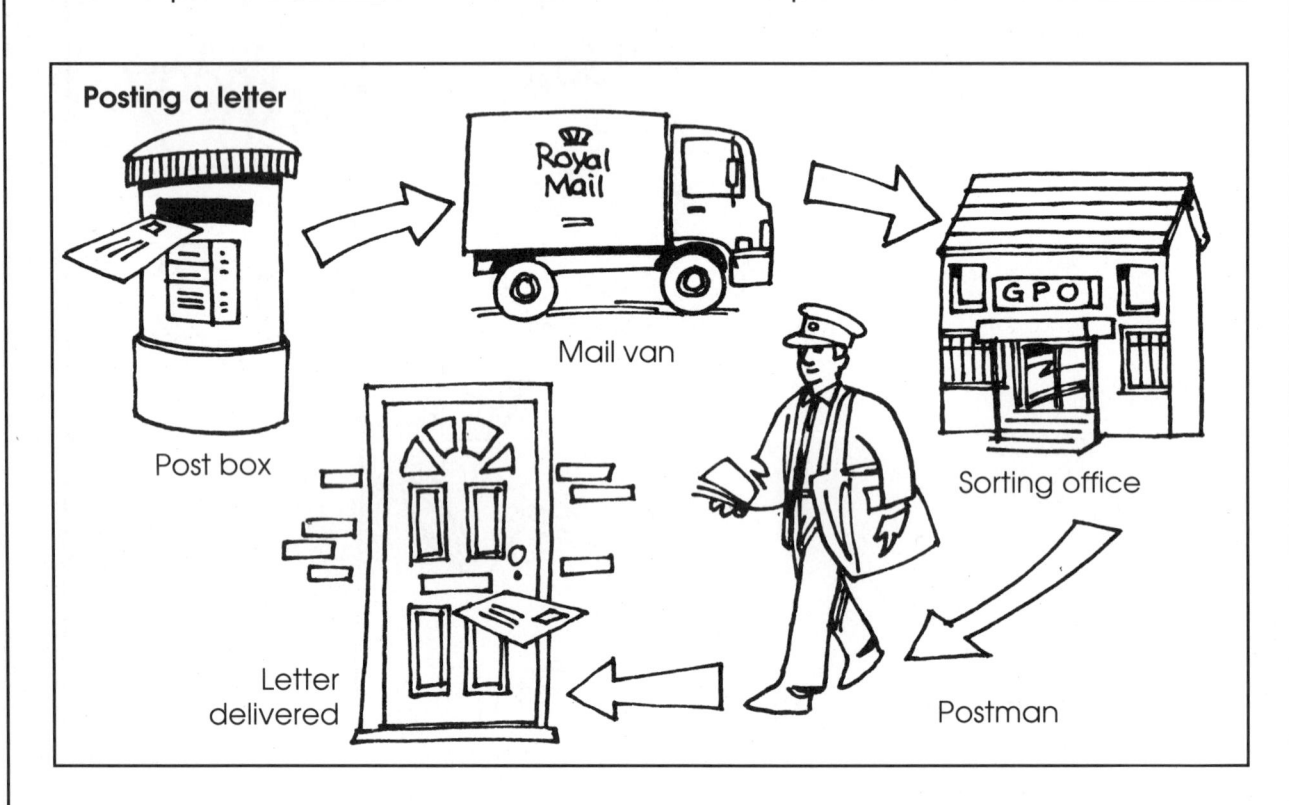

**Posting a letter**

Post box

Mail van

Sorting office

Postman

Letter delivered

The inputs are _____

The outputs are _____

# Pulley systems, page 121

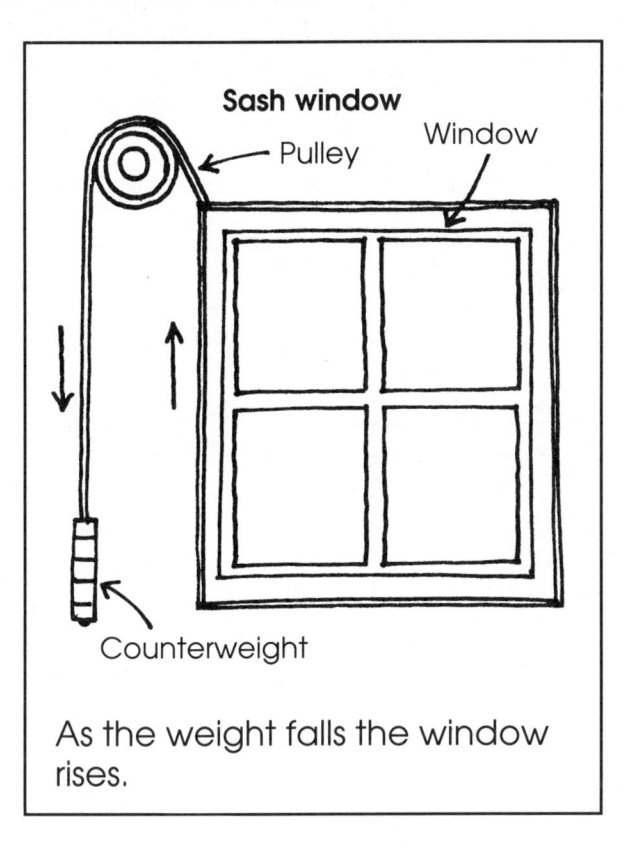

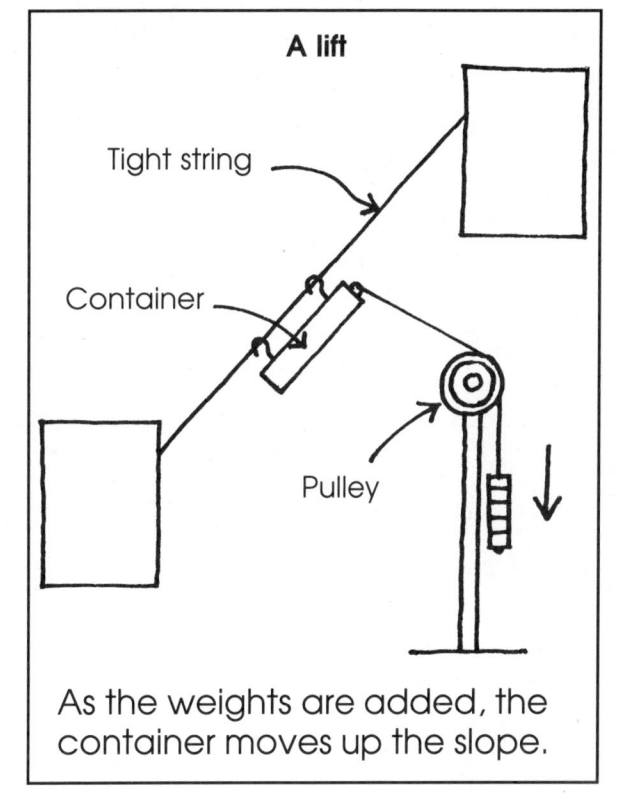

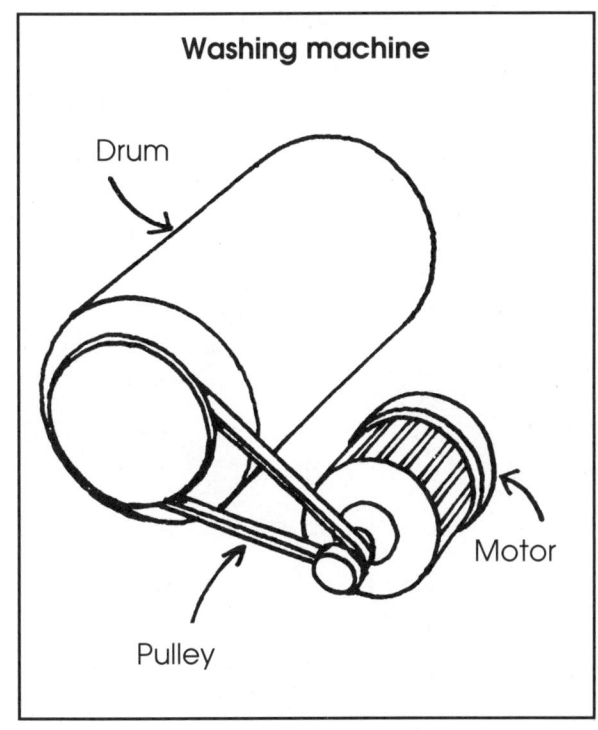

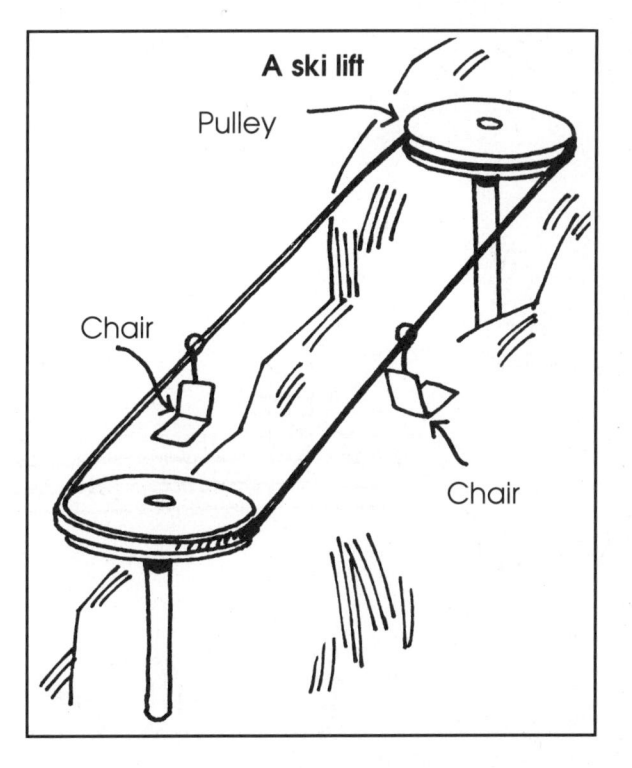

## Sash window
- Pulley
- Window
- Counterweight

As the weight falls the window rises.

## A lift
- Tight string
- Container
- Pulley

As the weights are added, the container moves up the slope.

## Washing machine
- Drum
- Motor
- Pulley

## A ski lift
- Pulley
- Chair
- Chair

# Making a pressure pad, page 131

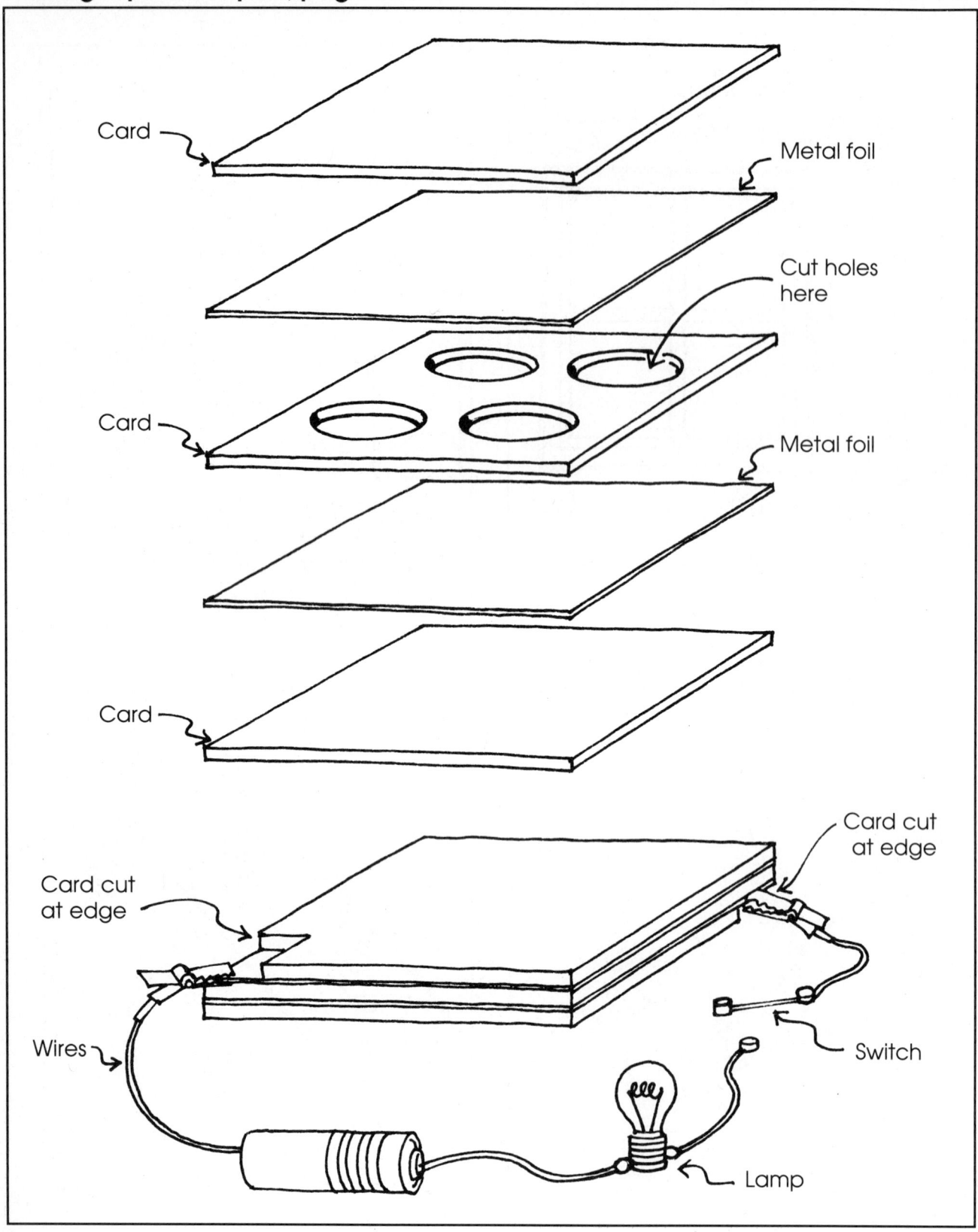

Card

Metal foil

Cut holes here

Card

Metal foil

Card

Card cut at edge

Card cut at edge

Wires

Switch

Lamp

*184*   Photocopiable pages

# Making different electrical circuits, page 134

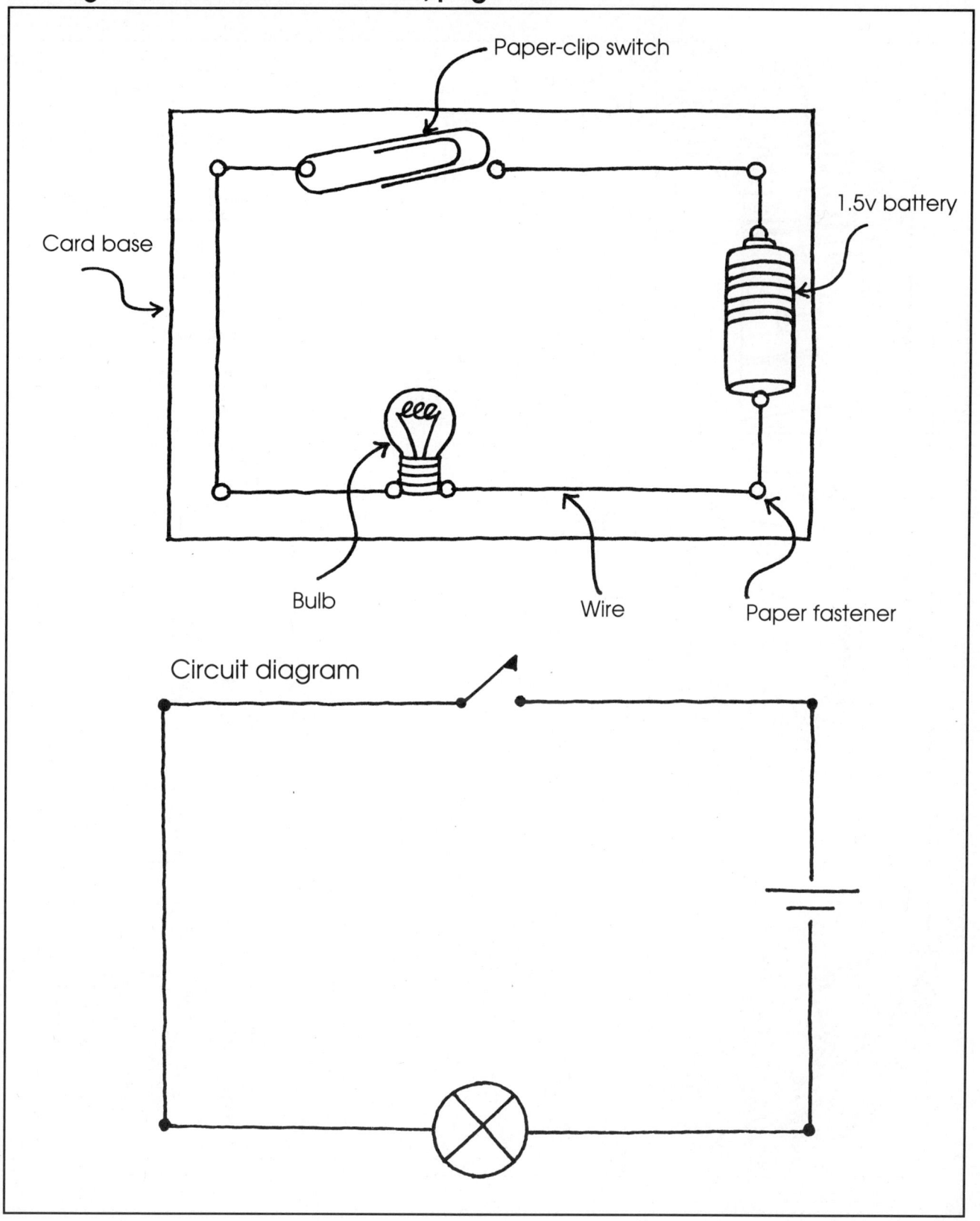

Paper-clip switch

Card base

1.5v battery

Bulb

Wire

Paper fastener

Circuit diagram

*Photocopiable pages*    **185**

# Controlling energy, page 141

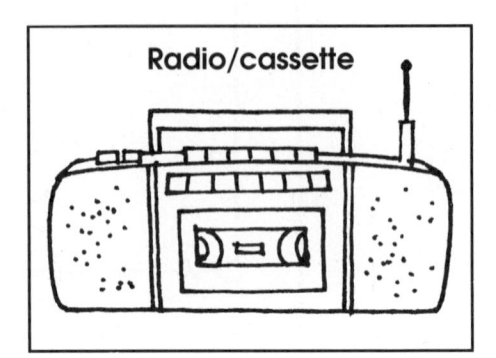

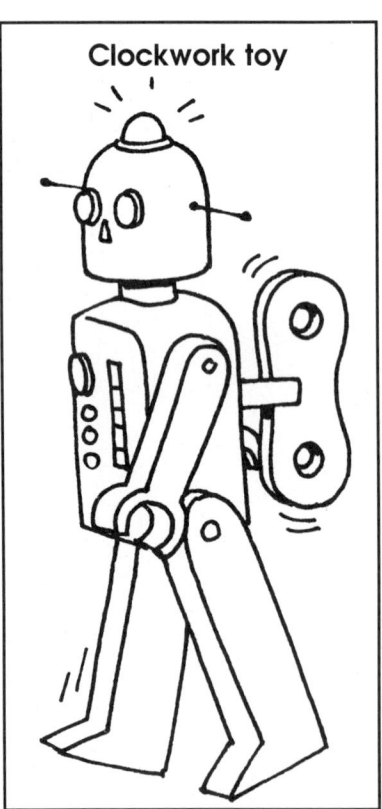

Cooker

Switch

Lamp

Telephone

Radio/cassette

Television

Clockwork toy

Car

Boat

Bicycle

# Balloon rockets, page 141

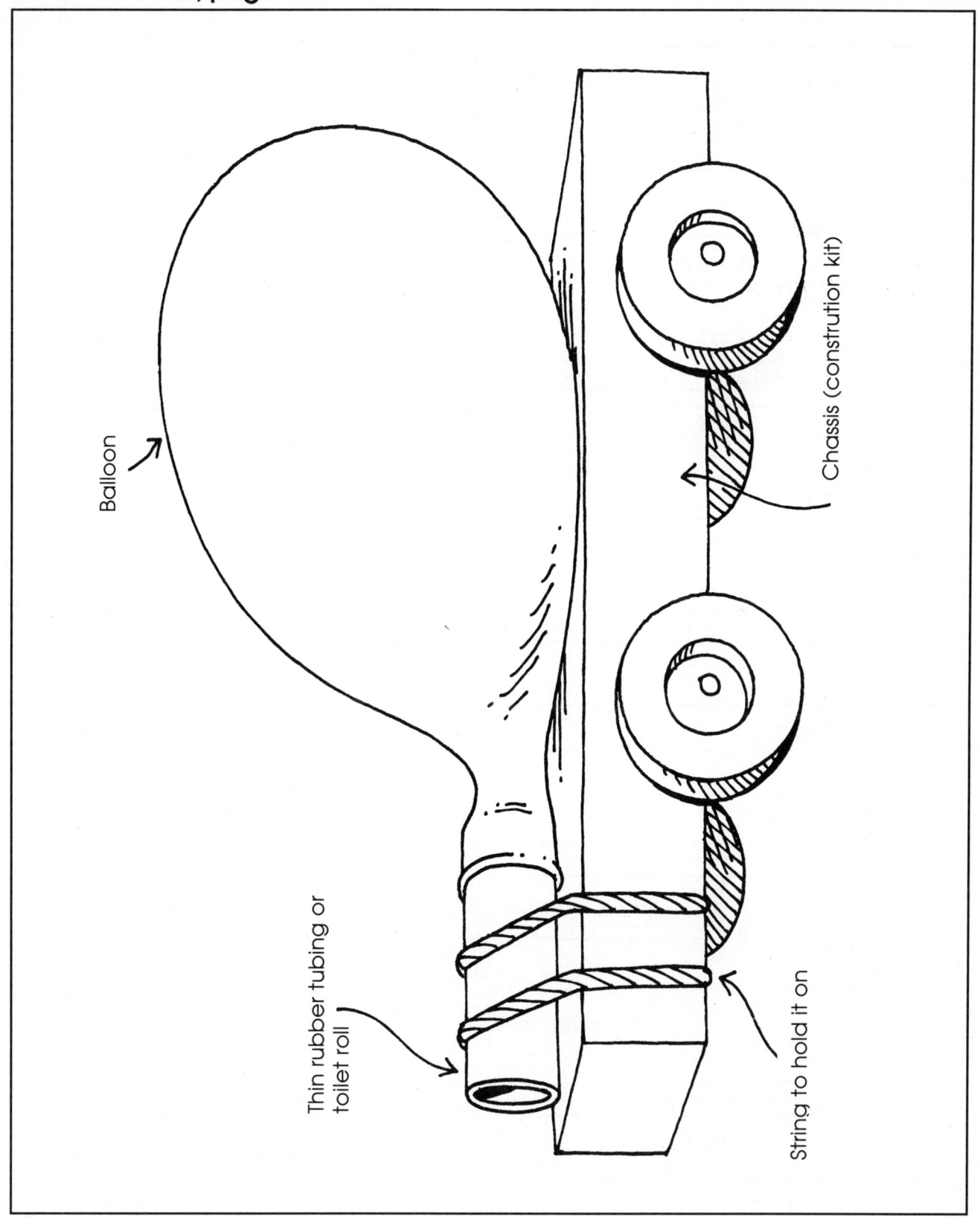

Balloon

Chassis (constrution kit)

Thin rubber tubing or toilet roll

String to hold it on

# See-saws, page 144

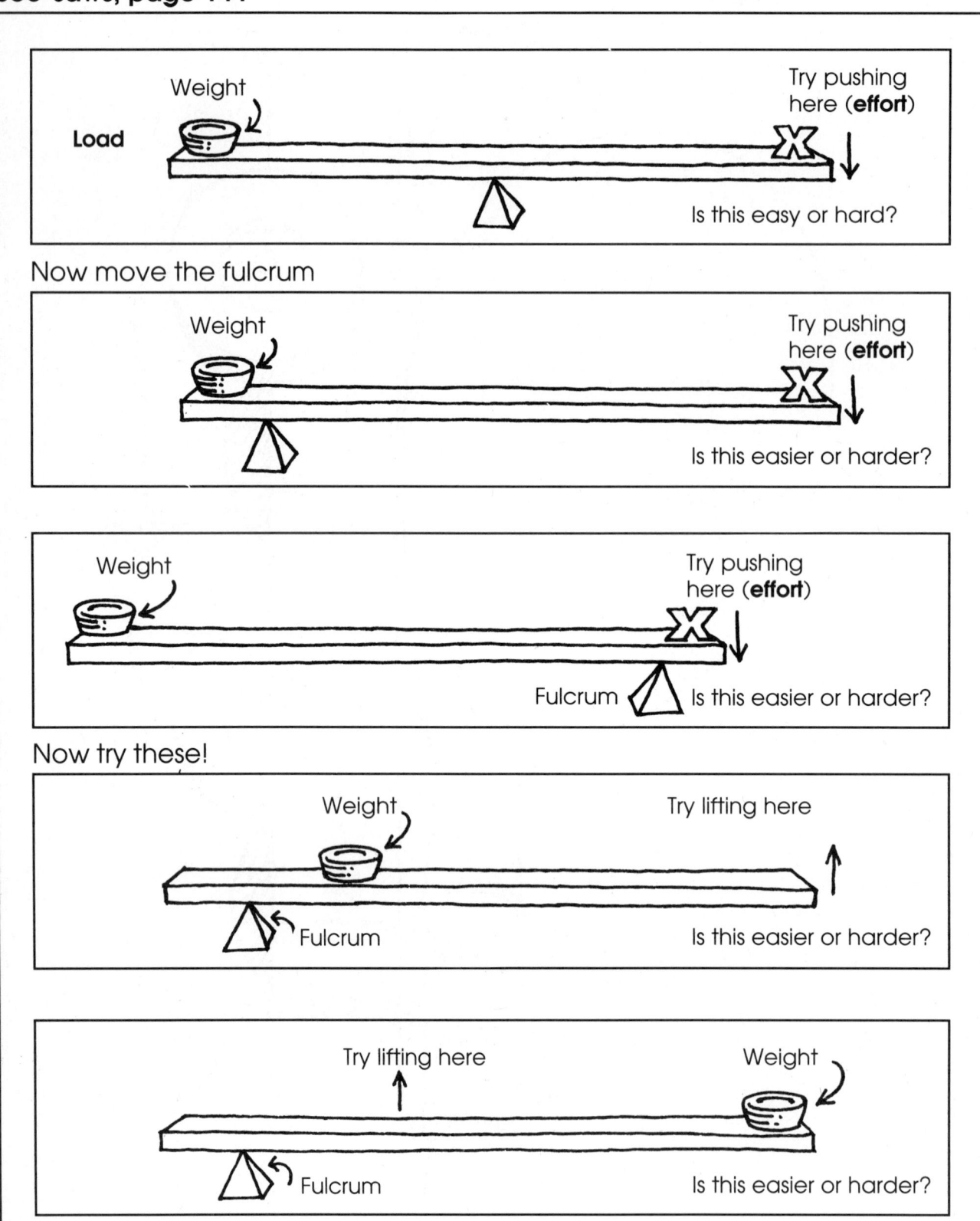

| Load | Weight | Try pushing here (**effort**) |
|---|---|---|
| | | Is this easy or hard? |

Now move the fulcrum

Weight — Try pushing here (**effort**) — Is this easier or harder?

Weight — Try pushing here (**effort**) — Fulcrum — Is this easier or harder?

Now try these!

Weight — Try lifting here — Fulcrum — Is this easier or harder?

Try lifting here — Weight — Fulcrum — Is this easier or harder?

*Photocopiable pages*

# Linkages, page 145

Try making these linkages. What do you think they might be used for?

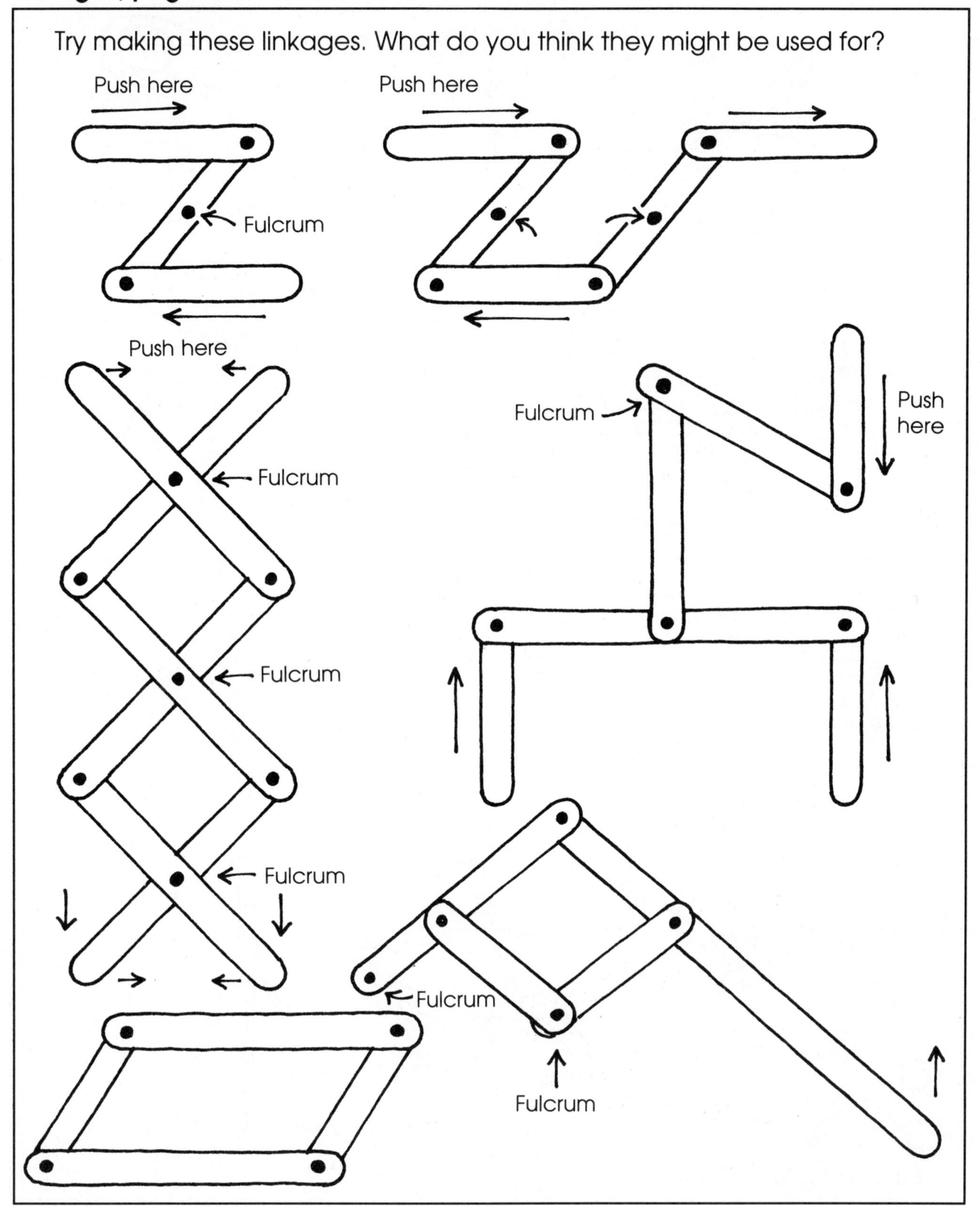

Push here · Fulcrum

Push here

Push here · Fulcrum · Fulcrum · Fulcrum

Fulcrum · Push here

Fulcrum · Fulcrum

*Photocopiable pages* **189**

# Looking at levers and linkages, page 145

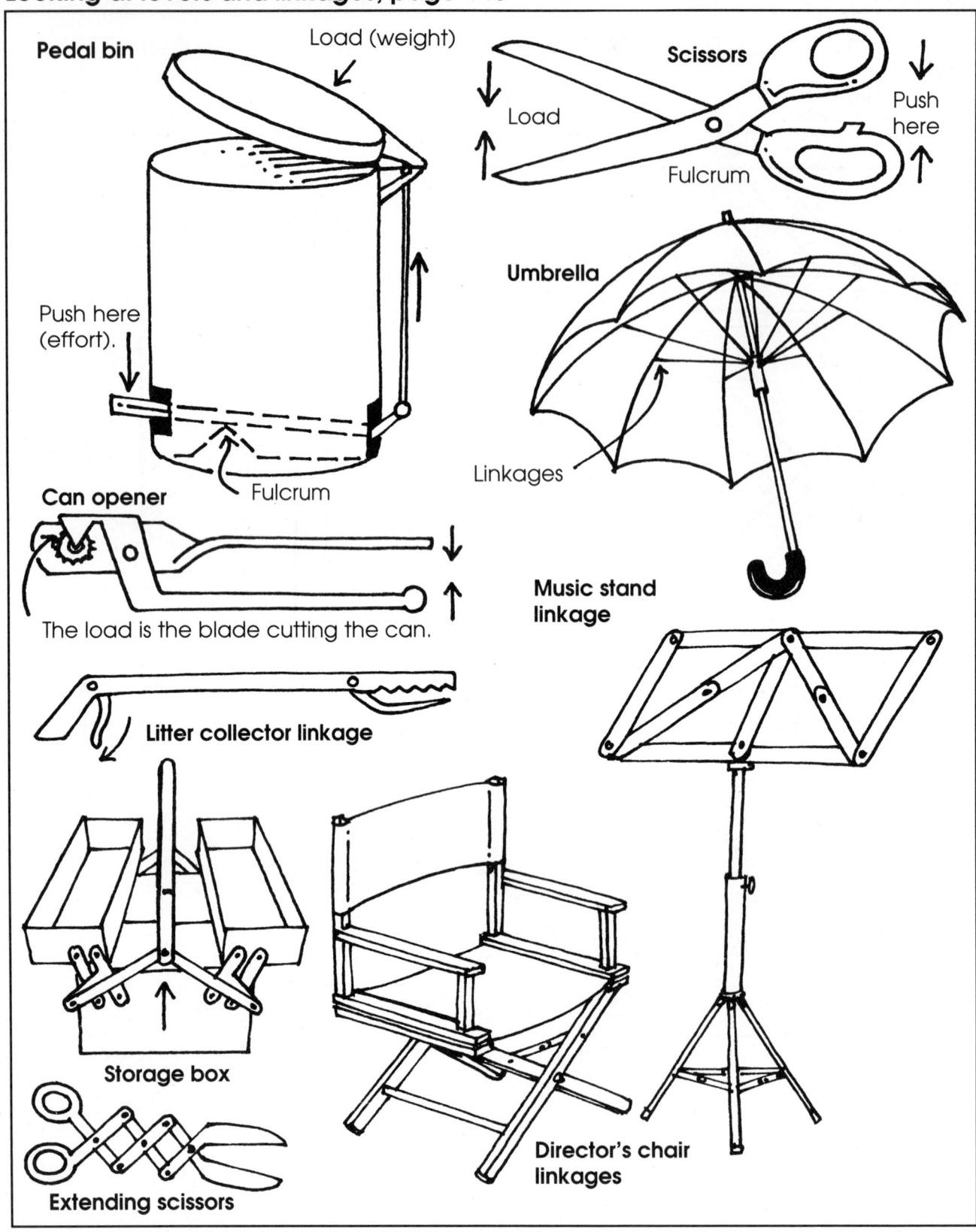

**Pedal bin** — Load (weight), Push here (effort), Fulcrum

**Scissors** — Load, Fulcrum, Push here

**Umbrella** — Linkages

**Can opener** — The load is the blade cutting the can.

**Litter collector linkage**

**Music stand linkage**

**Storage box**

**Director's chair linkages**

**Extending scissors**

# Introducing gears, page 153

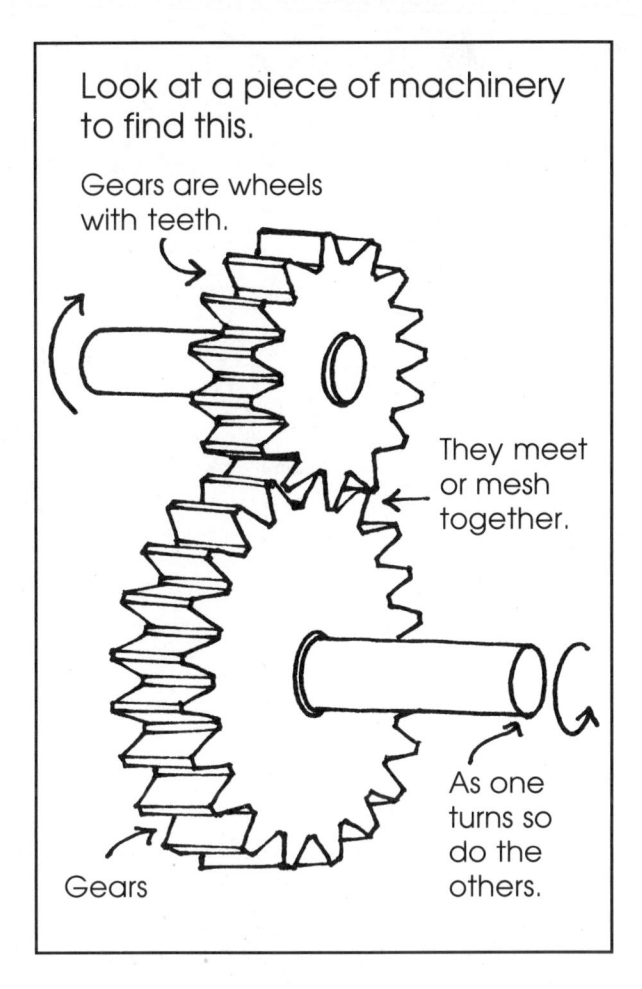

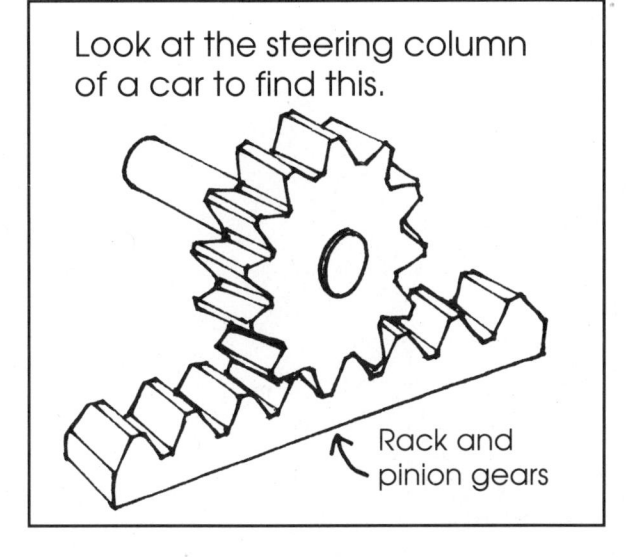

**Look at a piece of machinery to find this.**

Gears are wheels with teeth.

They meet or mesh together.

As one turns so do the others.

Gears

**Look at the heads on a guitar to find this.**

Worm gear

Worm wheel

**Look at the steering column of a car to find this.**

Rack and pinion gears

**Look at a hand whisk to find this.**

Bevel gears

*Photocopiable pages* **191**

# Turntables, page 154

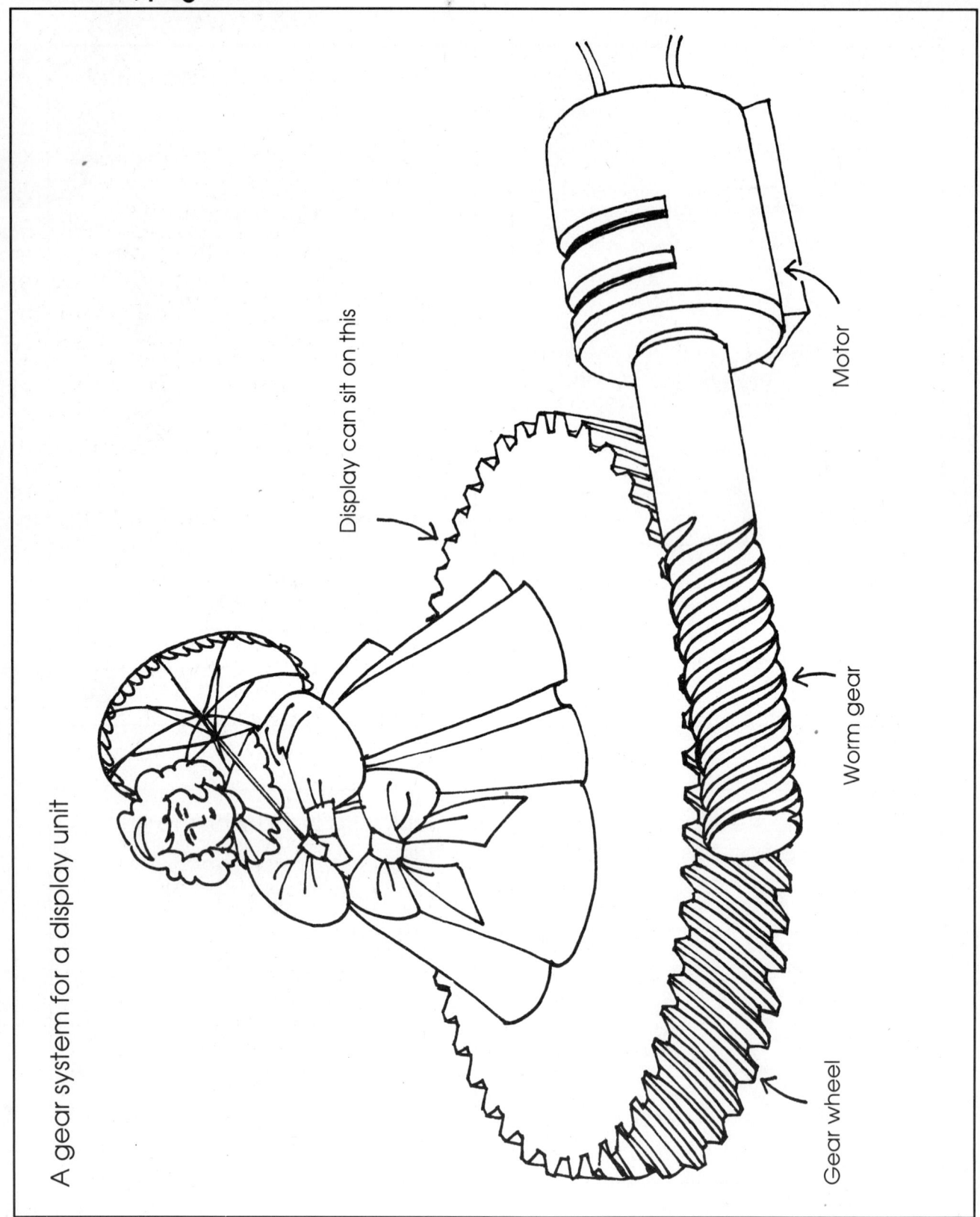

A gear system for a display unit

Display can sit on this

Motor

Worm gear

Gear wheel